BOBBY
BROWN

Best wishes.
Bobby Brown.

BOBBY
BROWN

A Life in Football,
From Goals to the Dugout

Jack Davidson

Best wishes Derek & happy wedding, Jack Davidson

pitch

First published by Pitch Publishing, 2017

Pitch Publishing
A2 Yeoman Gate
Yeoman Way
Worthing
Sussex
BN13 3QZ

www.pitchpublishing.co.uk
info@pitchpublishing.co.uk

ISBN 978-1-78531-301-1

Typesetting and origination by Pitch Publishing

Printed in the UK by TJ International Ltd, Cornwall

Contents

To the memory of Ruth Brown and to daughters Carolyn, Alison, Gillian and families; and to the memory of my father, George Davidson, who loved his football

Foreword

By
Campbell Ogilvie

I FEEL greatly honoured to contribute this foreword. I was
not fortunate enough to have seen Bobby play, but I have
known him since the early 1970s, when I worked at the
Scottish Football League, and later when secretary and director
of both Rangers and Hearts.

My dad, in his capacity as Rangers' club doctor since the late
1950s, certainly knew Bobby longer than I did. I had no idea
when he took me on my first trip to Wembley in 1967 – to that
unforgettable match – that I would one day become friendly
with the then Scottish team manager through my various roles
in the game.

Bobby's illustrious career spanned four decades, and I was
delighted to see him deservedly inducted into the Scottish
Football Hall of Fame in 2015.

My recollection of Bobby as a player, through photos and
film footage, is that of a blond-haired athlete resplendent in
a heavy yellow goalkeeper's jersey with a rollover neck. He
epitomised the standards expected and indeed demanded by
Rangers Football Club, and he was and still is a great example
to any aspiring professional player.

I always enjoy being in his company, listening to him recall the many tales of his playing days, and I was also privileged to have known many of his 'Iron Curtain' team-mates in that famous Rangers defence.

At 94, Bobby is as sharp as a tack, fit and still a keen rambler. He is always immaculate, usually in suit, shirt and tie with a pocket handkerchief.

I told my two daughters that I had been asked to write this, and they both recollected their conversations with him in the Blue Room at Ibrox and said, 'He is the nice man who always had time to chat with us.'

That is Bobby. A caring true gentleman who always has time for everyone.

Campbell Ogilvie,
SFA President 2011–2015.

Chapter 1

Wembley 1967

AS dream starts to new jobs go, even Carlsberg would have struggled to improve on Bobby Brown's. Appointed Scotland team manager only two months earlier, on 11 April 1967 he oversaw his team beating England, then reigning world champions, at Wembley, English football's impressive and emblematic stadium. It was his first full international in charge and England's first loss in 20 games. To defeat the world champions, Scotland's most intense and enduring rivals, in these circumstances was an outstanding achievement, like winning the Grand National on your debut ride or running a four-minute mile in your first race. The date is enshrined in Scottish football history as one of its most memorable days. In fans' folklore, it was the day when Scotland became 'unofficial world champions' by knocking England off their throne – and what could be sweeter for a Scottish fan? As Brown said, in his understated way at the time, 'It was a fairly daunting task for your first game in charge. I knew how important it was for Scotland especially after we had failed to qualify for the 1966 World Cup finals. We had a great team full of top players who rose to the occasion and did the nation proud.'

To appreciate fully the significance of this momentous victory, it is necessary to consider the backstory to this fixture. It is no exaggeration to say that at the time Scotland v. England was the biggest game in the annual British football calendar. Some would maintain that was largely only so for the Scots, but Scottish players of the era were convinced it meant as much to their English counterparts as it did to them. Certainly, English fans did not travel north to Hampden in the same numbers as Scots who made the bi-annual pilgrimage south. For years, Scots had been descending on Wembley in their thousands, giving the impression at times that it was a home fixture for them. In 1967, it was conservatively estimated that about 40,000 of the 100,000 crowd were Scottish supporters, although the noise they generated made it appear there were many more present.

Throughout the country, numerous small groups formed their own 'Wembley clubs' to organise their trips, with members contributing a weekly sum over two years to cover the expense. These 'clubs' would exist for years, with the same members making the exodus south year after year, many of whom took holidays to coincide with the game and enable them to spend a week or a long weekend on their trip. Off they would go in a sea of tartan, often accompanied by a piper and usually an enormous 'carry-out' to 'take over' London and affirm their Scottish identity in England's capital. Many photos of these expeditions can be seen capturing the mood of the enthusiastic fans, usually in a sizeable group, each grinning at the camera from underneath an outsize tartan 'bunnet', bedecked in tartan scarves, often with a cigarette in the mouth, a pint in one hand and the other arm wrapped in friendly embrace round a fellow fan's shoulder while apparently giving a rousing rendition of some old Scots air. Their visit undoubtedly signalled good times for London publicans, and although there was inevitably excess, for the most part they were good-natured, not a hostile invading army. Iconic landmarks, including Trafalgar Square and Piccadilly Circus, were favourite venues for them to congregate to vaunt their nationality and support, sometimes to a degree of consternation among the locals and usually entailing an increased police presence.

Apart from being an excuse for some considerable self-indulgence, it was also an opportunity, in the eyes of the Scots, to remind the English how innately superior they were at the national game. After all, was it not the 'Scotch Professors' coming down to play in England in the 1880s who laid the foundations of the English game, along with the likes of Perthshire's William McGregor, the founder of the English Football League and then FA chairman? The Wembley match afforded the opportunity for the classic case of the 'wee' neighbour to put one over the 'big' neighbour – the David v. Goliath syndrome. And how, in 1967, the fans relished it and how they celebrated it. Those celebrations were rendered even more jubilant because of England's status as reigning world champions, and at the same time doused the still keenly felt disappointment of a number of previous visits to Wembley.

This was the oldest international in world football, and, although by 1967 the World Cup, particularly, and the European Nations' Championship, to a lesser extent, were well established and high profile, Scotland v. England still rated as a very prestigious fixture. Although several unofficial games between the two countries took place between 1870 and 1872, at the Kennington Oval, the first official one was played on 30 November 1872 at the West of Scotland cricket ground at Hamilton Crescent, Partick, in Glasgow, ending in a 0–0 draw. This followed the FA's minutes of 3 October that year, recording, 'To further the interests of the Association in Scotland it was decided during the current season a team should be sent to Glasgow to play a match against Scotland.' Thereafter it became an annual match, usually as part of the Home Internationals until 1984, and thereafter until 1989 for the Rous Cup. After its inception, it quickly grew in importance, with its first 100,000-plus crowd in attendance at Hampden for the 1902 edition.

The construction of the Empire Exhibition Stadium, to give Wembley its full name, in 1923 was the catalyst for the Scots to travel south in ever increasing numbers for the game. As its name suggests, it was built for the purposes of the eponymous exhibition there, and no expense was spared. It was a landmark stadium, with its famous twin towers and the wide boulevard of Wembley Way leading up to it. Completed four days before the FA Cup Final that year, it hosted what became known as the 'White Horse Final', when a mounted police officer's horse distinguished itself on crowd control duties.

Ironically perhaps, regarding what is perceived to be such an English bastion, Scots were very much associated with its early days. The construction company which built it was Sir Robert McAlpine and Co, whose founder, Robert McAlpine, was a Scot, born in Newarthill, near Motherwell. The plan was to demolish the stadium after the exhibition, but Sir James Stevenson, a Scot from Kilmarnock, who was chair of its organising committee, opposed that proposal and campaigned successfully for it to be retained. And the first international goal scored there was scored by a Scot, Willie Cowan of Newcastle United – the winning goal against England in 1924. When constructed, it was considered the world's greatest sporting arena, and it continued to maintain its cachet, with the legendary Brazilian Pele, at a later date, describing it as 'the cathedral of football, the capital of football and the heart of football'. Curiously, and again ironically perhaps, Scotland's national stadium, Hampden Park in Glasgow, is named after an English politician of the 17th century, John Hampden, a famous parliamentarian and central figure in the Civil War.

Underlining the importance of this international, only Scotland played at Wembley against the home nation until 1951, when Argentina were permitted to play there, after which it became the regular home venue for all England's matches. Between the war years, the popularity of the match grew considerably, with a world attendance record being set at Hampden in 1937, when 149,547 were present. Two years later at the same ground, the figure had dropped to a mere 149,433! This emphasised the importance of this annual encounter between the world's oldest rivals, especially to the Scots.

By 1967, their enthusiasm for the fray had not dimmed, despite some severe drubbings dished out at Wembley in the not very distant past. A 9–3 humbling six years earlier has entered the annals as the low point from a Scottish perspective – their worst defeat by their southern neighbours. Frank Haffey, the Celtic goalkeeper playing that day for Scotland, bore the brunt of the criticism for that stinging loss, probably somewhat unfairly. His apparent carefree demeanour did not help in that assessment, with reports that he was singing in the bath after the match. His performance gave rise to quips such as 'What's the time? It's 9 past Haffey.' When Brown announced Ronnie Simpson of Celtic was to be Scotland's goalkeeper in 1967, the *Glasgow Herald* drily reminded its readers that the last time a Celtic goalkeeper represented the country, 'he conceded nine goals'.

In 1955, Fred Martin of Aberdeen was in goals as the English forwards put seven past him, with the Scots responding with a meagre two; while, in a wartime international in 1944, Scotland conceded six against two scored. Further back, in 1930, Hearts goalkeeper Jack Harkness, later a well-known football writer, picked the ball out of his net five times, again the Scots replying with two. There had been the occasional Scottish highlight, such as the 'Wembley Wizards' of 1928, when their diminutive artistes recorded a 5–1 win. In 1949, the Scots recorded a famous 3–1 win in a game often referred to as 'Jimmy Cowan's match' in deference to the Morton goalkeeper's brilliance that day. And in 1963 they gained a measure of revenge for the 9–3 thrashing two years before by winning 2–1.

However, despite such rays of sunshine occasionally piercing the dark clouds that seemed to hover over Scotland at Wembley, in 1967 the weight of history and form favoured the home team. In the corresponding match the previous year at Hampden, England had won 4–3, although informed opinion was the scoreline did not reflect their superiority.

In the meantime, they had gone on to win the World Cup on 30 July 1966, beating West Germany 4–2 at Wembley. Predictably, this success rankled with many Scots who cavilled at it, complaining that England, as host nation, did not have to pre-qualify and were allowed to play all their games at Wembley. They also perceived that the infamous Russian linesman Mr Bahramov had given them an unwarranted leg up by indicating that the ball had crossed the goal line for England's vital third goal, in extra time. Put briefly, the majority of Scots found it very hard to accept that England were world champions. They were also less than impressed by manager Alf Ramsey's 'wingless wonders' style of play, which they thought a negation of the true spirit of the game.

And what fuelled their occasionally less than gracious attitude to English success was that Scotland had not participated in the finals, the Scottish contribution being limited to a few non-league teams in the Borders providing warm-up opposition for some of the finalists. In their qualifying section for that World Cup, a stirring win over Italy in Glasgow in November 1965, thanks to a John Greig thunderbolt shot, raised hopes of qualification. What was required to clinch it was a win in the return game in Naples the next month. A depleted Scottish team, weakened by the non-availability of key players such as Law, Baxter, Henderson and McNeill, lost 3–0, and with that, Scottish hopes were trodden into the Neapolitan turf. The Scots' sense of grievance was compounded through England's memorable win. Scottish players based in England, 'Anglos' as they were referred to, had to suffer in dressing rooms as their English counterparts took delight in reminding them of their world champion status and how the Scots had not even made it to the finals. Denis Law, as proud a Scot as there is, admitted that he could not bear to watch the final, going to play golf instead. He claimed his afternoon was ruined when he heard the news of England's victory. Jim Baxter, another legendary Scottish player, did attend the final but was less than impressed by the English performance, expressing his surprise that 'that lot' had won it.

In the lead-up to Wembley '67, not many fancied Scotland's chances. Apart from the 'Wembley factor', this English team had played 19 consecutive games undefeated since 1965, including that famous final. In Scotland's corresponding number of games, they were undefeated in 13 of them, six of which were draws. The England team selected for this game was the same one that had won the World Cup, with the exception of Jimmy Greaves of Spurs replacing Roger Hunt of Liverpool, hardly weakening it.

This was to be their first match back at Wembley since then, and being defeated there as reigning champions, especially to Scotland, was not part of their agenda. They had a settled team and an experienced and proven successful manager, Alf Ramsey, at the helm, whose first game this would be since being appointed a knight of the realm. Adding spice to the forthcoming encounter was Ramsey's thinly disguised lack of affection for the Scots. When he arrived in Glasgow with his team for the previous year's match, the Scottish press greeted him with 'Welcome to Scotland, Alf', to which he replied, 'You must be bloody joking.'

In contrast, the 44-year-old Bobby Brown was new to international management. Well known north of the border as a former international goalkeeper, a position he had occupied with distinction for Queen's Park and Rangers, his management experience was limited to just over eight years in charge of St Johnstone, one of the country's provincial clubs. His profile in England was low, a factor which fed into pre-match coverage of the game by the English press. Although he was largely successful with the Perth-based club, he was having to operate on limited resources and, generally, low crowds. While he was manager, the club did not play in Europe, nor had he ever been exposed to international football as manager. He had never met a number of important players in the Scottish team, such as Denis Law, Jim Baxter and Billy Bremner, prior to the squad assembling in the days preceding the game. The international game undoubtedly required a different approach from club football, taking into account the fact that the players belonged to their clubs. Before Wembley '67, as on other occasions, Brown only had them with him for a few days before the game, making it more difficult to establish a rapport and ensure he got his message over to them.

Understandably, Scottish fans were unsure of Brown given that background, and he still had to prove himself in their eyes. That background did not in any way quell their eagerly felt anticipation for the game or diminish their passion for it. If anything, it served to ratchet up the tension to an almost unbelievable level. Although Scotland's ticket allocation was about 30,000, it seemed half the country was on its way to Wembley judging by the numbers of cars, buses and trains crossing the border on Friday afternoon and evening. Meanwhile, the English press were busy consigning Scotland's hopes to the dustbin and thereby adding to their motivation to upset the odds and beat the world champions.

Desmond Hackett in the *Daily Express* wrote, 'England will firmly relegate Scotland to their minor role in international football.' Geoff Green in *The Times*: 'This will be England's day.' Ken Jones in the *Daily Mail*: 'England's unbeaten run must end sometime but not today.' And Brian James in the *Daily Mirror* opined, 'The Scots have no chance – they have not learned as much about football as England.' While motivation to beat England on their home turf was never in short supply, such comments filled the tank to overflowing.

Despite the odds apparently being so stacked against Scotland, Brown maintains that he never felt negative about his team's prospects. He recalled, 'It was obviously a very big challenge. Playing England at Wembley always was, but this time the stakes were a bit higher with our opponents being the world champions. Although I was new to the job and obviously felt pressure, it was never overwhelming. As far as I was concerned, it was a great honour to be manager of my country and I had tremendous confidence in the players we had. I was fortunate in the calibre of player I was able to select, all of whom were really top drawer. A number of them played club football in England and had played with their clubs in Europe. And the home-based players included six Old Firm representatives who weeks later all featured in European finals with their respective clubs. We had no reason to feel inferior and nor did we.'

Brown was extremely diligent in his preparation. Following his final game in charge of St Johnstone on 18 February, he took up the reins with Scotland. During that period of just over six weeks to the Wembley fixture, he watched 24 matches in Scotland and England, clocking up a huge mileage in the process. Although he knew nearly all of the potential Scottish squad at least by reputation, there were several whom he had not seen play at first hand, and a few scarcely known to him but who had been recommended. He therefore undertook an extensive scouting operation, anxious to leave nothing to chance in arriving at his strongest eleven for his full international debut.

Prior to then, he was in charge of Scottish teams for two minor international fixtures, both against England. The first was an under-23 game at Newcastle on 1 March, a fixture the Scots had not won for six years. Brown's plan was to contain the opposition for the first 15 minutes and thereafter go on the offensive. It worked well, with the Scots going on to record a highly satisfactory 3–1 win following Jim McCalliog's 16th-minute opener, Peter Cormack and Jimmy Smith adding the others. McCalliog of Sheffield Wednesday, who had previously been capped once at this level, against Wales, had been attracting Brown's interest through his club performances and would go on to play a crucial part in the Wembley match. Others playing for Scotland that evening included keeper Bobby Clark, Pat Stanton, Eddie Gray and Tommy McLean. McCalliog met Brown for the first time at Newcastle and remembers being impressed by him: 'He was a lovely, happy, smiley man who obviously knew his football. He'd been a successful player himself and I was chuffed to meet him.'

The second match was between the respective league sides at Hampden on 15 March. One innovation introduced by Brown before that match was to convene a meeting of the seven club managers whose players featured in the team, to discuss their strengths and weaknesses and try to foster a spirit of co-operation with them. Present were Jock Stein (Celtic), Scot Symon (Rangers), Bob Shankly (Hibs), Malky Macdonald (Kilmarnock), Willie Cunningham (Dunfermline Athletic), John Harvey (Hearts) and Eddie Turnbull (Aberdeen). Brown stated that his objective was to win and score as many as possible.

Unfortunately, despite that intention, the English league won 3–0, with Geoff Hurst scoring a double and Allan Clarke the other. Only two players who would play at Wembley – Tommy Gemmell and John Greig – featured for the Scots. Others who played included Bobby Ferguson in goal, Billy McNeill, John Clark, Willie Henderson, Stevie Chalmers (travelling reserve for Wembley) and a certain Alex Ferguson, about whom the press wrote ahead of the match, 'Ferguson has a great future and if he is in form he could get the vital goals.'

Clearly it was not to be, and Brown had had his first setback. Alf Ramsey occupied the opposing dugout that evening and, contrary to the way in which he was often perceived, was magnanimous in victory towards Brown. As they made their way back to the dressing rooms, he put his arm round Brown's shoulder to say, 'Don't worry too much, Bobby. You'll suffer many disappointments as I did, the great thing is to learn from them.' Certainly, on that occasion, he was rather more loquacious than he would be after the Wembley game.

Brown deliberated long and hard about his team. Apart from his scouting activities, he had also studied a technical report, commissioned by the FA and written by Walter Winterbottom and Ron Greenwood, on tactics employed by the teams during the 1966 World Cup, including games against England. As a result, he became convinced that an attacking formation with an element of fluidity and a tight defence was the answer to combat Ramsey's rigid 4–3–3 formation. He wanted to have full-backs capable of going forward to exploit space up the flanks as auxiliary attackers, a midfield that operated not only there but also supported the attack, and forwards who would press the defence closely and hopefully score goals. Essentially, a fluid 4–3–3 that at times would convert to 4–2–4. With the personnel available to him, Brown felt he could make the English central defence of Jackie Charlton and Bobby Moore uncomfortable and that his attacking line-up could take advantage of Ramsey's 'wingerless' team.

Brown's selection was as follows: Ronnie Simpson (Celtic); Tommy Gemmell (Celtic), John Greig (Rangers, capt.), Ronnie McKinnon (Rangers), Eddie McCreadie (Chelsea); Billy Bremner (Leeds), Jim McCalliog (Sheffield Wednesday), Jim Baxter (Sunderland); Willie Wallace (Celtic), Denis Law (Manchester United), Bobby Lennox (Celtic). Travelling reserves: Bobby Ferguson (Kilmarnock – goalkeeper), Steve Chalmers (Celtic), Frank McLintock (Arsenal).

England lined up as follows: Gordon Banks (Leicester); George Cohen (Fulham), Jack Charlton (Leeds), Bobby Moore (West Ham, capt.), Ray Wilson (Everton); Alan Ball (Everton), Nobby Stiles (Manchester United), Martin Peters (West Ham); Jimmy Greaves (Spurs), Bobby Charlton (Manchester United), Geoff Hurst (West Ham).

Brown originally selected Jimmy 'Jinky' Johnstone as outside-right – an awesome dribbler on his day and capable of snatching a goal, having scored two in the previous year's fixture in Glasgow. However, he was injured the previous Wednesday night playing in a European Cup semi-final in Glasgow against Dukla Prague and had to be withdrawn. This was a blow to Brown's plans, because 'Jinky' could be a devastating player who was extremely difficult to combat. In his place, Brown called up Jinky's Celtic team-mate, Willie 'Wispy' Wallace. His team selection was subject to some criticism, particularly by the English press, who felt Johnstone's withdrawal weakened it considerably. They also expressed the view that not only was the manager inexperienced at this level, but so were a number of his players – Simpson and McCalliog were debutants, while Lennox, Wallace and Gemmell had only a handful of caps between them. It was pointed out that this was in sharp contrast to the home team, in terms of both manager and players.

Brown recalled the reasoning behind his selection. 'To my mind the midfield was absolutely essential to the game. Billy Bremner on one side and Jim Baxter on the other were key players in that area. Bremner on the right, who hailed from the Raploch, a tough neighbourhood in Stirling, I always thought of as like "ten stones of barbed wire". Although there was not much of him, he was a tenacious tackler with a high work rate, a "terrier" of a player. He was an important member of a then very successful Leeds United. On the left, Baxter was a complete contrast, a cultured, artistic player who could run a game. You could not expect much from him defensively, as he didn't do a lot of running. At this time he was playing for Sunderland and carrying a bit more weight, no longer the "Slim Jim" he had once been. He had left Rangers to go to Wearside and there was no doubt he was no longer the player he had been at Ibrox. But he still had bags of ability and great belief in himself. I thought he would most definitely be "up" for this game. Then I had to decide who would best combine with them and offer some fluidity in the formation by being able to go forward as an attacker and also cover back when required. This role called for a player with an excellent engine and a good measure of skill. Having been very impressed with young Jim McCalliog when I watched him in the under-23s and also for his club, I decided he was the man for the role. Some were sceptical of him, as he was only 20 and uncapped, but he had played in England since he was 15, at Leeds, at Chelsea and then with Sheffield Wednesday. His transfer fee from Chelsea to Sheffield Wednesday was a British record for a teenager – £37,500. He had also played at Wembley in an important game, the FA Cup Final in 1966, when his Sheffield Wednesday team lost 3–2 to Everton and he scored. As it turned out, he fully justified my decision. Once I was satisfied with my midfield, which I saw as the team's crucial hub, I turned my attention to the rest of the side.

'In goal I decided to give Ronnie Simpson his first cap for Scotland at age 36, making him Scotland's oldest ever debutant in this fixture. My choice was criticised in some quarters, but I felt confident about him. He was playing well for Celtic in big games at home and in Europe, was used to appearing in front of big crowds, and had previous experience of Wembley as he played there for the Great Britain team in the London Olympic Games of 1948. He had also taken part there in two FA Cup finals for Newcastle United in 1952 and 1955, collecting winner's medals each time. The other main candidate for the position was Kilmarnock's Bobby Ferguson (later of West Ham United) but I felt he was not at his best for the Scottish league against the English league about a month previous and I decided to make him travelling reserve. Ronnie had made his senior debut for Queen's Park as a 14-year-old in 1945 and had actually been my ballboy at times when I played for the Spiders. His father, Jimmy, had been a centre-half for Rangers who appeared for Scotland against England at Wembley in 1936, and so Ronnie was following in his footsteps.

'At right-back, I put in Tommy Gemmell, a strapping, athletic type of player, a strong runner who could set off on galloping runs up the right wing. He would run through a brick wall for you and had a terrific shot on him. Although he usually played on the left for Celtic, he could also play on the right. Again, some criticism came my way, as he only had three caps and according to some was playing out of position.

'In central defence I went for the Rangers club pairing of John Greig and Ronnie McKinnon. They were a tried and tested partnership who had combined well together for years, were well used to the big occasion, and I felt they could be relied on to do the job. Greig I made captain – he always gave 100 per cent and played for the jersey. McKinnon was a more reserved sort of individual who sometimes needed a little reassurance before going out on the pitch, but, as I say, the two of them dovetailed well together. I was under some pressure to field the Celtic duo of Billy McNeill and John Clark, a pairing whom I also rated highly, and I gave the decision a lot of thought. It was difficult, but I just felt that on this occasion the Rangers two should go in.

'At left-back I had no doubt that the best man was Eddie McCreadie of Chelsea, I think the finest left-back I've ever seen. He had the best and most cultured left foot of any left-back. He always tried to place the ball as well as being strong in the tackle. I thought he was ahead of his time actually, and would have no difficulty fitting into the modern game. In my book he was an outstanding player who had gone from fairly humble beginnings in Scotland with East Stirlingshire to excel in England with Chelsea.

'Up front, my original choice on the right, as mentioned, was the inimitable Jimmy "Jinky" Johnstone of Celtic, a mesmerising dribbler who could wreak havoc in opposing defences – but his injury meant he was not available. There is no doubt his absence was perceived as a weakness for us, but in his place I went for his clubmate Willie "Wispy" Wallace, a bit of a surprise choice in some eyes. He was relatively inexperienced at this level, with only three caps to his name, but I had seen him play a number of times and was impressed with his game intelligence as well as his overall play. He also carried a goal threat with his powerful shot, and was in form, having scored twice in that game against Dukla Prague. He had had big-match experience with Celtic, and I felt he could fit in well with the way I was approaching the game. I required him to drop back at times to help the midfield as well as contributing to the attack.

'Denis Law at centre-forward almost picked himself. At his best a truly wonderful player, and undoubtedly one of Scotland's all-time greats. He always brought a positive attitude, was confident in his own ability on any stage and always had a burning desire to beat England, particularly after 1966. And he was a superb finisher. For his club, Manchester United, I thought he was playing in a slightly deeper position than he should, but for this game I wanted him to be up close to the opposition central defenders. I wanted him to harry Jack Charlton and Bobby Moore, the captain, as I felt they were not used to having someone exerting so much pressure on them.

'On the left, I chose Celtic's Bobby Lennox – really a dream player to have in your team, a smashing lad. He could run all day, open up defences with his speed and skill and cut inside to score a goal. Again, some considered him inexperienced at this level, as he only had one cap, but for me he was a certainty to start. All-time English great Bobby Charlton thought extremely highly of Lennox, and that is about as good a reference as you could hope for.

'There were no substitutes then, but we could take travelling reserves. A goalkeeper was, of course, essential, and I picked Kilmarnock's Bobby Ferguson, who, despite not having his best showing against the English league, was a good, experienced keeper. As outfield players I chose Celtic's Stevie Chalmers and Frank McLintock of Arsenal. Chalmers, I felt, gave me options due to his versatility: he could cover a number of positions up front and drop back to midfield if needed. Again, he was a goalscorer and fitted the attacking pattern I had in mind for the team. And as for Frank McLintock, he was an experienced, solid defender who could also play in midfield and had played at Wembley previously in cup finals. That was the team I felt could do a job for us and I was delighted that it did!'

The home-based members of the squad assembled on the Wednesday before the game at Largs on the Ayrshire coast, where they stayed at the Queen's Hotel on the seafront, reserved for their exclusive use. Some light training was undertaken at the nearby Inverclyde Sports Centre, but Brown, being new to the job, used much of the time available familiarising himself with the players, some of whom he knew well and others less so. He made it his business to speak individually and collectively to them as he sought to foster a bond and positive spirit. Assisting him behind the scenes were trainer Walter McCrae and physio/masseur Tom McNiven. McCrae, a former goalkeeper at junior level, was an experienced trainer and also a qualified physiotherapist. A man of erect bearing thanks to his National Service in the Royal Marines, he commanded the players' respect, and Brown had a lot of confidence in him. He had served previous Scottish managers Ian McColl, Jock Stein, John Prentice and Malky Macdonald. Throughout his whole career, he was associated with his home-town team, Kilmarnock, as trainer, manager and general manager. Tom McNiven was also a former junior footballer and had been a successful sprinter. His career was also identified particularly with one club, Hibs, where he was trainer/physiotherapist for many years. He also provided valued support to Brown.

On the Thursday, the squad travelled down south, where they installed themselves in the upmarket Brent Bridge Hotel in Hendon, north London, about a 15-minute drive from Wembley. There the English-based players, the 'Anglos', joined up with the others and Brown began meeting the likes of Billy Bremner and Denis Law for the first time. He again spoke to all the 'Anglos' individually, to try to create a rapport with them, and placed great emphasis on developing team spirit.

After light training at the nearby Hendon Amateurs' ground, Brown outlined his tactics for the game. At that time, managers generally did not spend a lot of time on the minutiae of tactics. What was most important to Brown was getting his selection right and setting the framework in which he wished them to play. Little by way of motivation was required, given the importance of the fixture and particularly the attitude of the English press. On the Friday, another light training session took place, and, in the afternoon, the squad made a trip to Wembley to have a look round the stadium and a check of the playing surface, invaluable for those new to the arena. That evening, Brown and some players, by way of relaxation, went to watch Arsenal beat Dunfermline Athletic 2–1 at Highbury in a friendly. And various administrative tasks were attended to ahead of Saturday, including players' phone calls and the organisation of tickets for families and friends, as Brown did not wish such matters to be a distraction on matchday.

The build-up had gone well, and, although there clearly was pressure on the players, Brown never felt they were anything other than upbeat about their prospects. Although in managerial terms this was a step up from his time at St Johnstone, he never felt overawed – largely because he had great belief in the calibre of player at his disposal. He also felt his task was made that little bit easier as he had been an international himself, which helped win his players' respect.

On the Saturday morning, the squad did some light ball work for half an hour. Some players went for a stroll round nearby Golders Green, including keeper Simpson, whose calmness impressed Brown: 'He looked as if he was just going out for a walk with his dog on a Saturday morning!' Then, after the press photos had been dealt with and last-minute phone calls had been made, the squad sat down to a light lunch. Ronnie Simpson was delighted to have received a 'good luck' phone call from Old Firm rival goalie Billy Ritchie of Rangers, a nice touch from the Ibrox no. 1. Next it was on to the team coach for Wembley, which was met by police motorcycle outriders who shepherded them en route to the stadium, where they arrived at 1.30pm. Everyone on board became more and more aware of the sheer volume of Scottish fans as the bus threaded its way through them. Once the coach was on Wembley Way, the fans' presence was spine-tingling. Jim McCalliog recalled, 'It was absolutely amazing seeing all those fans thronging Wembley Way. They were all draped in tartan and shouting and singing, waving flags – an incredible sight. I realised this was a dream come true for me to be there, to play in this game. This is what I had spent hours and hours and hours kicking a ball about for as a kid, to make it to here. We were sitting there looking out the window, hardly able to believe our eyes. Occasionally our attention would be drawn to groups of fans and we would point them out to each other as we exclaimed, "Look at him, look at them!" and so on. It really was unbelievable.'

Brown echoed these recollections, being equally impressed by the number and 'betartaned' enthusiasm of the Scots fans on Wembley Way. 'It really was quite something and brought it home to you just how much this game meant to Scotland. In those days it was a real gala occasion, the undoubted high point of the season. Scottish fans took holidays to coincide with it and saved up over two years for this trip. And, of course, it had the added element this year: not only were we playing the "Auld Enemy" but also the world champions. I think the realisation of the enormity of the fixture began to hit the players as our coach made its way through the seething masses of our fans. They appreciated they were carrying a nation's hopes with them. In my recollection at that time, the mood among the players changed slightly as a kind of quiet descended on the bus while they all took in just how much this meant and several seemed lost in their own thoughts. You have to remember that it wasn't only their country or their clubs they were representing, but their families and friends, many of whom were down for the game. They were also conscious of representing those in their youth who had encouraged and shaped their early careers and the football-mad communities where most had grown up.'

Skipper Greig later wrote: 'On the surface we had no reason to feel confident but we thought we were unfortunate not to qualify for the 1966 Finals and we were desperate to make a point.'

Once in the stadium, Brown took his players out of the dressing room for a stroll on the pitch, to let them get a feel for it and soak up the atmosphere and acknowledge their amazing support. Back inside, the team first read the many 'good luck' telegrams that had flooded in from family, friends and fans, serving to underline further the occasion's importance. As warming up on the pitch was not permitted, it had to be done indoors. In the dressing room, the team went through their routine of stretching exercises, kicked a ball against the wall and prepared themselves physically and mentally for what lay ahead. McNiven gave the players a 'rub' while McCrae, in addition to supervising the warm-up, attended to players' individual needs, distributing items such as stocking ties, plasters, ankle bandages and the like where required. According to Bobby Lennox, in a book he later wrote, at Celtic and other clubs sometimes, if players asked, they would be given a small 'nip' of whisky before going out on to the pitch, to calm the nerves a bit. He remembered on this occasion, reserve and club team-mate Stevie Chalmers, mindful of this habit, had brought into the dressing room a small bottle of whisky from which Ronnie Simpson and one or two others helped themselves to a small 'nip'. It has to be emphasised: this was a minute quantity, not a tumblerful!

Brown gave a fairly brief talk on tactics, reminding his charges what he had already drilled into them at Hendon, and spoke individually to each player about his role. What struck him about them, particularly at this point, was how much belief they had and how little apprehension was apparent. Partly he attributed this to the fact that many of these players were household names, some in England. There they regularly faced up to their opponents that afternoon, and they knew they were at least on the same level as them, if not on a higher one.

McCalliog was impressed by the confident vibes from his team-mates. 'As a young 20-year-old coming in for his first cap, I was understandably a bit nervous at meeting up and playing with some of these famous names, guys like Law, Baxter and Bremner. Funnily enough, I had played against Law on the Monday night in a league game against Manchester United. But with the help of Bobby Brown, who gave me great confidence in myself, I soon felt at ease in the group. He was very good before the game in the dressing room, ensuring everyone knew their task and keeping things calm. The dressing room was actually disappointing for such a grand stadium – it was not very big, and all you got was a peg for your clothes! It was a concrete floor, so you had to be careful, walking about with your boots on, you didn't slip. However, the memory that sticks with me most strongly though was just how much confidence my team-mates seemed to have before the game. In training, it was fantastic to watch how they carried themselves, the way they could control the pace of the game and the outrageous pieces of skill they could come up with. Their attitude was "England had won the World Cup, so what?" In fact, they reminded me of the time when I was at Chelsea a couple of years earlier and manager Tommy Docherty gave some of us the chance to watch the Rest of the World XI train at Stamford Bridge before a special match against England at Wembley. There I saw people like Di Stefano, Eusebio, Puskas, Masopust, Santos, Denis Law, Gento and others close up, and it was fantastic to see what they could do with the ball. My Scottish team-mates in training were just the same. Law, Baxter, Bremner, Gemmell all had that streak of arrogance, and Greig had a strut about him, McKinnon too. It just made you think there was no way they were going to be second to anyone, and their confidence was infectious in the dressing room, like when Baxter announced, "This lot can play nane.'"

Five minutes before kick-off, Brown said a few more words, urging them to make their country proud. The bell rang for them to go out, and as they began to file out quietly, like men on a mission, Baxter bounced the ball a couple of times on the floor before the dressing room door slammed shut.

The teams were presented to the Duke of Norfolk just before 3pm, and, as stated in the FA's booklet of 'do's and don'ts', the match could not begin until the good Duke had resumed his seat in the Royal Box. Once he was sitting comfortably, the game kicked off amid ear-splitting roars of encouragement from the Scottish fans. An early earth-shattering tackle by Gemmell seemed to set the tone, and the Scots were soon on top. Jackie Charlton injured himself in about the 15th minute in a rash tackle on Lennox and spent the rest of the game up front. The Scots deservedly took the lead in the 28th minute thanks to Denis Law, who converted a rebound off English keeper Banks from a shot by Wallace. At half-time, the score remained at 1–0. In the dressing room, Brown was disappointed the scoreline did not reflect the run of play, as he felt Scotland were well ahead; he encouraged them to go for more goals. In the 78th minute, they went two ahead thanks to a Bobby Lennox goal, making him the first Celtic player to score at Wembley for Scotland. It was shortly after that when Baxter indulged in his now legendary bout of 'keepie-uppie'. McCalliog inadvertently set him up by backheeling the ball to him in the opposition half in response to his shout, prompting Baxter to exhibit his skills bouncing the ball off head, knee and instep, trying to humiliate the world champions. While this delighted the Scottish support, it did not have the same effect on Brown. 'I was standing on the touchline pulling my hair out at Baxter's antics and I was going berserk. I wanted them to drive on to get more goals, but there was no telling him, he could be a law unto himself.' Nor was Brown the only one upset at Baxter. Denis Law, who had suffered in the 9–3 reverse at the same ground in 1961, was determined to score more goals and rub English noses in it that way. Ronnie Simpson too was screaming from his goalmouth to 'get on with it', but Baxter was equally determined, as he put it, 'to extract the urine' from the opposition.

One commentator noted how when Baxter was indulging in this display, Nobby Stiles was nearby 'bobbing up and down trying to decide whether to tackle him at head or knee level'. In the 85th minute, Jack Charlton pulled one back for England before McCalliog notched a third two minutes later. Geoff Hurst scored a consolation second with his head shortly before the whistle blew for full time. Scotland were now world champions … according to some!

Alf Ramsey, at the end, shook Brown's hand and said in his own clipped way, 'Well done, you played very well today,' before disappearing up the tunnel. Brown reckoned that, inside, he was fuming after this defeat on his team's return to their scene of glory, and that to Scotland into the bargain. As is well documented, the Scottish fans celebrated wholeheartedly, a number spilling on to the pitch while some helped themselves to pieces of turf as souvenirs. They shouted repeatedly, 'We want Brown!' The centre spot in its entirety was removed, and many gardens in Scotland had their turf surprisingly supplemented the following week. The pitch invasion was good-natured, though understandably unwelcome from the authorities' point of view, and half an hour after full time mounted police had to clear it. Who can forget the famous photo of the two Scottish fans congratulating Baxter on the pitch, one of them with his arm in a headlock round the player's neck, unintentionally almost choking him, to his clear discomfort, as the fan's self-restraint succumbed to his euphoria? Interestingly, from today's perspective, both gents were in suit, collar and tie, although one would not readily regard either as being part of the establishment. A number of players had difficulty making their way to the safety of the dressing room through the exuberant fans. Some even tried to gain entry to the Scots' dressing room to celebrate with the team, but an alert Brown, commissionaire and police officer, prevented that.

Inside the dressing room, the atmosphere was electric. Brown was going round congratulating everyone and declaring, 'London belongs to you tonight, boys!' The players were ecstatic and high on cloud nine. Hugh Nelson of Arbroath, the chairman of the SFA international selection committee, and other Scottish officials came in to offer their congratulations. Denis Law shook Brown's hand warmly, saying, 'Congratulations boss, you've got off to a great start.' Speaking recently, Law commented, 'That was a fantastic win for us – to beat the world champions on their own patch was something else. It's a match that really stands out. I wanted to win so much, especially as I had been on the wrong end of the 9–3 score in '61. We should have scored more goals, but the supremely talented Jim Baxter started his "keepie-uppie" and taking the mickey. I was wanting to keep my great team-mate Bobby Charlton quiet after his World Cup win!'

Greig later wrote, 'It was a lifetime ambition of mine to play at Wembley so to go there as captain in 1967 and win the game as well was fantastic. Unofficially we were world champions and I think it's fair to say that's as close as Scotland will ever get!'

Brown, while delighted with the win, had one little pang of regret – that Scotland had not scored more goals. 'I felt we skinned them alive, we were so much on top. But instead of pushing ahead for more goals, Baxter, who controlled the play for us, slowed it down and wanted to make a fool of England. Bremner had the same attitude and he collaborated with him. It was hard to be angry with them given how they had played and the result we got, but still I thought it was an opportunity missed to have racked up a big score. I think we should have and could have scored five or six, given the pressure we had. In fairness, Banks did make two great saves late on from Law. Later I did confront Baxter about his antics but he just said, "Sorry boss, I wasn't trying to be cheeky!" That apart, I was really pleased that everyone did as they had been told.'

Alan Herron, veteran Scottish football journalist, was of a similar opinion: 'I thought we humiliated England, we completely dominated them. We should have scored more – I remember Bobby Brown being a bit perturbed after the game because of the way Baxter and Bremner mucked about at times, especially in the second half.'

They were nutmegging opponents and constantly teasing Alan Ball, the English midfielder, their man of the match in the World Cup Final. They would deliberately pass back and forward to each other, making him run from one to the other. They also wound him up by calling him the 'Clitheroe Kid', referring to a then well-known short, northern English comedian with a high-pitched, strongly accented voice, similar characteristics to Ball's. On other occasions one of them would walk casually away from the ball, as if going for a stroll, while the other would come to collect it, affecting an exaggerated ease in their play and underlining how England were struggling to deal with them.

While Brown acknowledged the excellence of Baxter's contribution generally, for him the Scottish man of the match was McCalliog. 'I thought McCalliog was, if you like, our unsung hero. He played a vital role in linking midfield with attack and scored an important goal. He carried out his instructions to the letter in a performance full of energy and guile, and was the perfect complement to Baxter and Bremner. A remarkable contribution when you consider it was his international debut and he was only 20, playing with and against all these well-established names. The other thing that helped us was that all the boys gelled very well together off the pitch. There were no cliques or prima donnas and the Old Firm players got on well.'

In McCalliog's opinion, Brown was due a lot of credit. 'Bobby Brown got his team selection absolutely right. I honestly thought the whole team played really well – everyone earned a minimum of an 8 out of 10 rating with some deserving even more. He was attentive, had a good way with the players and set out the right way for us to play. He gave me and others confidence with his approach. There were no big tactics talks, as was the case with most managers in those days, but once he made clear to us the framework we were to play in, it was up to us to use our football intelligence to make it work. One player whom I did not know really but who impressed me a lot was Willie Wallace. I thought he was very clever, particularly in his use of space to prompt attacks and also to combat English attacks. Although he was nominally a forward, he moved between midfield and attack, like me, and we would often cover for each other. We gave the English no chance to settle, and once we were in possession we did our utmost to keep it.'

Today, one could imagine such a momentous game being followed by a series of interviews with the players, but then the SFA rulebook did not permit them to 'comment on the match on television, radio or to the press after the game'. From Wembley they returned to their hotel to change before going to the banquet in the evening at the Café Royal in Regent Street, where they were to be joined by the English team. According to McCalliog, this was a welcome opportunity to socialise with the opposition, which was not normally possible in league football. His recollection was that both teams mixed well together, although Gemmell's was different. He later wrote that the English team sat sulking in a corner. Nobby Stiles thought Jim

Baxter was as entertaining there as he had been on the pitch that afternoon. Brown tried to engage Ramsey, telling him he had played against him during the war and after, but that elicited little reaction. As for the game, Ramsey only said to Brown that he had made a very good start. Although he was to meet the English manager several times more in the future, he never spoke once about the 1967 game. He thought the English manager generally courteous but 'hard to warm to. He didn't open out really, and it was as if it was costing him pounds each time he opened his mouth.'

Brown remembers at one stage of the evening going outside for a breath of fresh air. As he stood enjoying the evening breeze and reflecting on the day's events, he could see walking along towards him rather unsteadily, and singing loudly, a Scottish fan – tartan 'bunnet' askew – who had clearly been celebrating his team's success wholeheartedly. He made his way past the smartly dressed Brown with just a sideways glance at him and continued until he was about ten yards past, when he suddenly stopped, wheeled round and turned back. Stopping in front of him, he then proceeded to jab him in the chest with his forefinger while exclaiming loudly inches away from the national manager, 'See you, Scotland 3 England 2 – We beat you easily today, don't you ever forget it!', before continuing merrily on his way, much to Brown's amusement. During the evening, thousands of Scottish fans had taken over Piccadilly Circus, chanting, 'Sir Alf is on the dole!' and 'We all live in a tartan submarine, a tartan submarine!' and other less seemly ditties. Pieces of Wembley turf were on sale for ten shillings or a pound according to the size on offer.

Back inside, the party continued, with the Scottish team sticking together the whole evening. Some players recall meeting up at the Café Royal with fellow Scot Dave Mackay, the Spurs great who was not playing that day. He had appeared in a bar there with some family and friends from Edinburgh who had been at the match, and their table was covered with a large square of turf from Wembley, set like a tablecloth! The celebrations continued until late into the wee small hours at a number of parties after the Café Royal.

Back in Glasgow on the Monday, Brown attended the SFA offices for a debrief, after which he went out for lunch with some officials. When it was time to pay, the restaurant manager said to him, 'Mr Brown, you don't need to pay, this is on the house.' The feel-good factor in the wake of the result had certainly spread throughout the country, and Brown and his players were hailed as heroes.

Hugh Nelson made a statement to the press: 'Bobby Brown deserves the fullest recognition every Scot can give him – the Wembley win was his – he chose the team, he worked out the tactics, he put them over to the players. He kept us informed every step he took. I appreciated his courtesy phoning me to tell me his Wembley team the night before telling the press – he deserves all the credit he can get.'

The nation was definitely walking with an extra spring in its step. Brown recalls speaking to his father, a keen football fan, on his return. He told him that, on the day of the game, he had been so nervous about the outcome that he could not listen to it on the radio and instead had gone with Brown's mother to spend the afternoon in Callender, an attractive little town in Perthshire. They were walking along the riverside there, enjoying the peace and quiet, when suddenly, at about quarter to five in the afternoon, the calm of their surroundings was rudely shattered by a cacophony of car horns tooting loudly to signal the Scottish success – a sound that was music to his ears.

The tone of the English press after the game was for the most part in marked contrast to their pre-match comments.

Desmond Hackett wrote, 'The Scots command my highest praise for what they did to the World Cup winners. Remember history will only record a 3–2 win and that does not substantiate claims to have taken over the World Championship.'

Ken Jones: 'England were lucky to dodge a massacre. Scotland might have achieved the immortality of the Wembley Wizards … but they let England off the hook.'

Brian James: 'Tributes are due to Scotland; they were the better team and contained the more totally committed players. The truth is that in two years they have learned how to beat eight fit men whereas in 1965 they could only draw against nine[!].'

Peter Lorenzo: 'Let it be said firmly and fairly, Scotland thoroughly deserved their splendid triumph. But given eleven fit men I will stand unhesitatingly by the World Cup winners against Scotland and the cream of Europe.'

The latter two quotes clearly referred to Jack Charlton's injury, despite which he managed to score England's first goal. The reality was that the Scottish defence found him a handful up front and would have preferred to see him playing in his own position in defence. It is noteworthy that the Scots also suffered injuries. Gemmell was off the pitch receiving treatment when Law opened the scoring, and in the second half both Law and Lennox required treatment for injuries.

Ramsey himself was quoted as saying, 'I warned it would take a great team to beat us. Let's give them their due.'

The Italian sports paper *Stadio* stated, 'A well-deserved success; the Scots were much superior in midfield. We praise Scotland for their all-round strength. Individually and collectively this team shone brightly without any weaknesses.'

For Brown, this had been an unforgettable occasion, but he was keeping his feet on the ground. The match was also a qualifying game for the following year's European Nations'

Championship in Italy. With that in mind, he said, 'We didn't do any lap of honour because we're only halfway to our goal of qualifying for Europe. We should have had five or six goals. Every single player did his bit and a lot of the team's confidence was down to Baxter and Law. Without doubt it was the best managerial debut I could have been given.' Although in public he sought to keep the lid on fans' optimism, privately he was both relieved and delighted at the outcome of his first international in charge.

Although he was not to know it at the time, this was to be the one and only time he was able to field that eleven, because of injuries and call-offs – something that later would become a matter of particular regret.

Chapter 2

Early Days and Queen's Park

BROWN was born on 19 March 1923, at 30 Anderson Drive in the small village of Dunipace, which sits on the River Carron, about six miles south of Stirling and five miles north-west of Falkirk. Four years later, his younger sister, Agnes, known as Nan, now 89, was born. Their parents were James and Georgina, both of whose family roots were in farming in the area, the father's near Balfron, Stirlingshire. Shortly after Brown's birth, the family moved to live at 281 Stirling Street in Dunipace.

Coincidentally, Billy Steel, one of the most famous names in post-war Scottish football, was born six weeks later on 1 May, immediately next door to Brown in Anderson Drive. As well as being next door neighbours, they played together for Scotland, Steel winning 30 caps in total. His transfer fee of £15,500 from Morton to Derby County was a British record, while his £22,500 fee from Derby to Dundee was a Scottish record. They were pupils together in Miss Sproul's class at Dunipace Primary

School before the Browns left the village. Dunipace, previously known as the Milltown of Dunipace, adjoined the larger village of Denny on the other side of the river, and almost 50 years before Brown's birth the two came together to form a single burgh. There had been a village in medieval times at the foot of the Hills of Dunipace, and it was claimed that Sir William Wallace (of Braveheart fame) had been a frequent visitor there as his uncle was the local priest. Agriculture initially predominated, but industrialisation gradually changed the landscape.

When he was aged about six, Brown's family moved to Torwood, which was then a small hamlet several miles to the north. Both sets of Brown's grandparents lived there, and, as his mother was anxious to be near her own mother, the family made the move. Torwood was situated in the middle of open countryside a short distance off the main Denny-to-Stirling road. Within a radius of about ten miles there were foundries, coal mines and the famous Carron ironworks. The hamlet then had a population of only about 40 people and consisted of a number of scattered houses and three streets, with the partially ruined Torwood Castle half a mile to the south. It was a very quiet place and boasted little by way of amenities. The nearby main road had a small garage, and near there was a nursery where tomatoes and various types of plants were grown and sold. On the far side of the hamlet was a working sawmill that employed about ten men. For the children there was a small 'sweetie shop' that only opened at weekends, but in terms of facilities Torwood was fairly basic – there was no public house, community centre, football pitch, general shop or church, although there was a small village school. Brown's parents attended church, especially on communion Sundays, at Plean, two miles away. Villagers had to go to Stirling or Denny for shopping and other purposes, which usually entailed a bus trip. Cars were scarce at this time, although Brown recalls his uncle Alex from Leith in Edinburgh visiting occasionally in his 'big Rover'. The hamlet was on the site of an ancient settlement, an old Roman road ran nearby, and before the Battle of Bannockburn a section of Robert the Bruce's army camped here. The Browns lived in the last house in the village, about half a mile from the main road – a small cottage with an outside toilet, typical of the time. It had a large garden, which father James enjoyed tending and where he grew a lot of vegetables.

James had worked in the Plean coal mine as a young man, but after one of his brothers suffered a serious injury in an accident there he decided that mining was not for him. Instead he became an engineer at Bonnybridge Power Station, near Falkirk, which had been built in 1905 and continued to function as part of the Electricity Board until 1973, when it was demolished. During the 45 years he was employed at the power station, he only missed one half-day's work, something of which he was understandably proud. He cycled there and back every day, an eight-mile round trip. On his retirement, he was presented with a beautiful gold watch and chain, which was unfortunately stolen during a break-in to Bobby Brown's house some years ago. Mother Georgina, before she married, worked 'in service' as a housekeeper in large houses in the area, including one owned by the chairman of Nelson's the Edinburgh publishers, now part of HarperCollins. Once married, she became a full-time housewife.

Brown first attended Torwood Primary School, a single-teacher institution with about a dozen pupils whose ages ranged from five to 11. It was a typical small single-classroom country school of the period, with old-fashioned individual desks, each with its own inkwell and slate and chalk. His teacher, Miss Miller, is fondly remembered by him, although she was quite a firm disciplinarian and did administer the occasional clip on the hand with a ruler if his writing was not up to standard, admonishing him as she did so – 'Watch your writing, boy' – as he recalled. There was an open field behind the school where Brown and others kicked a ball about during break times. These early schooldays were essentially happy, and he enjoyed his upbringing in this close community. In common with many families during this difficult period of economic depression, money was not plentiful for the Browns, but they were more fortunate than some and always enjoyed the essentials of daily living. The countryside was on Brown's doorstep and ripe for exploration with friends, providing a natural playground. One of their favourite activities was to walk up the nearby Glen Burn for about half a mile, to where there was a shelf that impeded the trout going further upstream, and in the large pool there they could 'guddle' for them, i.e. feel for and then catch them with their hands underneath the stones. In the long summer days, he remembered roaming the countryside in bare feet and cousins coming to stay with his grandparents.

His father was a keen football fan and supported Falkirk, whose home games at the old Brockville ground he regularly attended. The young Brown would sometimes accompany him – he found this very exciting and began to take an interest in the sport. Slowly, the football bug was beginning to bite. Although the Torwood school was too small to have a team, he did acquire an old, irregularly shaped ball that his father used to mend from time to time, and which he used to practise with regularly by kicking it against an old farmstead wall and catching it on the rebound. In this way he learned the basics of catching and handling the ball, essential for a goalkeeper, although at this stage he had not thought about playing in that position.

It was by chance that his goalkeeping career began. In Torwood's long summer evenings, once the local men had returned home from their work at the various industrial sites in the area and had their evening meal, they would walk to nearby villages to play impromptu games of football. Brown recalled, 'The men would walk to the likes of North Bromage, about a mile away, or Plean, about two miles away, and have an informal "challenge" game against the men from these villages. Sometimes games took place in Torwood in the field behind the school. I was maybe about 11 or so when I started going with them, and I thought this was just great. There were no pitches as such, just grassy areas where the jackets were put down for goals. None of the men wanted to play in goals and they would say, "Put wee Bobby in!" I was quite short at that time – and so in I would go. I enjoyed it, and that's really how my goalkeeping started. I remember there used to be some tremendous arguments about whether or not a goal had been scored, because of course there were no goalposts or referees! The games would go on for what seemed like ages, but it was great fun being among the men and playing football with them.'

Once Brown had left Torwood Primary School, he attended Larbert Village School for two years until he was aged 14. This was about two miles from Torwood, and Brown travelled there by bus. Larbert was where he had his first taste of organised football under teacher Mr Campbell, who ran the school team. Brown played in goals from the start and would continue in that position for the rest of his football career. Games on Saturday mornings were keenly contested against other local schools such as Grangemouth Dundas and Carronshore, and attracted much local interest. The high point of his time in Larbert was winning the local schools' cup for their under-14 age group. He then attended Larbert Central School for a year.

Brown had also become a member of the local Falkirk and District Boy Scouts troop, which he attended on Friday nights. They met in the Scout Hall, near the Glenbervie golf course, on the way to Larbert, and Brown used to run the four miles there and back as a form of training. The Scoutmaster was Sir Ian Bolton, who lived in a large country mansion nearby, West Plean House. An inspiring figure for Brown and others, he had been seriously injured in the First World War, as a result of which he was disabled and required the use of crutches. He was decorated with the OBE for his contribution to the intelligence services during the Second World War and enjoyed a successful business career. A highly regarded figure in the community, he was a first-class Scoutmaster who instilled good values in the boys. Brown's sister, Nan, recalled he thought highly of her brother and in 1945, at the end of the war, went to Larbert railway station himself to collect Brown in his large car to take him home to Torwood.

Brown was a patrol leader of the Hawks and took part in the usual scouting activities such as map reading, tracking, learning first aid, camping, outdoor survival, signals and message sending, and cooking, as well as taking badges in sports such as athletics. They also occasionally fielded a football team, for whom Brown played in goals. He thoroughly enjoyed his time in the Scouts, particularly the annual camp. On Sir Ian Bolton's death, he bequeathed part of his Barrwood Estate to the Scouts for their use.

By now Brown was being taken by his father to watch games involving juvenile and junior teams such as Plean Juniors, Falkirk Violet, Shieldhill Thistle and Raploch Hearts, all based in surrounding communities. On these occasions, amid what he recalled as 'fans' vitriolic criticism of refereeing decisions', he would watch closely how the goalkeepers played, to try to learn as much as he could about technique. He did the same on his visits to Brockville and the Forthbank ground in Stirling, then the home of a Second Division team, King's Park. There he would stand behind the home goal and speak to keeper 'Pinky' Muir at moments during the game, asking him questions, and, as Brown recollects, 'I was in awe, just in awe, and began to fancy myself as a keeper.' King's Park folded just after the war, to be replaced by Stirling Albion, whose own Forthbank stadium is about half a mile from the site of the original, which was largely destroyed in a Luftwaffe attack.

While his enthusiasm for football was growing and his talent as a goalkeeper emerging, his parents were careful to instil in him and his sister the importance of a good education. They did everything to encourage them in this regard, and Brown remembers his father in particular always ensuring there was a fire on in the house on Sundays to facilitate their studying. At that time in Scotland, when pupils reached their early teens, they sat what was known as the 'Qualifying' examination to determine whether they would then pass on to a junior secondary school or a senior one, the latter offering a higher standard of education and the opportunity to sit leaving examinations known as 'Highers'. Brown passed his 'Qualifying' and as a result progressed to the senior secondary, Falkirk High School. His sister, Nan, benefitted too from parental encouragement in education, following in her brother's footsteps to Larbert Central School and then Falkirk High. After that she studied at Glasgow University, graduating with an MA degree, before going to Moray House Teacher Training College, Edinburgh, and qualifying as a teacher. As money was tight then, she had to make sacrifices, and Brown recalls she sometimes went without lunch to be able to buy books she needed. To arrive in Glasgow for her 9am lectures meant an early rise, a bus trip from Torwood to Larbert for the Glasgow train, and once there a tram to university.

His time at the High School was to have a lasting influence on his future football career, as it was there he came under the wing of his PE teacher, Hugh Brown, father of Craig, one of Brown's successors as national team manager. Hugh Brown played for Partick Thistle at one stage and during the war was an RAF wing commander in charge of physical education for the Force based at Cosford, Wolverhampton. Some years after the war he would become principal of the Scottish School of Physical Education at Jordanhill College, Glasgow. At Falkirk High School, where football was considered an important part of the curriculum and encouraged by the headmaster, he was in charge of the school team. Bobby Brown remembered, on his first day there, being taken along with other new boys to meet their PE teacher and being earnestly asked if any played football. He was instantly impressed by Hugh Brown's obvious passion for the game, and his ability to encourage and communicate. Soon he was in the school team, after having to perform the delicate task of replacing the incumbent goalkeeper, Jimmy Hogg, son of the headmaster!

Through his PE teacher, Bobby Brown learned the importance of discipline, good habits and building team spirit. Hugh Brown ran the school team almost along professional lines. He insisted on boys having highly polished boots and spotlessly clean strips, for which they were responsible. Bobby Brown's boots were 'Hotspurs', which when new were rigid and needed to be softened up in hot water before use. The squad, but not the team, for the Saturday morning game was announced on the Friday, when the boys would assemble in the school gymnasium to listen to Brown's instructions. When they appeared in the dressing room for Saturday's game, the team was announced and strips were hung up on individual pegs before Brown's final pre-match talk. Everything was done in meticulously organised fashion, to emphasise to the boys the importance of the game and their importance to the team. In many ways, his approach mirrored what Bobby Brown would experience in the future at Rangers under iconic manager Bill Struth. The team spirit that Hugh Brown inculcated meant they gave him maximum effort, and Bobby Brown can remember how he could tell by Brown's gait as he moved up and down the touchline during games if he was content or not with the team's play.

The team was winning its games quite easily against local opposition such as Falkirk Technical School and St Modan's High School. To increase the level of competition and improve standards, Hugh Brown applied successfully for Falkirk High to join the Glasgow and District League, where games would be more competitive against schools such as St Aloysius Academy, St Mungo's Academy, Queen's Park Secondary and Our Lady's High School, Motherwell, which were among the country's leading teams. There was a lot of interest then in these schools' fixtures, which would attract sizeable crowds. Bobby Brown responded well to this step up and his game continued to improve, aided and encouraged by Hugh Brown's post-match one-to-one analysis sessions with him about how he had played.

This led to selection as goalkeeper for the Falkirk and District Schools team, which played in the Scottish Schools Cup. Others in that team who would go on to have successful careers in professional football included George Young, future captain of Rangers and Scotland and one time cap record holder, of Grangemouth Dundas; David Lapsley, from Bainsford, by Falkirk, who would captain St Mirren to Scottish Cup success in 1959 and represent the Scottish league; and Eddie Turnbull of Carronshore School, a future star of the great Hibs team of the 1950s and member of their 'Famous Five', Scottish international and highly acclaimed manager of Aberdeen and Hibs.

Six teachers from the area picked the team, which reached the final, where they played Lanark and District Schools. The away leg was drawn, but the Falkirk team convincingly won their home leg 5–0 at Firs Park, home then to East Stirlingshire, in front of an impressive crowd of over 5,000.

Brown reflected, 'That was a great occasion when we won that Scottish Cup. We had a great team and all the boys got on well. Through it I made lifelong friendships with George Young, whom of course I played with later at Rangers, and Eddie Turnbull. Young would sometimes have a good-natured dig at me about my style of play, but I knew how to deal with him, as an aunt of mine had taught him at school and let's just say George had more talent on the pitch than in the classroom! Long after our playing days were over and I had finished with football, if I was in Edinburgh on business I would sometimes take the then wheelchair-bound George to meet up with Eddie, and sometimes Lawrie Reilly, and enjoy a reminisce. On the run to that Schools' Cup Final, we played Markinch Schools in an earlier round, during which their centre-forward and I collided. As was usual then, there were nails in his studs and when we came into contact my hands were cut. Every time after that when I met Eddie, even latterly, he would always ask me, "How's your hands Bobby?"!'

In the background, as Brown was becoming known for his goalkeeping prowess, his father was quietly encouraging and they enjoyed a close bond. Although not a particularly demonstrative individual, he was keen for Bobby to develop his talents to the maximum, but not to do so at the expense of his education; he therefore applied himself academically too, with reasonable success. A keen outdoors man, James was an enthusiastic cyclist and walker. He was a member of the Stirlingshire Roads and West of Scotland Clarion cycling clubs; and he, two of his brothers, Dan and Joe, and others, would meet every Sunday at the Drip Road, Stirling to go off on a 25- or 50-mile run. Joe was successful at district level, winning several medals in road racing. James also started to go out cycling with his son, who recalled buying his first bicycle for £6 7s 6d, now around £6.35, in instalments from the Coop store in Falkirk. Keen for Bobby to learn about Scotland and its stunning scenery, during school holidays he took him cycling all over, as far as John O'Groats in the extreme north and, among other places, to Glenshee, Braemar, Deeside and his own particular favourite, the imposingly captivating Glencoe. They would also go walking during these excursions, and, at night, depending on their whereabouts, they would either camp or stay in youth hostels, which cost 6d per night, just over 2p. One summer, when aged about 16, Bobby and a school chum, Adam Veitch, who also played in the school football team, went touring together in the West Highlands on a tandem that they were given by one of Bobby's uncles. Adam, a retired chartered accountant and still a close friend, recalled, 'We had great fun on that trip. Neither of us had used a tandem before, but we got into it quite easily. We had a Primus stove with us and used to stop by the side of the road for a "drum up", a cup of tea. I remember another holiday when Bobby and I and some classmates spent a week at a forestry camp doing voluntary service at Achaglachgach at West Loch Tarbert, where we were given scythes and put to work! These were great days.' In his final year at school, Bobby took a holiday job at an outdoor centre in the Cairngorms as an instructor on hillcraft, map reading and related activities. These experiences imbued Bobby with an everlasting love of the outdoors, which has continued to the present.

During another summer holiday when aged about 17, Brown worked for several weeks in the local sawmill. His main job was to take a horse and cart into the woods just outside Torwood, where the woodcutters were working, to load it up with the cut tree trunks and convey them back to the sawmill for fashioning into pit props and other uses. This entailed his going early in the morning to the sawmill to feed the horse, then harnessing it up to the cart, on which he would then sit to guide it through the woods. He usually did two of these trips every day while helping out with other tasks in the sawmill. At the end of the day, he was responsible for feeding and watering the horse and getting it ready to be stabled for the evening. Brown recalled, 'That was a great life – I really loved that job.'

* * * * *

On the football pitch, meanwhile, Brown's goalkeeping skills were attracting wider attention, resulting in his being selected for the Rest of Scotland Schools in their annual match against Glasgow Schools for three years in succession, a notable achievement. In 1940, his school team won all their matches in their section of the Glasgow District League, earning promotion to the top tier, another impressive feat and testimony to Hugh Brown's coaching expertise. The following year, they went one better, winning the League Shield, the overall league title. The proceeds of the Rest of Scotland's 1940 match were allocated to the Stirlingshire War Relief Fund, and a press report of the game, which the Rest won 3–0, stated, 'Outstanding among the Rest was Brown, the Falkirk High goalkeeper. He had a complete understanding with his full-backs Muir and Robertson from the same school.' In the next year's game, Brown was reported to have put on 'a splendid display. He was a "life-saver" on many occasions and is a lad well worth watching.'

As a result of the press attention he was beginning to attract, the young Bobby began collecting cuttings for his scrapbook, a habit he maintained throughout his football career.

By now, Brown was invited occasionally to train with his local club, Falkirk, whose manager, ex-Ranger Tully Craig, showed interest in signing him. Although the idea of a career in football appealed, Brown at this stage was reluctant to commit himself to Falkirk. He also entertained the idea of wanting to play for Queen's Park, where, it being an amateur club, he thought he might be given more opportunity to progress. In his final year at school, he discussed with his father what he might do on leaving. When he suggested he might like to become a PE teacher, his father responded, 'But you won't be able to get up the wall bars when you're 60!' His father went on to propose that he join the police force, adding there was a good pension to consider. And he also, only half in jest, mentioned becoming a minister as a possibility, remarking that 'they only work one day a week!' Influenced by his mentor, Hugh Brown, Bobby began thinking more and more about the idea of doing a PE course.

On the morning of Saturday 13 April 1940, just over three weeks after Brown's 17th birthday, he was playing for his school at their ground, Bleachfield, against St Aloysius in a Glasgow Schools League match. He recalled it was a lovely spring morning and Falkirk won 3–1, the opposition goal being scored by Jimmy Farrell, later a well-known Glasgow lawyer and Celtic director. At the end of the game, two men he did not know ran on to the pitch and announced to him that he was required to play that afternoon for Queen's Park at Parkhead against Celtic in a league match.

This came as a 'bolt from the blue', without any prior warning, and would be a momentous event in his life, as it essentially flagged up the starting point of his senior football career. After further discussions with the gentlemen and Hugh Brown, it was confirmed they were indeed representatives of Queen's Park, who desperately needed a keeper due to their problem filling this position. Their main custodian over the preceding seasons, Mustafa Mansour, an Egyptian student at Jordanhill PE College, had returned to his native Egypt after the outbreak of war. A flamboyant player, he made his debut against Hearts in April 1937 and was their principal keeper thereafter. Interestingly, his predecessor was Desmond White, later better known as Celtic chairman. Another keeper, Gordon

Hamilton, from Greenock, who had played occasionally for the first team, was a lieutenant in the Territorial Army and had been called up for war service. No other keeper was available. Brown did not have much time to consider the request, but readily agreed. In a state of considerable excitement and shock, he was driven by car to Hampden Park, where he met his team-mates for the first time, signed his registration forms for Queen's and thereafter went with them by coach to Celtic's ground at Parkhead.

Although Queen's Park now play in Scotland's lowest league in front of several hundred fans, at this time – despite being an amateur club – they were considered a force in the land. The oldest club in the country, founded in 1867 and remaining amateur throughout their existence, they have enjoyed a long and distinguished history. In the early days of the game in Scotland, they were the country's pre-eminent club and regularly provided the backbone of the national team. They were instrumental in establishing the Scottish Cup, and through that, the game's governing body, the Scottish Football Association. In the first 20 years of the Scottish Cup they won it ten times, and they also participated with distinction in the FA Cup several times, twice reaching the final in the 1880s. In addition, they played an important role in the development of the game and its rules, and helped promote the first international between Scotland and England in 1872. They built and owned Hampden Park, the national stadium – once holder of the world's record crowd, as has been noted – and played their home games there. In 1898, they undertook their first foreign tour to Denmark in evangelical spirit to spread the football gospel.

By April 1940, they were no longer at the summit of the national game but were still a highly respected team. In every season in the decade prior to the outbreak of war, they were members of the old First Division, playing to the seventh highest average crowds in the country. Only ten years previously, a crowd in excess of 95,000 had trooped into Hampden to watch an early-round Scottish Cup tie between them and Rangers.

On his debut for Queen's, his first game of senior football, Brown's team-mates were, in 2–3–5 formation: D. Clyne, H. Dickson; A. Cross, R. Cross, W. Buchanan; J. Gray, A. Aitken, A. Sleigh, W. Browning, W. Wright.

He recalled, 'To say I was nervous is an understatement. In the Parkhead dressing room, the Queen's trainer, Bert Manderson, a former Rangers full-back and Irish international, told me just to play my "normal" game! Easier said than done when you run out in front of thousands of opposition fans, having just met my team-mates for the first time and having left my schoolmates a little earlier – it was quite an experience. This was the Celtic team that two years previously had won the Empire Exhibition Cup by beating Everton in the final. And I couldn't have got off to a worse start. Within a couple of minutes, Celtic right-winger Frank Murphy swung over a high, curling cross towards my far post. As I went to collect it, the next thing I knew was I found myself in the back of the net clutching the ball, and Celtic's John Divers on top of me saying, "I know yir just a boy, son, but you dinna' catch these ones, you punch them o'er the bar."'

In those days the goalkeeper did not receive the protection he does now, and a shoulder charge into the net with ball in hand was legitimate. John Divers was the father of the player of the same name who enjoyed a successful career with Celtic in the 1950s and early 1960s. After that rude introduction, Brown settled down and in the circumstances had a decent game, which ended in a 4–4 draw. Bobby Cross scored two of the Queen's goals, with one each coming from Andy Aitken and Andrew Sleigh. Celtic's marksmen were Divers, Murphy, Kelly and Lynch. Queen's were pleased with his debut and told him to submit his expenses claim, for which he recalls receiving 4s 11d, i.e. 25 pence!

Afterwards he went with the Queen's party for the post-match meal before returning to Torwood. There he recalls 'Wee Bobby', as he was still affectionately called, receiving a warm welcome from friends and neighbours, which, together with his own pride at the day's events, made him 'feel like a king'. He was delighted to have made his senior debut, and for the remainder of the season he turned out for his school on Saturday mornings and Queen's in the afternoons. By then he had played another seven league games – against Motherwell, Rangers, Airdrieonians, Morton, Hamilton Accies, Albion Rovers and Kilmarnock – as well as a Merchants Charity Cup tie against Clyde. Despite the abrupt nature of his introduction to the senior game, Brown had coped well, had adapted to it, had impressed with his form and was enthusiastic about playing for Queen's, where he had bought in to the club ethos.

Apart from the league side, the club ran three other teams: the Strollers, the Hampden XI and the Victoria XI. After games on a Saturday, all the players and officials would come together for a 'Scotch high tea', an early-evening supper often consisting of fish and chips, tea and cakes. They met in Reid's Tearoom in Gordon Street, central Glasgow. The officials and committee who ran the club sat at a type of top table, with the players in front of them. The president, Willie King in Brown's initial season there, would always say a few words on the team's performance in that day's league game, and there would be brief contributions on the minor teams' games. General chat about the day's games would then ensue. There was a strong sense of togetherness and tradition about the club, which Brown found very appealing. They were well supported, attracting average crowds of about 10,000. When Queen's attacked, the fans in the stand would encourage them by stamping their feet on the wooden floor and shouting 'Queen's, Queen's!' It was a happy environment in which to play, especially for a relatively inexperienced youngster, as Brown then was. He received good support from his more experienced team-mates, a number of whom were professional men. These included Herbert Dickson, David Clyne, Wally Wright, Joe Kyle, Willie 'Buff' Browning, brothers Alex and Bobby Cross, and Andy Aitken.

Dickson was a full-back who had been with the club for about ten seasons. According to Brown, 'He had a great left foot and kicked everything above grass level! He was what you might call vociferous! But he gave me a lot of good advice. In one early game, I remember losing a goal at my near post and him pointing out to me I should never lose a goal there, something I never forgot.' Clyne was a fine right-back who had been a member of the league side for two years. Sadly, in 1944, he was killed while on service with the RAF. Wright, from Clydebank, was a gifted forward full of artistry. Joe Kyle was an exciting centre-forward with a cannonball shot, who had played for Great Britain in the 1936 Berlin Olympics and would later become a noted amateur golfer. He had been with Queen's for seven years. Bobby Cross, a doctor like his brother Alex, was a half-back with five years' experience of first-team football, while Alex was a midfielder with two years in the first team. Browning was a talented left-sided attacker who had played with the club for seven years. Aitken was an inside-forward who had been in the first team since the start of that 1939/40 season. And one of the ballboys was a young Ronnie Simpson, later of course capped by Brown at Wembley in 1967.

At school, the dashing, blond-haired Brown was a standout figure popular with everyone, and his final year had been a very successful one. Not only had he excelled between the posts, but he also held the prestigious position of school captain and did well academically, securing four 'higher' and one 'lower' examination passes. His 'highers' were in Mathematics, English, French and Art, while his 'lower' was in Geography. On top of that, he was school sports champion, winning the 100 yards, the 220, the half-mile and the high jump, and was a member of the winning five-a-side team. On all fronts, everything had gone as well for him as he could have hoped. In a feature on him in the local press, he was quoted as saying, 'I've had three very happy years at Falkirk High. Mr H. Brown the sports master became one of my best friends and his coaching was instrumental in my gaining the honours I have done. The school football team is the very best I'll ever play with and I loved playing for it.' These comments demonstrated the depth of the affection Brown had for the school and its football team, which he considered the catalyst of his career in the game. It was also an appropriate and heartfelt tribute to the invaluable input of his mentor, Hugh Brown, to whom he was very close and who later would be best man at Brown's wedding.

Despite his father's reservations about PE teaching, Brown still remained keen on pursuing it. He loved his football, and was an all-round sports fan and an outdoors enthusiast. Having secured his examination passes, he applied for a place to study physical education at Jordanhill College in Glasgow, beginning in September 1941. Thanks to Hugh Brown's excellent reference, he was admitted, although the total number of applications had exceeded the number of places available.

Chapter 3

Jordanhill College and War; International Debut

WHEN Brown began his studies at Jordanhill, the war had been under way for almost two years. Due to wartime restrictions such as blackouts and rationing, day-to-day living was very different. The country had lived on a knife edge through the Battle of Britain, as it brought its daily dose of casualties and devastation. Throughout there had been considerable fear and anxiety over a possible German invasion, and daily radio news bulletins and newspaper reports on the progress of hostilities were followed with apprehension. Everyone had friends and family members who had enlisted in the forces. Communities were deeply conscious of the absence of the many young men and women on active duty. Significant casualties had already been sustained, and an uncertain future faced all involved in the war effort. Munitions factories were desperate for workers to help increase their vital output, and

'Dig for Victory' appeals were to be seen everywhere urging people to make the most of their land by changing its use to food production. In brief, the atmosphere in the country in September 1941 was much changed from two years previously.

At the same time, the government had considered it necessary, in the interests of national morale, for civilian life to continue as normally as was possible in the circumstances. While it was initially thought all football might be suspended during wartime, it was soon realised that the sport had a positive role to play in providing public entertainment. To accommodate wartime conditions, the league was reorganised into regional divisions to minimise travel, and the Scottish Cup was suspended for the duration. Several high-profile players joined the forces and were considered excellent role models, doing 'their bit for King and country'. As part of their duties, they often took part in special representative games, to entertain people at home and troops overseas and to raise funds for the war effort. Of necessity, a limit was put on the size of attendances at games, taking into account the potential danger from air raids. At Hampden Park, this was initially set at 15,000, but was later increased to 50,000 to cater for representative and derby matches.

In the case of Queen's Park, wartime difficulties in keeping a club afloat were exacerbated by their financial predicament, as they had taken out a sizeable loan from the SFA in 1937 to finance ground refurbishment. More generous repayment terms were renegotiated, and, with the spectre of having the ground closed during hostilities lifted, the club was able to continue in action, albeit with difficulty.

Brown combined his PE studies with playing for Queen's, taking up where he had left off at the end of the previous season when still a schoolboy. He was enthusiastic about his course and integrated well with his 20 or so classmates from all over Scotland, none of whom he previously knew. Jordanhill had been established in 1931 as the national college for training PE teachers, and the principal when Brown joined was Mr Frank Punchard, whose main interest was gymnastics. Brown's daily routine involved travel to and from his home at Torwood. This called for an early rise and a bus to Larbert train station, a train to Buchanan Street station in Glasgow, and from there a tram to Jordanhill in the city's west end.

The day's activities were varied, beginning with the students changing into their tracksuits and doing an hour's general gym work. This was followed by lectures on various subjects, including the theory of exercise and recreation; the mechanics of human movement, health and hygiene; on the rules of different sports and teaching methods; and – at the John Anderson College of Medicine – on anatomy and physiology. Alongside the academic work, there was also practical work in gymnastics and in the swimming pool, and participation in a number of sports, along with mock teaching practice. Brown and his classmates also took part regularly in Scottish country dancing practice, without the benefit of lady partners, taken by a well-known teacher, Miss Milligan, who always prefaced her instructions to the class by announcing, 'Now, gentlemen …'. In free time, Brown often practised his goalkeeping skills on the football pitch, with fellow students shooting in against him. Thanks to this regular physical activity, Brown achieved and maintained a good level of core fitness – there was little opportunity to train with Queen's due to wartime conditions. And in the evenings he did the journey in reverse, arriving back at Torwood at about 7pm. The routine was tiring, but one on which he thrived.

His first appearance in the previous 1940/41 season, in his final school year, had been on 10 August against Hibs at Easter Road, a 3–2 win for the Edinburgh side. Five weeks later, he played in front of 20,000 against Celtic at Hampden. After that, he was an ever-present until the 21 December home match against Falkirk, a 3–1 loss. At this point, he was the subject of some criticism, suggesting that he was 'too frail and immature' for this level of senior football. That followed a particularly poor November for Queen's, when they shipped five goals in each of five consecutive matches. However, after the first of those, a 5–0 humbling by Rangers, a press report stated, 'The conditions were atrocious. Alex Venters scored an outstanding goal for Rangers, almost beating the entire Queen's team before walking the ball into the net. Brown I believe is still at school but in this game he kept goal more like a master than a pupil.'

Earlier matches also attracted favourable press comment, for example against Hearts ('Queen's have a grand keeper in Brown') and against Hamilton Accies, a 3–1 reverse ('Bobby Brown was mainly responsible for keeping the score down, he pulled off many fine saves.').

For reasons Brown is unable to recall, he did not feature in the league side from 21 December until the last league game of the season, against Hearts on 3 May. It may have been that his form shaded a little, a reaction to having been subjected to too much top-level football too soon, and the difficulty of combining schools football with the senior game. At Hampden, Brown received no formal coaching as such, just some pointers here and there from senior players and occasionally Bert Manderson. Specialised goalkeeping coaches were years ahead then.

It had been a difficult time for Queen's, who had lost players to war service and only won a few of their fixtures. Although this represented a steep learning curve for Brown, adapting from schools football to playing regularly in front of big crowds against Rangers, Celtic, Hearts and Hibs, he had gained tremendous experience and his appetite was whetted for more.

His opening game of the 1941/42 season was against St Mirren in a 2–1 home defeat, after which he played every match until a League Cup tie against Celtic on 28 February. Brown continued to receive good reviews. After a match against Celtic, it was rather colourfully reported, 'Young Brown is coming on like an oil tank on fire.' And, after a Rangers game, he was credited with 'great goalkeeping. Brown's anticipation, daring, and coolness not only created a confidence throughout the defence but proved he has made such improvement as to be rated among the very best in the country.' While football was going well, Brown's thoughts were turning towards the war.

During the Celtic League Cup tie, he sustained a fractured wrist when it struck the bar as he saved a goalbound shot from Johnny Crum. This led to his being out of action for six months, making his comeback against Partick Thistle in a Glasgow Cup tie in August. A few more games followed before what would be his last game for the Spiders for some time, against Dumbarton on 31 October 1942.

Brown and his friends at college had been aware for a while that many of their contemporaries had already enlisted, and there was a growing feeling among them that they should also do so. After discussing it among themselves, Brown and several others decided to leave Jordanhill together to enlist in the Fleet Air Arm. They did so on 2 November 1942, Brown becoming the 29th Queen's player to join up. However, given the continuing importance of football to public morale at this time, Brown was given frequent leave most weekends after his induction period, to travel to Glasgow to play for Queen's and return south afterwards.

The Fleet Air Arm was responsible for the operation of naval aircraft and had been created in 1924, initially as a unit of the RAF before becoming subject to the jurisdiction of the Admiralty in 1939. Brown and his colleagues went to Dartmouth Royal Naval College, in the town of the same name in Devon – the Royal Navy's officer training college, first established in 1863. There they began the training they hoped would result in their qualifying as naval pilots in due course. The college was a long, imposing building, with an impressively symmetrical front elevation and central clock tower, sitting on a high position overlooking the town of Dartmouth and its attractive bay below. Suitably apprehensive on arrival, Brown soon realised his mindset was understandable.

'I can tell you it was very much a rude awakening we had. There were petty officers shouting at you all over the place, do this, do that! It seemed we were doing drill constantly and the discipline was very strict. Kitbags had to be kept in good order and locked all the time. Our hair was cut extremely short, down to the wood you might say. We were kitted out in naval uniform, with a white band round our hats signifying our rank as naval airmen class 2. There were about 30 or 40 of us together. One of the first things they did with us was to take us to the swimming pool and order us up to the highest diving board, from where we had to jump in about 20 feet to the water below. Some guys couldn't even swim, and once they started thrashing about the officers would pull them out with long poles. We were given lots of physical training, including cross-country runs, and some mornings we were woken up at five o'clock to go out on the quarterdeck, where a PTI put us through a half-hour exercise session. We were monitored over a month. This was part of an induction process really, to help determine who was considered fit to progress to Elementary Flying Training School at RAF Sealand near Chester. Some guys simply were not up to it or fell foul of the strict discipline and were not selected for flying training. They would go on to serve as ordinary seamen. On the plus side, the food was good and the guys from Jordanhill stuck together well.'

Brown and colleagues completed the induction successfully, which meant they were transferred to HMS *St Vincent*, a land base at Gosport across the bay from Portsmouth. There, for several weeks, they studied navigation and the theory of flying, and received instruction on flying Tiger Moths, the biplanes on which they would learn in the next stage of their training. Again, Brown and friends completed this part successfully and moved to RAF Sealand for the 'hands-on' flying training.

Tiger Moths were used as the trainer aircraft for this purpose. This initially involved flying with an instructor seated behind the trainee pilot, with the two in radio contact and dual controls available to the instructor. Although Brown had never flown before, he recollected 'not having any qualms' about his maiden flight. He understood what he had to do and was confident in his instructor, who 'was regularly bawling out instructions into my ear'.

With the benefit of the theoretical input and the practical instruction, he found the take-off reasonably straightforward, initially going up to 500 feet before going higher to 1,000 feet. Learning to fly straight and level was another important skill. Landing could be complicated, requiring good judgement of approach speed vis-a vis proximity to the ground, to avoid spinning or stalling or, if too fast, bumping off the ground and having to go up again. After about 15 hours of practice, Brown had completed take-offs against the wind, steep turns while airborne, awkward landings, gliding and cutting, and restarting the engine.

Next he had to perform his first 'solo' flight, without the instructor, which consisted of completing two circuits of the airport at 1,000 feet before making a satisfactory landing. Once he had done that, he undertook flights to destinations such as Wolverhampton and back, accompanied by his instructor, who, if he was satisfied with his performance, arranged for a senior officer to accompany the trainee on one of these flights. If he in turn considered that satisfactory, the next stage was to complete a triangular cross-country flight. Brown had progressed with his instructor to doing cross-country flights twice from Sealand via Bolesworth Castle to Northwich and back to Sealand, each about an hour long. He was next required to do the trip a third time, but on this occasion on his own.

This solo effort did not go so smoothly. He flew into a cloud on his way back and became disorientated. As he had been trained to do, he lowered the nose of the Tiger Moth and emerged from the cloud, still unsure of where he was. He saw a train on the railway below and remembered his instruction during training to use landmarks like the railway or canal to establish your bearings. He knew the rail line ran to Chester and therefore followed it until he saw the spire of Chester Cathedral, which confirmed his location for him, and went higher before landing safely.

Although all ended well, he almost found himself in trouble over it. Later he was summoned to meet the station officer, who had received a complaint from a member of the public about Brown flying low. When he exited the cloud, he had been temporarily at about 1,200 feet, which was below the prescribed minimum height permissible. Having admonished him over this, the senior officer then congratulated him on the use of his initiative in navigating his way back safely.

* * * * *

Another testing experience for Brown had occurred during an exercise in stalling the aircraft and emerging from the stall. This required the pilot to fly at a certain altitude straight and level and then switch off the engine, leading to a loss of power and the plane starting to dive. To pull it out of the dive, the engine had to be switched back on and the stick pulled back, which raised the nose to enable it to resume its position. He had done this manoeuvre several times with his instructor behind him when he was instructed to do it on his own. As he recollected, this caused him a degree of anxiety, and he tried to compose himself mentally, rehearsing the sequence of steps he had to follow. As he did so, the instructor unceremoniously barked 'Get on with it!' It was a much-relieved Brown who successfully completed the manoeuvre.

Notwithstanding these experiences, Brown satisfactorily passed the various flying tests he had undertaken. This meant he was selected to progress to more advanced pilot training for the Fleet Air Arm at their principal training base at HMS *Daedalus*, near Lee-on-Solent in Hampshire, about four miles west of Portsmouth.

Others of his group were sent to Pensacola in Florida to train on the Seafire, a plane similar to the Spitfire, and others went to courses at HMS *St Vincent* for navigators.

At HMS *Daedalus,* Brown trained on the Fairey Swordfish under the guidance of a number of instructors. The Swordfish was a biplane, principally a torpedo bomber, nicknamed 'the string bag', as it could carry a variety of weaponry. It was also used for reconnaissance and convoy escort duties. It had an excellent reputation and played an important part in sinking the *Bismarck* and crippling the Italian Navy at Taranto. While considered a relatively easy plane to fly, launching torpedoes effectively from it called for a degree of expertise. They had to be dispatched at a distance from the target, with the Swordfish being flown straight and level at low altitude.

Before Brown started his Fleet Air Arm training, several Fairey Swordfish had been engaged in an attack on the German battleships *Scharnhorst* and *Gneisenau* in the English Channel as they made their way from French ports back to Germany to prepare for the invasion of Norway. A number were shot down, incurring heavy casualties and Lieutenant Commander Eugene Esmonde was awarded a posthumous VC.

Brown readily achieved a basic mastery of the Swordfish and, with a navigator on board, engaged in training patrols in the Channel, going on exercises to Southampton, the Isle of Wight and other destinations.

As we have seen, throughout his training, Brown had been given permission to continue playing football, initially with Queen's Park. When he was based at Sealand, he turned out occasionally for Chester and also played in various services fixtures. Once at *Daedalus*, that pattern continued, although an increase in the services' representative matches meant he was missing parts of his Swordfish pilot training. Fixtures such as the Trafalgar Cup Final between the Royal Marines and the Royal Navy, and a combined Army and Royal Air Force team against a combined Royal Navy and Royal Marines team, in both of which Brown kept goal for the Navy, required him to take time off flying training. Playing in other less high-profile services games also bit into his flying training. This led to a degree of tension between him and his commanding officer at *Daedalus*, whose principal concern was Brown's flying duties.

* * * * *

Brown felt he was in a dilemma, being tugged in one direction by flying and in the other by football. The solution would come from an unexpected source. He excelled in another representative match for the Navy when they lost 2–0 to the Army in a War Charities game at Ipswich in front of almost 20,000 spectators. Despite being on the losing side, Brown thought this 'the best game I ever played'. There were three fellow Scots in his team: Tom McKillop and future Jordanhill colleague Billy Williamson of Rangers, and Willie Corbett of Celtic. Present in the crowd were A.V. Alexander, First Lord of the Admiralty, Mr Stanley Rous, secretary of the FA, and Mr George Graham, secretary of the Scottish FA Match report headlines supported Brown's opinion on the standard of his play, e.g. 'Keeper Brown, Navy Star', 'The Genius of Robert Brown', and 'Great Display by Brown'. One report claimed, 'He is probably the best player in his position seen in British football for several years.' It was one of these games where everything went right for him, and he could not be faulted for the loss of the goals.

Afterwards he was summoned to meet Alexander, who congratulated him on his outstanding performance and asked if he might 'guest' for Chelsea, where he was a director. Brown agreed to this and in the course of further conversation mentioned to the Sea Lord his dilemma over flying and football. He also explained how he had studied at Jordanhill and was keen to resume his PE course there at the end of the conflict. Alexander suggested that, as there was then a shortage of available PTIs, Brown should be relieved from flying duties to become a PTI at the Royal Navy School of Physical Education at Portsmouth. This appealed to him, as it would facilitate what he saw as his future career as a PE teacher and enable him to continue playing football at the same time. Alexander agreed to have the necessary arrangements put in place.

He then transferred from *Daedalus* to barracks at Portsmouth to start as a PTI at the college. While there, he fitted in a couple of games for Chelsea, and a few for Portsmouth at Fratton Park. Portsmouth had sustained a lot of bomb damage, and at times Brown felt that being there 'was like living on a knife edge'.

Despite that, he thoroughly enjoyed the life of a PTI at the college. After several months there, he and two colleagues were summoned to the principal's office, where they were informed of their forthcoming transfer to HMS *Foliot*, a land base near Plymouth. Along with gunnery and sailing instructors, and other specialists who would be involved, their duty would be to prepare landing craft crews' physical fitness for the forthcoming

Normandy landings. A total of six student PTIs were to take part alongside another three more experienced instructors. At *Foliot*, they were told to subject the men to hard physical training, and the commanding officer, Dixon, informed them that during the hours of daylight he did not wish to see any of the extensive playing fields lying empty. The men were given standard physical training classes, and took part in unarmed combat, cross-country running, football, rugby, hockey and swimming under the direction of Brown and his colleagues. The playing fields were in constant use.

* * * * *

It was at *Foliot* that Brown met his future wife, Wren Ruth Knight, who was in the Signals regiment. She delivered him his signals, messages informing him when and where he was to play in representative games, and they got to know each other. They also played against each other in regular Sunday games of mixed hockey, she at left-back and Brown at outside-right, and soon they began going out together. Commander Dixon found it hard to accept Brown's frequent football commitments, at one point declaring, 'Till my dying day, Brown, I'll never understand how the First Lord of the Admiralty wants to see you playing football while we're engaged in a life and death struggle with Germany!' His relationship with Ruth developed, and he was invited to meet her family at their home in Billacombe, about six miles from Plymouth. By now they were courting seriously.

After the Normandy landings, the intensity of Brown's duties at *Foliot* reduced and he was able to revert to a normal PTI's timetable, a standard 9-to-5 routine, until the end of the war. By this stage, the Allies were pinning Germany back, and there was growing confidence about the final outcome. He received permission to live with Ruth's family and travelled by bus each day to and from the base. In this rather low key way, he saw out the end of the war before his final transfer to Port Edgar, the naval base near South Queensferry, where demobilisation awaited, to be followed by a return to civilian life.

As has been noted, his football involvement continued during wartime. One of the most significant moments in his playing career occurred when he was selected to represent Scotland for the first time, in a War Charities match, against the RAF at Sheffield Wednesday's Hillsborough ground, on 25 November 1944. The news of his selection was relayed to him via a telegram from Queen's Park while he was based at *Foliot*, which was delivered to him by Ruth. He actually received this when on top of a haystack at Tamerton Farm, where he assisted the farmer, Jack Ferris, in his free time. Although his excellent form had been attracting attention, he was nevertheless surprised to receive word of his selection but 'thrilled to bits' at the prospect of his Scottish debut. The Scots team contained a number of well-known figures, including captain Matt Busby, then of Liverpool, Jimmy Delaney of Celtic, Billy Liddell, also of Liverpool and Andy Black of Hearts. The RAF also included well-known players such as Stanley Matthews, Raich Carter, Ted Drake and Stan Mortensen.

In the build-up to the match, one press report pondered, 'One wonders if Brown will seize this chance to make the goalkeeping position his own – he can very well become the Scottish keeper for years to come. He is filling out, now 6 feet tall and weighing 12 stones. He has a phenomenal strength of wrist and has it also in temperament.'

In front of a crowd of 40,172, Scotland defeated their opponents resoundingly 7–1, with Brown playing an outstanding game. He was delighted, particularly so as his mentor Hugh Brown and his father were among the spectators for their first 'real view of him in a big match', as Brown later entered in his scrapbook. He also noted in his book the factors that had made for an unforgettable day as follows: 'Hugh's intense satisfaction at my showing and my dad's pride too. Matt Busby was a great captain whose brilliant generalship was always a striking feature. The jubilation which heralded our victory. We players, committee men, pressmen etc. were ever so gay[!].'

One newspaper headline stated, 'Youngster Brown never made a mistake'. Another newspaper said, 'Bobby Brown, Queen's Park's 21-year-old keeper is an outstanding discovery.' 'Scotland owed a big debt to their 21-year-old Navy keeper who never made a mistake,' wrote another. And journalist Jack Harkness, Scottish goalkeeper for the 1928 Wembley Wizards and also a former Queen's keeper, wrote, 'He had a youthful confidence I liked, I had a quick word with him before the game, he's the first amateur to play for Scotland since myself.' And team-mate Andy Black was quoted as saying, 'I have never played in a team with a better keeper.' Days later, Brown maintained his good form in shining for Plymouth Argyle in a 2–2 draw against Exeter City, crowning what was described as 'a brilliant display' by saving a penalty. Around this time, he made further appearances for Argyle against Southampton, Coventry City and Derby County, in the last of which BBC radio commentary was provided by the well-known Corinthian player and amateur international F.N.S. Creek.

Brown has particularly fond memories of his time playing for the 'Pilgrims'. 'We used to get decent-sized crowds, and everyone was very encouraging. Parts of Home Park, their ground, had been devastated by bombing during the war, as had large parts of the city. I remember we used to change in an old tramcar at the far end of the ground once we were able to use it. Regular league football was suspended and we played, I think, in a regional league with games often held at Millbay. There was a big appetite for football then, especially with the prospect of war coming to an end. I remember special trains taking fans to the games were run from Penzance. I had a great time with Argyle and was grateful to the club for giving me the chance to play for them.'

* * * * *

The next highlight for Brown was selection to play two games for a Scotland XI in Belgium on 6 and 7 January 1945, his first trip to the Continent. The first game was to be against the Belgian national side in Brussels and the second against a Flanders XI in Bruges, and it was hoped the games would be a big attraction for British troops based there. The party assembled at the Russell Hotel in London before being flown by the RAF to Brussels in an eventful flight. Bad weather forced their return when within 15 minutes of their destination, before they made it successfully on their second attempt. Matt Busby was unavailable, but the squad included Sammy Cox, later of Queen's Park and Rangers fame, Tommy Pearson of Newcastle United, and a future manager of Aberdeen, 'Jock' Dodds of Blackpool, as well as Black and Liddell. One innovation was the introduction of tracksuits for the Scottish players, complete with Lion Rampant badge, described as being similar to 'those worn by American athletes'.

Despite a snow-covered pitch at Daring FC Brussels and a plummeting temperature, the Scots, in front of thousands of troops, prevailed 3–2 against the Belgians, with Brown again claiming the plaudits, having pulled off three 'impossible saves' in the second half. George Graham, secretary of the SFA commented, 'I would like to say what a splendid performance our goalkeeper put up. He was grand.' A press report headline announced, 'Brown a hero in Scots victory, brilliance of Brown thrills 15,000 in Brussels duel.' Once more Brown rose to the occasion and added to his growing reputation.

He wrote in his scrapbook, 'My most vivid memories are of the terrific reception from the troops, the icy condition of the field, the wearing of tracksuits and the clean sporting spirit of the Belgian players and spectators.'

After those heights, the 6–4 defeat suffered the next day in Bruges was something of an anti-climax, although the icy conditions in which the Brussels game had been played exacted its toll of injuries on the tourists, who were playing their second game in successive days. It did not dampen the Scots' morale: as Brown summarised, 'The tour was a great success with the escapades of players and officials in Brussels always a living memory.' Given his outstanding display, Brown was considered a certainty to play for Scotland against England the next month at Villa Park, Birmingham.

He was duly selected for the match on 3 February in a line-up that read: Brown; Harley, Stephen, Busby (capt.); Thyne, Macaulay; Delaney, Fagan, Dodds, Black, Liddell. The English team was: Swift; Scott, Hardwick; Soo, Franklin, Mercer (capt.); Matthews, A. Brown, Lawton, Mortensen, L. Smith. The Scottish support was high on expectation following the convincing win against the RAF, which had featured several England players. They were optimistic this match could turn the tide of five successive defeats by the 'Auld Enemy' in wartime matches since 1942.

The game had aroused huge interest and was a 66,000 sell-out, leading to a black market in tickets. Brown, himself needing some stand tickets, was told that a 'guinea' seat would cost four times that amount and did not pursue his interest. When he arrived on the Friday afternoon by train from Plymouth, Birmingham was awash with Scottish fans in high spirits. After booking in to the team's Queen's Hotel in the city, his first task along with his team-mates was to visit wounded servicemen in the Queen Elizabeth hospital, where they spent two hours. In the evening, there was a tactics discussion led by skipper Matt Busby, and Brown prepared to go to bed at 9pm to the tune of an eightsome reel being enjoyed by his countrymen outside the hotel.

Kick-off the next day was preceded by almost an hour's mixed musical programme provided by the South Staffordshire Regimental band and an American Army one, the two combining at the end to play 'The Star-Spangled Banner'. The teams, led on to the pitch by respective captains Busby and Mercer followed by Swift and Brown, were presented to the Lord Mayor of Birmingham and A.V. Alexander, First Lord of the Admiralty. Brown felt rather nervous on taking the field as he saw the crowd, and initially found the game very fast. A long passback from Busby and a save from Lawton helped settle him down. In an exciting match, England took the lead through Charlton's Albert Brown before Delaney countered. Brown then set up Mortensen to put the hosts ahead, after which Dodds drew Scotland level. With 20 minutes left, Mortensen scored the winning goal after Brown could only parry his shot.

Despite the result, heaps of praise were lavished on Brown, whose performance avoided a much bigger defeat. One report commented that after Mortensen's second goal, 'Brown went berserk – he saved ten shots, any one counted a winner by the crowd, and became the hero of the game. He punched them out, he kicked them out, he took injury, he took pains to ensure Lawton did not get his goal and stopped Stanley Matthews scoring twice when he was 10–1 on a goal.' The *Daily Record* headlined their report 'Bobby Brown Our Hero' and continued, 'The real hero was the ever smiling Bobby Brown – the boy went through the whole repertory of goalkeeping technique, some saves were positively uncanny; several times he had to dive low for a ball and when he had reached full stretch seemed to telescope himself another foot or so to get it; the save from

Tommy Lawton's header was a masterpiece, Lawton stood staring in amazement and admiration. When he ran off the field at the finish he was pursued by many who wanted to pat him on the back.' Another report claimed, 'This boy Brown has played himself into the Scottish team as long as he has a leg to stand on.' And Jack Harkness added, 'Our star above them all was Bobby Brown.'

Brown and his team-mates were slightly disappointed with the result in the immediate aftermath, and he reproached himself for not holding the shot from Mortensen that had led to the winning goal. Later they recognised that the better team had won. That night in the hotel, Brown enjoyed meeting for the first time the famous sports broadcaster Raymond Glendinning, who congratulated him on his outstanding display and 'christened' him 'Boy Brown' to distinguish him from Albert, the English scorer. The 'Boy Brown' had certainly covered himself in glory, and his name was on everyone's lips that night in Birmingham.

He created such an impression that Tommy Lawton, the outstanding English centre-forward of his era, wrote later in his autobiography, *Football Is My Business*, 'This will perhaps go down as Bobby Brown's match. Not for many years have I seen such an inspired display as this young keeper gave, particularly the last twenty minutes. It may have been Frank Swift's advice but whatever it was Bobby Brown made ten herculean saves in these last twenty minutes when Scotland had been run ragged, each from shots that had goal written all over them. Young Bobby Brown looking like a schoolboy in a large sized too big green sweater and long pants should remember this game for a long long time. A pal said to me after the game Bobby must have had a horseshoe in his goal these last twenty minutes. And I could point out to him he did. It was given him by a Scottish paratrooper who ran on to the field as the Scots were warming up. Bobby stuck it just inside the net and carried it to the other end at half-time.'

Brown was particularly proud of his showing, as his father had been present at the game, having cycled all the way to Birmingham from Torwood, about 350 miles! Being a self-contained, reserved individual, he did not trouble his son for a ticket but managed to obtain one himself. Other fond memories Brown retained of that game included the spontaneous welcome to both teams from the crowd; his feeling of pride in the preliminaries and the presentation to the dignitaries before kick-off; his first introduction to the renowned English keeper Frank Swift, whom he thought a terrific fellow, an undoubted personality and a first-rate sportsman; his first game against Tommy Lawton, also a sportsman and player of tremendous quality; and, finally, Villa Park itself, which he thought one of the best grounds he had played on and beautifully kept. The next morning, Brown caught the train back to Plymouth to rejoin his unit.

Important matches were now taking place regularly, with the next one on the calendar another meeting between Scotland and England, this time at Hampden on 14 April 1945. Brown, as expected, was chosen, and as this was his first representative game in front of a home Scottish crowd – and also against England – it was of very special significance for him. And of course, adding to the occasion, Hampden Park was his 'home' ground. He travelled from Plymouth in the company of Ruth, now his fiancée, and who should he meet en route on the train at Birmingham but his opposite number, Frank Swift, heading to Glasgow with his wife. Hugh Brown, then a senior RAF officer, travelled north from Wolverhampton specially to watch his former protégé. Accommodation for the Scottish team had been arranged in the North British Hotel in the city's George Square, while their counterparts were housed in Central Station Hotel nearby.

With war coming to an end and the game seen as an opportunity for the home team to reverse its losing trend against England, interest in it was huge, and Hampden could have been sold out twice over. Scottish optimism was not overflowing, but it was realistically thought that the country had a reasonable chance. A cartoon epitomised the home fans' outlook, declaring, 'WE'VE BOY BROWN – and 10 good men – and the Hampden Roar!' Brown's profile was growing.

An event took place the night before the game, which would be almost unimaginable today. Joe Mercer and Matt Busby, the two captains, accompanied by some team-mates, visited Glasgow's Barlinnie Prison to take part in a football quiz with inmates and give brief talks. The resident padre joked that they should keep Tommy Lawton locked up over the weekend. Had he known how matters would unfold, that would certainly have been a very smart move, at any rate from a Scottish viewpoint!

On the morning of the match, the heavens opened, and from then on there was a steady downpour. Brown and team-mates had a tactical discussion in the hotel, the main thrust of which Brown recalled was a determination to set about England with 'abandon' and 'keep chasing every ball'. Another recollection was, 'We also told SFA Chairman Douglas Bowie OBE we would do our best.' Next they attended the Grosvenor Restaurant in Gordon Street at 12 noon for lunch, consisting of fish and buttered toast, with SFA officials and guests. After lunch, something else barely imaginable today happened: once the home team had boarded their coach, it set off to collect the English team from their hotel to travel with them to Hampden.

As the teams arrived, the atmosphere was already building up, with thousands already there in and outside the stadium. It was awash with tartan and tam-o'-shanter 'bunnets' as the Boys' Brigade and Glasgow Police pipe bands, parading up and down the pitch, entertained the fans and sought to inspire a home win. In memory of the American president, Franklin D. Roosevelt, who had died two days previously, a Boys' Brigade bugler played 'The Last Post' before a band struck up 'Abide with Me', with the fans singing heartily. As a further mark of respect, both teams walked out to the pitch together wearing black armbands. Brown was not the only Queen's player in the Scottish team, as he had been joined by centre-forward Tony Harris, a dental student, who had come in for the injured Jock Dodds. The other Queen's Park connection was that Scotland's trainer was Bert Manderson.

* * * * *

The Scotland team was: Brown; Harley, Stephen; Busby (capt.), J. Harris, Macaulay; Waddell, Bogan, T. Harris, Black, Liddell. One of the reserves was Brown's old schoolboy team-mate and future Rangers colleague George Young. England lined up as in the previous fixture except for one change, Carter replacing Mortensen.

By now, 133,000 fans, undeterred by the miserable conditions, had squeezed into the ground, loudly exhorting the home team to victory. The continuous rain had made the pitch heavy and greasy. After only two minutes, Scotland lost debutant Tommy Bogan of Hibs, injured in a collision with Swift, who was photographed holding him in his arms awaiting the attention of trainer Manderson. Thereafter Swift was booed every time he touched the ball, which he later admitted upset him, as the collision had been purely accidental. In an eventful game, which controversially saw three goals disallowed and Busby miss a penalty, and which had to be stopped three times for dogs to be ejected from the pitch, England pulled away in the last 15 minutes to record an ultimately emphatic 6–1 win, their biggest ever win at Hampden. Carter scored the opener, which was then equalised by Johnstone of Clyde, who had replaced Bogan, with Lawton and Albert Brown notching two more to give England a 3–1 half-time lead. Then, in the last quarter of an hour, Scotland collapsed, allowing Matthews, Smith and Lawton, again, to score. The Scottish press was unsurprisingly critical of Scotland's players. Absolved from blame were Brown, who was faultless with all the goals, and Rangers winger Willie Waddell, future Ibrox manager and team-mate of Brown's. Brown himself, despite losing six goals, was reasonably pleased with his play – especially his handling, which was difficult in the conditions, although he had reservations about his kicking.

Referee J.S. Cox of Rutherglen was generally considered to have had a 'bad day', and that proved to be his final game at first-class level. There was a certain irony in Busby's missed penalty. Swift had been his team-mate at Manchester City when Busby had advised him on how to save penalties, his good deed coming back to haunt him. Apart from the penalty miss, Busby did not play well, and he retired from international football aged 36 after the game. The Scots gathered for dinner that evening in the North British Hotel, where they licked their wounds. The next day, Brown and his fiancée returned to Plymouth. The defeat had been a chastening one, but at least Brown had emerged from it with his reputation unscathed.

A further charity match followed three weeks later, just three days before VE day in May, when a Scottish Services XI with Brown in goals played Hibs at their Easter Road ground in aid of the Soldiers, Sailors and Airmen's Families Association. A crowd of 18,165 attended, raising £1,500 for the charity. Hibs were supplemented by two Hearts players, McCrae and Kelly, and featured the inimitable Gordon Smith among their number. The Services team congregated for lunch at 12.30pm at Littlejohn's restaurant in nearby Leith Walk before the match. The Massed Bands of the Royal Dragoons and King's Own

Scottish Borderers played prior to kick-off amid the military displays also taking place. Again Brown stole the headlines for a wonderful game. It ended 2–2, with the Services' goals netted by Inglis of Falkirk and the Army, and Juliussen of Huddersfield Town and the Army, who would later play for Dundee and Berwick Rangers. Hibs' goals were scored, ironically, by their two Hearts imports, McCrae and Kelly. After the game, the players retired to the North British Hotel in Princes Street for 'high tea'.

Headlines included 'This Was Brown's Game', with the report adding that had it not been for 'Scotland's brilliant keeper', Hibs would have won easily. His first-half display was 'attractive' and his second half 'superb'. Another headline ran, 'This Fellow Brown?', and George McLachlan's report continued that Brown was a 'goalkeeping genius' and that when he became too old to be known as 'Boy Brown', he should be called 'sticky fingers'.

A couple of Summer Cup appearances for Queen's Park followed, against Clyde and Morton, in the latter of which his old Dunipace schoolmate Billy Steel displayed little sense of camaraderie by rifling a 20-yard shot past him to clinch the tie!

Another charity game took place shortly after, when Queen's Park, with Brown in goals, played the RAF national team in aid of their Benevolent Fund at Grant Street in Inverness, home of Highland League club Clachnacuddin. This was the RAF's sixth match of a north of Scotland tour, in the course of which they raised £1,700 for their fund. Their team was a strong one featuring Bill Shankly, of future Liverpool managerial fame, Franklin, Soo, Matthews, Mortensen, Albert Brown and Smith, all internationals. They overwhelmed Queen's 5–1 with three goals from Middlesbrough's Micky Fenton and two from Mortensen. Brown felt there was nothing he could have done about any of the goals.

The next morning, while his team-mates were enjoying a dip at the local swimming pool, Brown was being interviewed at the town's Cummings Hotel by BBC Radio about his career and thoughts on the sport, reflecting his increasing public profile. The interview was broadcast the following Wednesday evening on *Scottish Half Hour*, during which Brown advocated more encouragement for schools football and argued that rugby-playing schools should also offer football. He reiterated the debt he felt he owed to Falkirk High School for the coaching and facilities there. During the interview, he struck listeners as unassuming and unspoilt by all the publicity he was receiving.

In the afternoon, he joined his team-mates for a coach trip along Loch Ness to Fort Augustus. Because it was Sunday, there was nowhere open for the party to have a snack, but a local lady and her two daughters invited them into their house for an afternoon tea, with Brown and the Queen's Park president doing the washing-up afterwards, another very unlikely occurrence nowadays.

During their subsequent tour of the famous Abbey Boarding School in the village, a photograph of Desmond White, the former Queen's keeper and future Celtic chairman who had been educated there, was pointed out to them. They returned to Inverness before heading back to Glasgow, having enjoyed a very pleasant weekend despite the result.

The final services' charities game of the summer was between the RAF and the Royal Navy at Hampden Park on 14 July, Brown again in goals for the Navy. The RAF fielded the same strong team that had defeated Queen's easily in Inverness shortly before, with only one change, Carter for Mortensen. It was officiated by well-known Scottish referee Peter Craigmyle, from Aberdeen, in front of a crowd of 30,000. The RAF won easily 7–1, Carter claiming four of the goals. He, Matthews – known as 'The Prince of the Potteries' – and Shankly ran riot, giving the opposition a torrid time. But, once again, despite conceding seven goals, Brown was highly praised for how he played. 'Superlative keeping by Brown prevented a cricket score' was one newspaper's summation.

The same evening, Brown switched sports, again for War Charities, when he took part in a cricket match between the Scottish Police and a Footballer's XI at Clydesdale Cricket Club's ground at Titwood in Glasgow. Also donning the pads were former Rangers players David Meiklejohn and Arthur Dixon. The English players Soo, Matthews and Carter were down to play but had to withdraw at the last minute. Brown distinguished himself by opening the batting and scoring 28 runs in half an hour, and later diving full-length for a left-handed catch to dismiss the Police skipper. He had certainly spent a very busy Saturday.

The next week he attended an SFA Coaching Course for trainers and players at Ibrox. It was led by Frank Punchard, the Jordanhill College principal, who was assisted by Squadron Leader Walter Winterbottom, later England's first manager, and Tom Mitchell, manager of York City and others. Brown's group included future Rangers and Scotland team-mate Sammy Cox and Clyde's Peter Galletly, along with a number of trainers and other players. This was a pioneering initiative by the SFA consisting of a mix of theoretical classroom and practical work, which Brown found very useful. With the war over, speculation was beginning to mount about Brown's future, although he had not yet been demobbed from the Navy. For his part, he maintained he would continue with Queen's Park, but rumours suggested he might be heading to Ibrox.

Back at Plymouth, Brown further demonstrated his sporting versatility, this time on the athletics track. He won his unit's sports championships, with successes in the 100 yards, 220 yards and high jump, and a second in the long jump. His 100 yards time of 10.4 seconds was very accomplished for the era, considering he did not train for the event and was running on grass. The last Scottish 100 yards championship prior to the outbreak of war was won in 10.3 seconds.

With the conflict now over, Brown, like many others, was keen to resume 'normal life' and return to his PE studies and playing regularly for Queen's. First he had to pass through the demobilisation process, which he intended to accelerate by claiming category 'B' status, applicable to school teachers and similar, providing for a quicker release. To support this, he asked for his previous Jordanhill studies and his practical experience as a PTI to be taken into account. By mid-September 1945, the first step in the process had been completed, with his transfer to Port Edgar, the naval base at South Queensferry. Resumption of studies, a career in football and marriage began to be at the forefront of his mind.

Chapter 4

Post War and Queen's Park

BY September 1945, Brown was back in Scotland and able to resume playing regularly for Queen's Park, his first game being a 1–1 draw with Partick Thistle at Hampden on the 22nd of that month. In taking his place in the team, he ousted a 15-year-old Ronnie Simpson. Rumours had been circulating about Brown's future, but he was in no doubt that in immediate terms it lay at Hampden with the Spiders.

Two weeks later, Brown played his part in helping Queen's win the Glasgow Cup, then a prestigious trophy, for the first time since 1898. Two other members of the team were still in uniform: Ken Chisholm and David Letham. Queen's had required two games to dispose of a stuffy Partick Thistle in the semi-final but, with both of the Old Firm clubs eliminated, were optimistic about their prospects in the final against Clyde. In front of a 40,000 crowd, they fulfilled expectations, winning 2–0 with goals from Tony Harris and Andy McGill. Brown had only two testing shots to deal with and did so comfortably.

An enjoyable evening at Reid's Tearoom followed, with the beautifully crafted silver cup in pride of place on the top table.

Brown continued to collect plaudits for his form. After an exciting 3–3 draw at Tynecastle on 27 October against Hearts, he was reported to have put on 'a masterly display'. The report also stated that 'Scotland need have no worries about a goalkeeper with Brown enhancing his reputation at Tynecastle'.

On the Tuesday following that Tynecastle game, Queen's flew to Germany to play a fixture against the BAOR (British Army of the Rhine) team. A break-in to Hampden the night before they were due to fly, when boots and other items of kit were stolen, might later be thought to have set an unfortunate marker for the excursion. Adding to their woes, on the morning of their departure from Prestwick Airport they were held up for over an hour as treasurer Tom Sneddon was refused permission to travel as his passport was not in order. The team chosen was that which had won the Glasgow Cup, which meant Brown in goals and future Hibs manager Walter Galbraith at full-back, with Brown's fellow international Tony Harris leading the attack. An RAF Transport Command Dakota was provided for the four-hour flight to Hanover, with its radio officer Newman acutely aware that the last time he had flown there he had been on a bombing mission. On arrival, they were met by former player Joe Kyle, now in charge of the opposition, and George Graham, SFA secretary.

Once they were on the pitch the next day, another familiar face awaited them as the BAOR goalkeeper was former Spider Gordon Hamilton, whose call-up into the army near the beginning of war had paved the way for Brown's senior debut. The home team won fairly comfortably 3–0, with Whittinghame of Chelsea, Lewis of Arsenal and Westcott of Wolves scoring, in front of 20,000 fans, mostly troops. Brown had a decent game, but overall Queen's were second best.

Their journey home made the mishaps at the start seem trifling misfortunes. As the *Evening Citizen* put it, without a hint of hyberbole, 'This was one of the biggest muddles in football history.' On both Thursday and Friday mornings, the party rose early to go to Wunsdorf Airfield for the flight, but on both occasions poor weather conditions put paid to flying. On the Saturday, the party left their Hanover hotel at 6am to go to the airfield, but apparently no plane was available. The absence of any senior officers resulted in their enquiries being bounced on from one junior officer to another. Eventually a mid-morning telephone call indicated a Dakota aircraft was on its way to Wunsdorf for them, but it arrived later than intended. Queen's officials, conscious of their league match against Queen of the South that afternoon at Hampden, made calls to try to cancel it, unaware that their colleagues in Glasgow had already decided to field what was effectively a Strollers XI in their place. The plane finally took off early in the afternoon, depositing a decidedly weary and hungry squad of players and officials at Prestwick at about 5pm.

For Brown, the delays were exasperating. 'We did, however, manage to fill in our time well on the Thursday and Friday between going riding, doing some yachting, playing table tennis and a tour of the city of Hanover.'

His next important game was the first Victory International, in celebration of the Allied success in the war, on 10 November against Wales at Hampden, for which caps were not awarded. Beforehand there was considerable speculation as to the team the SFA Selection Committee, now reduced from 14 members to seven, would pick. Several reports expressed the opinion that Brown was the only certainty, and he did take his place in goals in a team that included Jock Shaw and Waddell of Rangers, Smith of Hibs and Liddell of Liverpool. Goals from Waddell and Dodds secured the win for the Scots, with

'Brown's astute positioning behind a good defence making it look fairly easy'.

Within a week, he was back in Germany, as goalkeeper in a Scottish Select team that played two games against the Combined Services. Again the flight was by Dakota, with the same pilot as on the Queen's trip, but on this occasion all the travel went smoothly. The first match was on 17 November in Celle, just north-east of Hanover, where the Select won 4–2. Apart from Brown, who had a 'grand' game, team-mates included Sammy Cox; Partick Thistle pivot Jacky Husband, who now has a stand named after him at Firhill; Celtic's Jimmy Delaney; and Hibs' Gordon Smith. Their trainer was Hugh Shaw, also from Hibs.

The second game was the very next day, at the Bahrenfeld Stadium in Hamburg in front of a crowd of 40,000, mostly troops. This was built up as being the bigger game and was more accessible for the troops, with the result that roads to the ground were soon clogged up with lorries and buses ferrying thousands of soldier fans. Once more old team-mate Joe Kyle was in charge of the servicemen and had his men fired up for the challenge. It was a keenly disputed fixture, featuring several meaty challenges, which ended in a 1–1 draw. A dinner was held in the evening at Steits Hotel in the city, at which Colonel Blackie, a Glaswegian and senior officer in the area, gave a speech thanking the Select on behalf of the many Scottish soldiers based there for having made the trip to play these games. Two lasting recollections for Brown and team-mates were the extent of the destruction of Hamburg and the sight of small children entering the stadium after the final whistle to pick up discarded cigarette ends.

It was back to league business thereafter for Brown with Queen's, who were enjoying a good run towards the end of the year with wins over Aberdeen at home on Christmas Day and Partick Thistle at Firhill four days later. In a review of the football year, one journalist wrote, in the contemporary style, that in judging who the fans' number one favourite for the year might be, 'I believe if I put down Bobby Brown's name I wouldn't be far out.' Shortly before the end of the year, Brown had considered entering the famous New Year Powderhall Sprint, but concern over his amateur status and the forthcoming Festive Season fixtures decided him against it, although his best time of 10.2 seconds for 100 yards would have put him among the favourites.

By January 1946, he had been demobbed and had resumed his studies at Jordanhill. On the 23rd of that month, he earned his first full cap against Belgium at Hampden, none of his previous international appearances having been deemed to merit one. The conditions were appalling, the pitch being covered in snow while a thick fog swirled around, hampering visibility. Despite this, nearly 50,000 fans turned up, demonstrating again the post-war hunger for the game and desire for spectacle. Unsurprisingly, fans resorted to snowballing resulting in two casualties being taken to the Victoria Infirmary for treatment, one a Belgian soldier! In the circumstances, it was surprising that these two casualties were not joined by some injured players. Brown's team-mates included Jock Shaw, Gordon Smith and Jimmy Delaney. A Delaney opener put Scotland in the lead, but that was cancelled out by two Belgian goals, the second of which was blamed on Brown through his failure to hold a high ball. A Delaney penalty thereafter secured a draw for the hosts. Although at fault for a goal, Brown was praised for the rest of his showing, with headlines announcing, 'Bobby Brown saved us against the Belgians' and, 'Bobby Brown unquestionably stood between Scotland and humbling defeat'. In a newspaper interview after the game he was quoted as saying, 'I never got the feel of that sodden ball all day.' In appearing for Scotland, he set a record that is set to last in perpetuity: this was the last international in which an amateur player – Brown – represented the full Scottish international team. In the evening, a dinner was held in the Grosvenor Restaurant for all the players and officials, at which gifts were exchanged, Brown and his team-mates each receiving a crystal ashtray.

Perhaps the last word on the game should go to Aberdeen's Archie Baird, who received his only cap that day, as an inside-forward. He wrote in his autobiography, *The Family of Four,* 'It should never have been played. Snow covered the ground to a depth of several inches and the top surface was like sheet ice, more like a skating rink than a football pitch. The fact that Belgium had travelled so far – and a foreign team was a rarity in Scotland – must have influenced the decision to go ahead with the game. An international match would never be played today in these conditions. As well as the snow and ice, there was a lot of fog. Unable to see the goals from the centre circle as the rules say, we could scarcely make out players a few yards away. For spectators the whole thing was farcical; few if any saw the four goals scored that day. Certainly the keepers never saw them and how on earth our selectors saw anything to help them pick their next team I have never understood.'

Despite these difficult spectating conditions, the selectors claimed to have seen enough to justify changing the front five in its entirety by picking Waddell, Hamilton (Aberdeen), Dodds, Chisholm and Liddell for the Victory International against Ireland at Windsor Park, Belfast on 2 February. Brown retained his place in goal, and he and his team-mates sailed to Belfast on the *Lairdsburn* steamship from the Broomielaw dock in Glasgow. There was huge interest in this game, the first time the Scots had played there in eight years, and several thousand Scottish fans made the trip across the Irish Sea. Prior to kick-off, the presence of 12 press photographers in the centre circle reflected the level of interest, as did the record crowd of 53,000 shoehorned into the ground.

In a physical game, the home team fielded Arsenal winger Dr Kevin O'Flanagan, who had played rugby for Ireland the previous week in an international versus France. His jousts with full-back Jock Shaw reverberated round the packed ground. The Scots eventually prevailed 3–2, with Brown described as having a 'grand game', one save from Belfast Celtic's Bonnar particularly standing out – 'Our blond headed keeper was just Bobby Brown at his best – the Bonnar save was a wonder.'

In the meantime, he continued as an ever-present in goals for Queen's, amid consistent speculation that he was going to turn professional and probably with Rangers. For his part, he was not sharing his thoughts with the media, other than to indicate he was enjoying his season with the Spiders, who were doing well. He had resumed his PE course at Jordanhill College and was giving that and his Hampden duties priority over becoming involved in conversations about his future playing career. Brown and his Queen's team had recorded some excellent results, including convincing wins over St Mirren, Aberdeen, Motherwell and Falkirk, with arguably the best being a 3–1 League Cup win against Celtic in front of 34,000 at Hampden.

On the international front, the biggest fixture of the year was the Victory International against England at Hampden Park, to be played on 13 April. Given recent experience against the opposition, the 'Seven Pillars of Wisdom', as the Scots selectors were nicknamed, were under pressure to come up with a strong team. Here was their choice: Brown (Queen's Park); D. Shaw (Hibs), J. Shaw (Rangers, capt.); Campbell (Morton), Brennan (Airdrie), Husband (Partick Thistle); Waddell (Rangers), Dougal (Birmingham), Delaney (Manchester United), Hamilton (Aberdeen), Liddell (Liverpool). England lined up as follows: Swift (Manchester City); Scott (Arsenal),

Hardwick (Middlesbrough); Wright (Wolves), Franklin (Stoke), Mercer (Everton, capt.); Elliott (West Bromwich), Shackleton (Bradford Park Avenue), Lawton (Chelsea), Hagan (Sheffield United), Compton (Arsenal). Baird was originally chosen for Scotland, but an injury sustained against Partick Thistle the previous week meant he had to withdraw, his place going to clubmate Hamilton. Of note was the fact that three of Scotland's team were from the small mining village of Annathill, near Coatbridge: the Shaw brothers at full-back and centre-half Frank Brennan, later of Newcastle United.

The Scots gathered for two days before the match in comfortable retreat at the Forest Hills Hotel at Aberfoyle in the Trossachs, where they attracted attention training on the local amateur team's pitch. Although interest in the game again was all-pervading, that did not equate to a groundswell of optimism in the Scottish ranks. One visitor of interest to Glasgow for the game who was spotted by the Scottish press on her arrival at Central Station from Plymouth was Ruth Knight, Brown's fiancée. She added to the intrigue surrounding the keeper's future playing plans when she informed reporters that she 'was looking forward to taking up permanent residence in Scotland'. They were to marry on 6 July in her home county of Devon.

As with any build-up to a Scotland–England game, especially then, it was intense in the lead up to kick-off. Brown recalled feeling highly emotional as he stood in front of the enormous 139,468 crowd during the national anthem, his thoughts straying to fallen comrades while tears ran down his cheeks. When play got under way, it soon became apparent Scotland were the better team but unable to convert their superiority into goals. As the game drew to a close, the hosts at last made their breakthrough with less than a minute remaining. A Husband free kick into the box was headed on by Waddell to Delaney, who sidefooted home. The crowd erupted in celebration, having assumed the game was going to finish in a goalless draw, their recent lack of success against the 'Auld Enemy' fuelling their delight. There was only time for England to kick off and make a couple of passes before Peter Craigmyle blew his whistle, signalling the start of one long party. In a fitting cameo, the last two players off the field were keepers Swift and Brown, the latter with his arm sportingly round the shoulder of the former, who had been knocked out at one point during the 90 minutes. The Goalkeepers' Union appeared in good fettle. Brown's performance had been summarised in one of the Sunday newspapers as 'debonair, distinctive and safe'. That night, he and other members of the Scottish party celebrated with gusto in the city's North British Hotel in George Square. Although it was not known at the time, this would be his last international appearance as a Queen's Park player – for shortly after he would renounce his amateur status and sign for Rangers, as had been widely predicted.

His transfer would be part of an end-of-season exodus from the Spiders, an occupational hazard for the amateur club. Others who left at the same time included Archie McIndewar, who accompanied Brown to Ibrox, Andy McGill and Walter Galbraith to Clyde, Johnny Aitkenhead to Hibs, Tony Harris to Aberdeen and Ken Chisholm to Partick Thistle. An excellent eighth-place finish in the top tier – on the same points total as Hearts in seventh, whose goal average was better – at least cushioned the blow. Indeed, an extra two points would have secured them fifth place. A further blow at the end of April was the death of long-serving trainer Bert Manderson, who had been ill for some time.

Brown had been weighing up his options for a while, and, with the war over, studies almost complete and marriage pending, it seemed the right time to make the move.

Chapter 5

First Year at Rangers

BROWN was aware that as an amateur player, were he to sign for a club as a professional, he would be entitled to keep whatever transfer fee could be negotiated for himself. Given that he was due to marry in July, he knew that this could help secure his financial future. His star had been in the ascendant, particularly since his debut for the Scotland XI against the RAF two years previously, and many clubs were interested in securing his signature. One newspaper report went so far as expressing the opinion that he could sign for any professional club in Britain, such was his standing in the game. One club that did advance its interest was Manchester United, whose new manager, Matt Busby, a former international captain of Brown's, held talks with him about joining up at Old Trafford. Brown recalls they met towards the end of the 1945/46 season for about an hour in the North British Hotel in Glasgow, where Busby explained his vision for the future of his club and Brown's potential part in it. He held Busby in extremely high regard, and was not surprised later that he went on to carve out an iconic career in management. While discussions were affable and the prospect tempting, Brown's focus remained on concluding his PE studies and continuing to play in Scotland. He therefore declined the offer while expressing his appreciation.

Frequent links were being made between Brown and Rangers. It was common knowledge that the Ibrox side's custodian, 'Jerry' Dawson, known as 'The Prince of Keepers', was nearing the end of his time with the club. Although his first name was James, he was affectionately known as 'Jerry' after the famous 1920s Burnley and English keeper of the same name. He had been at Ibrox since 1929, and between 1935 and the outbreak of war was the country's regular number one, earning 14 caps, an impressive haul at that time. He had enjoyed legendary status with Rangers, where he was a very popular figure with the club and its fans. But he was now 37, and the Light Blues were having to look to the future.

The first positive indication Brown had that Rangers might want him to replace Dawson came in a conversation with his former school football coach, Hugh Brown, by now commanding officer at RAF Evanton in Ross and Cromarty. Bobby Brown, of course, was interested, and Hugh Brown set up a meeting with Rangers manager Bill Struth at Ibrox to discuss the possibility. The meeting took place in the manager's office about the beginning of April, with Hugh Brown also present. Bobby Brown can remember feeling 'overawed' at meeting Struth for the first time. Although he knew of him and had played at Ibrox, he had never met him, far less been in his 'inner sanctum'. Struth was 'Mr Rangers' – an iconic figure in the club's history, credited with setting the highest expectations and standards of its players on and off the pitch. He was a stickler for discipline who dressed immaculately and who lived and breathed Rangers Football Club.

Curiously, he had no football background but had been a professional athlete who figured frequently in the early 20th century in the prize lists over distances ranging from sprints to the mile at the New Year Powderhall event, the country's premier professional meeting. After his running career finished, he became trainer first to Hearts and then Clyde, before he was appointed assistant manager at Rangers. When manager William Wilton drowned in a boating accident in 1920, he stepped up to replace him, becoming only the second manager in the club's history. His influence permeated all aspects of the club, and he became synonymous with it. He lived in a flat nearby in Copeland Road overlooking the ground, enabling him to indulge his love of gardening in his greenhouse behind the 'Celtic end' – which, surprisingly, was never vandalised. When presented with his portrait by the club on his retirement, in summarising what being 'a Ranger' meant, he stated, in almost Churchillian tones, 'Let the others come after us, we welcome the chase. It's healthy for us, we will never hide from it. Never fear: inevitably we shall have our years of failure, and when they arrive we must reveal tolerance and sanity. No matter the days of anxiety that come our way, we shall emerge stronger because of the trials to be overcome; that has been the philosophy of Rangers since the days of the gallant pioneers.'

Ibrox Stadium was one of the outstanding football grounds of Britain and indeed Europe, bearing in mind its record crowd of 118,567 at the 1939 Celtic New Year game, its Archibald Leitch-designed main stand and red brick facade, its fabled marble staircase and its opulent Blue Room for directors' use, complete with wood panelling from the *Queen Mary* and Italian marble fireplace. It lacked for nothing in terms of contemporary design and comforts, with furnishings and fittings more commonly seen in transatlantic liners of the period. The team was the most successful in Scotland, having won the league title six times in the nine seasons preceding the outbreak of war as well as winning the Scottish Cup four times during the same period. At the time of the meeting, they were on their way to winning the first post-war league title. As he sat in Struth's room admiring its understated elegance and well-ordered neatness, Brown appreciated that if things worked out he would be joining an institution with a success-drenched past and high expectations for continued success. It was difficult for him to avoid feeling overawed until Struth put him at his ease.

Brown recalls the manager saying to him, 'How would you like to come to Ibrox Stadium?' And he himself feeling 'thrilled to bits'. 'He had an aura about him, a real presence. and he left an indelible impression on you,' he added. Struth knew Busby had pursued him for Manchester United and did not want him to slip through his fingers. He was also aware that Derby County had invited Brown to 'guest' with them on their summer tour of Czechoslovakia, with a view to securing his future signature. In the event Brown, although flattered to be invited, declined the invitation. In conversation with Struth, he explained how he wanted to complete his teaching studies as he was aware of the need to have an alternative career should football not work out. There was general conversation about Brown's family, his Fleet Air Arm service and his forthcoming wedding plans – but, at that stage, no discussion about terms. Struth suggested having another meeting, at which he wanted Brown's father to be present as he wished to meet him.

That took place soon after, with club secretary James Simpson also in attendance. After some pleasantries, terms were discussed. There were no agents in those days, of course, but Brown trusted Struth implicitly and 'hung on his every word'. His father was keen that his son obtain his PE qualification, but apart from that was content to let Bobby make his own decision. When Struth mentioned the signing-on fee he would receive, it seemed a 'fortune' to Brown. He realised that if he did not re-sign for Queen's by 26 April 1946, as an amateur, he would become a free agent and be entitled to keep the signing-on fee. With marriage in the offing, this was a big incentive to turn professional. Struth and Simpson advised it would be beneficial for tax purposes that it be spread over five years. At the same time he was informed that wages would be £20 per week with a £2 win bonus, while every week £25 was put aside for each player to be paid at Christmas and the end of the season in two lump sums, net of tax. That made Rangers players the best paid in Scotland, if not Britain, as the maximum wage constraint in England did not apply. It was an extremely attractive package. Brown and his father were allowed to think things over while a third meeting was arranged, at which, hopefully, agreement would be reached.

In reality there was little for Brown to weigh up: he was already convinced about the move. He did, of course, consult with fiancée Ruth, who was completely in favour. They had already decided they would set up home to live in Scotland, and Brown had been in discussion with a housebuilder, Duncan Ogilvie of Stirling, about building a home for him and his new wife. Brown had known Ogilvie for some years through football, as he had been a winger for Motherwell. Ogilvie had identified a plot of land in the village of Cambuskenneth near Stirling as a suitable site, which appealed to Brown and Ruth. This would be the first house built by Ogilvie's company. When Brown returned for his third and final meeting with Struth, he explained the position regarding this and requested a £500 advance to cover initial outlays, which Struth was happy to endorse. The paperwork was completed, and Brown was now a professional player for Rangers. He was delighted with his new status.

Two days later, on 4 May 1946, he made his debut for his new club against Airdrie in the Victory Cup, a competition that effectively replaced the Scottish Cup in the immediate post-war aftermath. An all-ticket crowd of 21,600 crammed into Airdrie's compact Broomfield ground. A fellow debutant was Sammy Cox, a former Queen's Park team-mate and international colleague. The Rangers team was: Brown; Gray, Cox; Watkins, Young, Symon; Waddell, Thornton, Smith, Williamson, Caskie. He had played with Young at schoolboy level, and with Waddell and Thornton at international level. Scot Symon, of course, would later replace Struth as a decorated Rangers manager and was a dual Scottish international at football and cricket. Brown's recollection is of meeting up with his team-mates for the first time at midday over a light lunch in the St Enoch's Hotel before travelling to Airdrie by coach. At this stage, he had not even attended a training session at Ibrox.

Rangers won the tie 4–0, and Brown's Ibrox career was off to a great start. George McLachlan wrote, 'Apart from one lapse, Bobby Brown was the perfect keeper. With Cox he gave the Ibrox defence a more solid appearance than it has carried for some time.' The lapse referred to an Airdrie 'goal' subsequently chalked off for offside. Another report stated, 'Bobby Brown was top class and pulled off many brilliant saves.' Interviewed afterwards, Brown said, 'I enjoyed it all. I was sorry to leave Queen's Park, but am happy to be a Ranger.' He had been under pressure for his debut, aware of the expectations on his shoulders, and was pleased and relieved to emerge with credit marks.

Although he was by now an experienced keeper who had played in a number of important fixtures, including internationals, establishing himself as the Rangers number one in the footsteps of the hugely accomplished and highly popular Jerry Dawson was a demanding prospect. To go from playing in front of decent-sized crowds at Hampden to massive ones at Ibrox represented another big step up. Brown not only hoped he would continue as he had started at Broomfield, but was determined to do so.

The next public appointment Brown had was at the 24th Annual Display of the Glasgow Lifeboys on 7 May in Pollokshaws Church Hall, at which he was 'guest of honour', described in the programme as 'Bobby Brown of Queen's Park', it clearly having been printed prior to his transfer.

Eight days later, Brown earned his first cap as a Ranger in the international against Switzerland at Hampden on 15 May. The Swiss party arrived at the Central Hotel two days beforehand and took part in a training session at Hampden the day before the match. Courtesy of the Clyde Trust, they went for a sail down the river that afternoon, before being entertained to a dinner by the Lord Provost at the City Chambers that evening, which Brown and his team-mates also attended.

The Scottish team only showed two changes from the English match, with Thornton and Tommy Walker of Hearts replacing Dougal of Birmingham City and Hamilton of Aberdeen respectively. The game attracted a British record crowd for a midweek game, outwith the holiday period, of 113,404, an incredible figure given that the opposition were not a recognised force in the game and were part-time players. The public appetite for football at this time, particularly in Scotland, was insatiable. The Swiss team consisted of players from clubs such as Grasshoppers, Lausanne, Servette and Young Fellows of Zurich whose occupations included police officer, merchant, cinema owner, mechanic and watchmaker.

Despite an early Swiss goal, for which Brown was considered possibly at fault by one newspaper, the Scots pulled away to win comfortably by 3–1, with a brace of goals by Liddell and the other by Delaney. The press was critical of the visitors' style of play, accusing their players of 'pushing, holding and obstructing', which nowadays sounds pretty much par for the course.

A month later, Brown was back at Hampden in big-game action, this time the Victory Cup Final against Hibs, Celtic having been disposed of in the semi-final after a replay. The cup had originally been gifted by the SFA to the Scottish Football League for the new League Cup competition, but instead it was diverted to this competition, with the winners being allowed to keep it in perpetuity.

The game was preceded by entertainment from a massed band of over 300 pipers and drummers, many of whom were veterans of El Alamein and the North Africa campaign under Field Marshal Montgomery. In front of a crowd of 88,000, Brown won his first trophy as a Ranger, the Ibrox outfit beating their Edinburgh rivals 3–1. This signalled the start of what would be a trophy-laden career at Ibrox. That evening, Brown and several team-mates celebrated their success at the Rangers Supporters' Association annual dance at the well-known city-centre restaurant, the Ca'D'Oro.

By now, preparations were under way for his biggest match, his wedding to Ruth Knight, who had joined the Wrens to be a Signals officer after completing her training at Balloch Castle, near Loch Lomond. It was Ruth who brought him the telegram informing him of his selection for a Scotland team for the first time, the game against the RAF in 1944. Her family were Devonians, and the wedding took place on 6 July 1946 at St Mary and All Saints Church in her home town of Plymstock. Her father, Bert, was a furniture restorer, and mother Carolyn a housewife. The best man was Hugh Brown, and ushers were David Letham, a Queen's Park team-mate, and Stanley Knight, Ruth's brother. Among the various family guests who attended was Billy Williamson, another Rangers player and fellow PE College student. They spent a memorable honeymoon in St Ives in Cornwall, later naming their Cambuskenneth house after it. Brown recalled things getting off to a mildly embarrassing start as they waited at the station for their train. He went into his pocket for a handkerchief and unthinkingly pulled out a load of confetti, much to fellow travellers' amusement.

A busy summer soon gave way to a new league season, starting on 12 August with Brown and team-mates chalking up a fine away win against Motherwell. It had been observed that Brown's form with his new club had been variable and not up to his usual consistently high standard. He recognised this and thought it attributable to a number of factors, as he recalled, 'It was a period of adaptation making the change from Queen's to Rangers. It had been a fairly high-profile move and there were big expectations on my shoulders. I was replacing a legend in the form of Jerry Dawson, I had a new defence round about me used to a different style of play. At that time keepers rarely came off their line to deal with cross balls but I liked to do so and dominate my area. Initially this led to some misunderstanding and tension with defenders like Young and Woodburn because I thought they were getting in my way. Inevitably this led to a few words being exchanged, but Mr Struth told me just to respond in the same fashion. Gradually they came to respect my wish to control my area and play the way I wanted to. Another factor was there was a degree of resentment towards me in the dressing room, as it was known I was being paid my own signing-on fee, having joined as an amateur, but that did not last for long. Also, playing for Rangers meant long periods of inactivity, as they usually dominated games meaning your concentration levels had to be really high. And it was also a time of change in my personal circumstances. I had married in the summer and was busy off the pitch with my studies and having a new house built.'

Indeed, Brown was quoted in the press as saying, 'I've not played as well as I'd like to for my new club.' He was the target for some barracking from a section of Rangers fans. But the majority of fans supported him at this difficult time. One fan, when interviewed, stated, 'The defenders hang around in the area too much ... they obscure Brown's view ... they should leave him to clear his own lines.' Letters streamed into Ibrox from all over the country addressed to him, telling him to disregard the barrackers as they were not true 'Light Blues fans'. The Supporters' Association also wrote expressing their confidence in him. An anonymous letter dated 4 November, bearing to be sent from 'twenty miles out of Glasgow', two days after a win over Morton, expressed the following sentiments: 'Congratulations on a superb display on Saturday. You had a great game ... one and all agreed your exhibition could not have been bettered. Let me wish you all the best and many years at Ibrox Park ... keep it up Bobby play the game ... that was such a masterly performance you provided in your most recent outing. From only one of your countless admirers content to sign himself "Well-wisher".' That and other messages boosted Brown's morale, and his form gradually picked up and reached its previous level.

A first league encounter against his former team, Queen's Park, resulted in a satisfactory 2–0 win, with a young Ronnie Simpson wearing his old shirt. And he made his debut in an Old Firm league match at Parkhead, a 3–2 win for the Light Blues, an unforgettable occasion given the intensity of the atmosphere. He remembered, 'The Celtic games were always special, there's no doubt about it. There was definitely a hike in the level of tension in the dressing room before kick-off. They were undoubtedly the games I was most nervous before. Although we were expected to win all our games, you felt you really had to win these ones. It was the only time that board members would come into the dressing room to wish you luck and congratulate us afterwards if we won. There was definitely something extra in the air at the time of these games.'

Although it is well documented that at this time Rangers operated a discriminatory policy of not signing Catholic players, Brown maintains there was no overt anti-Catholic bias in the dressing room or in the club generally. The Rangers players always got on well with their Celtic counterparts on Scotland duty, which Brown also found to be so when he was national manager. However, it was suggested to him not long after arriving at Ibrox that he join the Freemasons, which he felt in the circumstances he ought to do. He did not feel obliged to do so, but equally felt he should do. At this remove, he cannot recollect who suggested it, but as a result he joined the Bannockburn Lodge. He attended a few meetings, but decided it was not really for him and discontinued his link. Some years later, while a guest at a Masonic function, he heard a former well-known referee recount how he had officiated many Rangers matches and was proud of never having once refereed a losing Ibrox side! Perhaps the terrace cry of 'Who's the Mason in the Black?!' did have some currency back then!

On New Year's Day, a British record crowd of 85,000 for a club game that season crammed into Ibrox to watch the Old Firm draw 1–1 in a very physical match featuring 50 free kicks. It was not only those 'derbies' that attracted large crowds. At Tynecastle, 45,000 watched Rangers beat Hearts 3–0; over 41,000 saw Hibs draw with them at Easter Road; and at Ibrox, 60,000 watched them defeat Aberdeen. Hibs had emerged as their closest challengers, as they would be in succeeding years, but they maintained their form throughout the season to win the league title from their Edinburgh rivals by two points.

This season saw the introduction of the League Cup, a gift from then league president Mr John McMahon, which Rangers also had the honour of winning by defeating Aberdeen in the final 4–0 in front of 82,684 fans. In the semi-final, an incredible attendance of 125,154 witnessed Rangers beat Hibs 3–1. The

Scottish Cup was less successful for the Ibrox men. Having won 2–1 in the first round against Clyde in front of 74,000 at home, they were drawn against Hibs in the second round. After a goalless draw at home with 95,000 in attendance they succumbed 2–0 at Easter Road, watched by a record crowd of 48,816.

Brown's first full season at Ibrox had been highly successful, gaining two winners' medals, in the league and the League Cup. After an inconsistent start, he had gathered momentum and recaptured his old form. Reflecting this, he headed the season's appearances list, having played in every league and cup game except one sectional League Cup tie against Morton, when reserve keeper John Shaw played his only game ever for the senior team. Skipper 'Tiger' Shaw recorded the next highest number of appearances.

He had completed his studies at Jordanhill and been appointed by the Stirlingshire Education Committee as a peripatetic teacher to give classes in schools at Bannockburn, Plean, Cowie and Denny. His new house at Cambuskenneth, with its extensive grounds, had been completed and Brown and his wife were now living in it after being in temporary accommodation in Stirling. And, courtesy of Mr Struth, he and three other players – much to their surprise – had been given the opportunity to buy cars.

'One day after training – it was during school holidays, as I trained full-time then – trainer Jimmy Smith told me, Willie Waddell, Sammy Cox and Jock Shaw that "the boss" wanted to see us in his office. I can tell you we went up the marble staircase rather nervously in some trepidation, as naturally our first thought was we were in trouble of some sort. He opened the door to us as immaculately dressed as ever, looked us up and down as usual, then told us to take a seat. He then asked us individually if we would like a car. Everyone said "yes" till he reached me and I had to tell him I couldn't drive. To which he replied, "It's high time you did, Bobby!"

'At this time, post-war there was a five-year waiting list for cars, but somehow he had managed to bypass that and arrange for these Austin A40s to be made available for us through Carlaw's motor dealers. I started taking lessons and arranged to sit my test in Stirling in an old Armstrong Siddeley, which was not the easiest to drive, as it required double declutching. Having slipped back during a hill start, which caused a passing workman to slip on the icy road, scattering his tools everywhere, I asked the examiner "tongue in cheek" if I had passed, to which the answer was a resounding "no". Thankfully I passed on the second attempt, driving the Austin, which was an easier car to drive.'

Normally Brown trained three nights a week at Ibrox with another 20 or so part-timers. This usually meant his catching a train from Stirling to Glasgow, then a tramcar to the ground. As was standard then, running formed a large part of the training programme, and this was done on the track surrounding the pitch. There was also general gym work, but, as Brown spent each and every day in a gym, not much was required of him in that respect. He also did some one-on-one goalkeeping training with assistant trainer Joe Craven, who would throw balls at him to catch and fire in shots at him. For outfield players, the ball was 'for Saturdays' only, the emphasis being on running. After training, he undertook the journey in reverse, all of which added up to a punishing schedule but one which he embraced.

Always respectful of 'Mr Struth', still referring to him as such today, he had by now become used to his ways. On matchdays, players had to appear in suit, collar and tie and were regularly reminded they were Rangers both on and off the pitch.

'He was not someone who took much to do with tactics, like all managers then, expecting the captain to take the lead, but he had a good eye for a player and how to fit them together into a successful team. He did succeed in creating a great spirit of togetherness, which was underpinned by club social events involving not just the players but wives too. The club dances were a grand affair, with the players in dinner suits and wives in ballgowns. Often after home games, players and wives would socialise together in the Blue Room, and everyone mixed well. He took an interest in players' personal lives, and you really felt good about being part of this wonderful institution and successful team.

'On home matchdays, his routine never varied. If it were a particularly important game or a cup tie, we might gather at the St Enoch's Hotel. Otherwise we'd meet at the stadium, where we had to report by 1.30pm for the then-normal 3pm kick-off. Punctuality was important to him, and being late was not a good idea. Players would start their warm-up routines, which then were done indoors, in the gym and running area beneath the main stand. Once I had done some running to loosen up, I would go into the gym and practise my handling and do some shot-stopping.

By just after 2pm, we were all back in the dressing room. At 2.15pm on the dot, "Titch", a ground staff member, would carry in Mr Struth's own swivel chair and position it in the centre of the room, the signal that he was on his way. Once he came in, always impeccably dressed and carrying his walking stick, the hubbub of noise and chat would die away as the manager would look round the dressing room, eyeing us, taking everything in. He didn't have to say a word for it to go quiet. His presence really was amazing. He would usually say a little about how he wanted us to play that day in general terms and ask the captain, usually initially Jock "Tiger" Shaw, to contribute, with others chipping in occasionally. There was no tactics board or any sophisticated briefings such as happen nowadays. He would speak individually to players, reminding them of their role and encouraging them.

'Your white shorts were always last to be put on before going out on to the pitch, to ensure they were spotlessly clean. As in everything, Mr Struth was a stickler for his team turning out immaculately and would check their kit. Finally, just as we prepared to leave the room, he would remind us that we were playing for Glasgow Rangers and that thousands had come to see us play our very best. "And, don't forget, you're playing for your ham and eggs," he would add. With that he would throw the ball to Jock Shaw and say, "Lead them out, captain."

'Although he had a reputation as a strict disciplinarian, he was never a manager who shouted at or bullied his team. I only saw him once lose his temper with a player, with Willie Woodburn. We were playing Queen of the South when one of Willie's bootlaces broke and he had to leave the field to replace it. Inevitably, of course, when he was off the pitch, Queen's scored. Well, at half-time, Mr Struth tore a strip off Willie, he really didn't miss him. I hadn't been all that long then at Ibrox and it certainly made an impression on me. So much so that after that, I was determined it would never happen to me, and each time I played from then on I put brand new bootlaces in! Another area apart from tactics where Mr Struth differed from his modern-day counterpart was that he always watched games from the stand, not the dugout. I can only once remember him being on the touchline, and that was during an Old Firm Glasgow Cup tie. Two Celtic players had been sent off and a third was injured, meaning they were effectively down to eight men. We were leading 2–0, and with 15 minutes remaining the atmosphere in the ground was particularly volatile, especially because of the expulsions. At that point Mr Struth came to the line to tell skipper "Tiger" Shaw we should "just keep possession and play the game out", as it was feared serious crowd trouble could break out. Thankfully it never did, as we followed his instructions.'

Brown's team-mates were, as has been mentioned, aware in general terms of his financial arrangements with the club and curious about his new house. Not long after its completion, the team had played against Dundee at Dens Park, and, during the return journey to Glasgow, Jimmy Smith, now the trainer, suggested they go to have a look at it. The coach was diverted to Cambuskenneth, where the team were suitably impressed by 'St Ives' and its two acres of garden ground. Soon an impromptu seven-a-side game was under way, with jackets down for goalposts, and as the word spread in the locality a healthy-sized crowd soon ringed the 'pitch'. After that, the Rangers party enjoyed a high tea at St Ives, courtesy of Ruth, before heading off to Glasgow. This type of event was redolent of the family atmosphere that Brown and his team-mates enjoyed under Struth then at Ibrox.

Over the coming seasons, Brown was to enjoy considerable success – but, in the later years of his time at Ibrox, there would be a degree of disappointment.

Chapter 6

Rangers 1947–52

OVER the next five seasons, Brown would play 245 games for the Light Blues, making him easily the player with most appearances during this period, an impressive achievement by any standards but particularly so for a part-timer. He played in every single league game bar the final one, on 19 April 1952, when reserve keeper George Niven deputised. In addition, he kept goal in all Rangers' cup games, both Scottish and League Cups, throughout those seasons. If his first full season of 1946/47 is thrown into the equation, his total of games up to the end of season 1951/52 amounts to 293, a remarkable record of consistency. During these five seasons from 1947 to 1952, he collected six winners' medals: two in the league, three in the Scottish Cup and one in the League Cup. Yet in his last four seasons with the club, 1952–56, he played in only 41 games, and did not qualify for any medals from the two league titles and one Scottish Cup won during that time. This represented a significant reversal in his fortunes, largely because of one game – the opening match of season 1952/53, a League Cup tie against Hearts, which will be considered in detail later.

Hibs would prove Rangers' biggest challengers in the next five seasons and set out their stall by winning the title in 1947/48, relegating the Ibrox club to runners-up by two points. They were a stronger attacking force, outscoring Rangers by 22 goals. Three of the forwards who would compose their 'Famous Five' line-up were featuring at this time, namely Gordon Smith, Eddie Turnbull and Willie Ormond. Turnbull would later manage them, as (briefly) did Ormond, who was also a successor of Brown's as national team manager.

A landmark match took place on 20 September 1947, when Rangers beat Celtic 2–0 at home. It was the first time their famous defence, nicknamed the 'Iron Curtain', played together in a competitive match: Brown in goals; George Young and Jock Shaw at full-back; Ian McColl, Willie Woodburn and Sammy Cox at half-back – all Scottish internationals. The nickname arose because of the difficulty opponents had in penetrating them, in satirical reference to the famous Winston Churchill speech in America in 1946 when he talked about 'an iron curtain descending across the continent of Europe', in relation to the separation of the communist east from the democratic west. The 'Iron Curtain' would underpin the team for years to come and provide the backbone of their success.

Brown's recaptured good form led to another international appearance against Ireland, in a goalless draw before 98,766 fans at Hampden. His display was rated as 'good and worthy of his place'. There was some controversy beforehand as Brown and three of his club's international team-mates, Willie Thornton, Jimmy Duncanson and George Young, were permitted to attend the Rangers FC Dance, with wives, at the Grosvenor Restaurant the night prior to the game. A newspaper photograph of them appeared, headlined 'The Four Truants'.

In a far-sighted move, Rangers took a midwinter sunshine break to travel to Portugal for a challenge match against the national champions, Benfica. The Portuguese outfit were not the cracks they would later become, and the visit of Rangers, then considered a particularly big name, attracted huge interest, with a crowd of about 5,000 waiting to welcome them at Lisbon Airport before they transferred to the Palace Hotel in Estoril. Their journey involved a stop at Bordeaux prior to continuing on to Lisbon, causing director and ex-player George Brown to complain the journey had been 'too long' and was 'boring'! The home fans clearly thought highly of Torry Gillick, the Rangers and ex-Everton inside-forward, as they made a point of chanting his name as the Ibrox party passed through the airport. Brown recalled, 'The accommodation was luxurious, we really were treated like royalty. It was the type of hotel that was only for "those and such as those". You have to remember there were no European competitions then, and this was something unique that created a huge amount of interest, particularly there and also at home. This was my first club game abroad for Rangers. I remember Torry fondly, he was a good friend of mine, an exciting and talented player. He maybe wasn't the world's best trainer, but over a distance of 30 yards or so he was like greased lightning.'

The Benfica president was not optimistic about the result, expressing the hope that they could restrict the losing margin down to three goals. Echoing that pessimistic note, the local press headlined their photographs of the Glasgow side with the nickname 'Super Tigers'. Apparently the possibility of a return match in Glasgow depended on the standard of the Portuguese team's performance, of which Rangers would be arbiter! The game was played at the National Stadium in Lisbon, which Jimmy Smith, the Light Blues trainer and former centre-forward, described as 'the loveliest stadium Rangers have ever played in'.

The match was not a classic, but, in front of a 60,000 crowd, Brown kept a clean sheet as his team ran out comfortable

3–0 winners thanks to late goals. In the evening, their hosts entertained them to a high-class banquet featuring lobster, champagne and port at the Imperium Restaurant in the Portuguese capital. Willie Woodburn repeatedly toasted the hosts 'Viva Benfica' so often that his team-mates thereafter nicknamed him 'Ben'. It was also a memorable trip for Willie Waddell, as he met his future wife, who was an air hostess on one of the flights. Brown fondly remembers the trip and the generous welcome and hospitality afforded them. Back then Rangers were truly a force in the football world, seen to be doing almost evangelical work in what was perceived to be a lesser football nation. Almost 70 years on, the balance has shifted considerably.

Although the Easter Road side took their title, Rangers did have the satisfaction of eliminating them from the Scottish Cup at the semi-final stage thanks to a Thornton goal. Their cup run had started with some surprising difficulty against lowly Stranraer away, where a single Thornton goal squeezed them through to a second-round tie against Leith Athletic, whose goalkeeper was Lewis Goram, father of future Rangers and Scotland keeper Andy. They won comfortably 4–0, thereafter beating Partick Thistle and East Fife to take them through to the semi against Hibs.

An incredible Hampden crowd of 143,570, unsurprisingly a record for this stage, watched this game. The demand for tickets was overwhelming, and there were scenes of complete chaos at Glasgow Central station as thousands of fans stampeded their way through to the platforms to try to secure a place on one of the 17 special trains to Hampden. Such was the squeeze that people were falling from platforms on to the lines and many were injured. At Hampden itself, things were little better, with 50,000 reported present an hour before kick-off. By kick-off, almost three times that number were in place, with women and children regularly being passed down as in a relay above the heads of spectators, to reach places of safety to avoid crushing. To make matters worse, it was a warm day, which resulted in people fainting and the first aid services being kept fully occupied.

As for the game itself, it could be said to be a 'Tale of Two Goalkeepers' in which Brown came out on top against Hibs' George Farm, future Scottish international and FA Cup-winning keeper with Blackpool. Brown was widely praised and referred to as 'brilliant', with one report stating, 'Brown has certainly no superior in goalkeeping today. He won the tie for Rangers just as the unfortunate Farm lost it for Hibs.' This and other good performances led to a clamour for Brown to be reinstated in the Scottish goal for the upcoming game against England in April at Hampden. On the same day as Hampden was bulging at the seams for this semi-final, on the other side of the city the second semi-final between Celtic and Morton was being played in front of (only!) 80,000 fans, meaning that on the one day in Glasgow more than 223,000 fans watched two matches!

Morton won that tie and took their place in the final, with Rangers established as firm favourites. However, Brown, as he readily admits, did not distinguish himself when the Greenock side scored their first goal. In the second minute, he misjudged their skipper Jimmy Whyte's 35-yard high curling free kick, which, aided by a strong wind, left him out of his goal as it sailed over his head, just under the bar and into the net. 'He caught me completely cold and I made a bad mistake. We had been warned before kick-off about the strong wind by Mr Struth, and to make allowance for it, but just a moment's inattention by me led to the loss of an important goal.' Much to his relief, Torry Gillick equalised ten minutes later. At half-time, Struth made his displeasure known to Brown, administering a sharp blow across his rear end with his stick while admonishing him, 'Pay attention to your work, boy!' After that potentially costly error, Brown went on to play well, keeping his team in the match with some top-drawer saves.

As it ended one apiece, a replay took place the Wednesday evening afterwards in front of 129,176, a record for a midweek tie, with an estimated 20,000 locked out – making a total attendance over the two games of 261,151, a phenomenal figure. Brown's fellow PE teacher Billy Williamson was brought into the team for this game, a shrewd selection as he notched the winning goal in extra time with a diving header five minutes from full time, sparing Brown's potential blushes arising from the first tie. In any event, Brown achieved some redemption, playing excellently in the replay. When Williamson reported for duty at his school, Lenzie Academy, on the Monday morning, he was reportedly accorded a 'hero's welcome' by pupils. Brown recalled, 'Before the final we had heard that Morton were on a £200-per-head bonus to win the cup. Today that seems very little, but then it was a lot of money. This made some of our team think we should be on a similar bonus, as ours was a lot less. Jock Shaw, our captain, was persuaded to go up the marble staircase and speak to Mr Struth about it. Suffice to say he returned with his tail between his legs. Mr Struth apparently said "Now, John, have a seat and tell me what's on your mind." Once Jock did so, he was reminded in straightforward fashion how well paid Rangers players were, win or lose, and that we were in finals regularly, whereas Morton didn't reach many finals. And "John" was left in no doubt there would be no increase in our bonus!'

Brown's second season at Ibrox could be considered reasonably successful. The 'Iron Curtain' defence, of which he was a crucial part, had embedded itself in the team. They had won a Scottish Cup, run a very good Hibs team a close second in the league and reached a semi-final in the League Cup. They were expected to win that tie against Falkirk, who had old favourite Jerry Dawson in goals, but an uncharacteristic Woodburn error with two minutes remaining let the Bairns in to score and clinch the win. Featuring well in the three competitions was creditable but would be eclipsed by the following years' achievements, when Rangers swept all before them.

The 1948/49 season, during which Brown was the only ever-present in all games, is recognised in Rangers' history as groundbreaking as it was the first time a club won the mythical 'Treble' of league, Scottish Cup and League Cup in the one season. The league campaign began in rather muted fashion, with a 1–1 draw at Motherwell followed by a high-scoring match against Falkirk with Rangers scoring the odd goal in seven to secure the points, Dawson again being the Bairns' netminder. An Old Firm win at Parkhead lifted spirits, but a month later consecutive defeats by Hearts at Tynecastle and Hibs at Ibrox dampened the mood. Then five consecutive wins eased them into second place, a point behind Hibs, at the halfway mark.

Meanwhile, they shared a difficult League Cup section with Celtic, Hibs and Clyde. In the penultimate fixture, 76,466 watched them beat Hibs at Ibrox. In the final game against Celtic at home, which they had to win to qualify, 105,000 – Britain's biggest crowd of the season – saw them defeat their fiercest rivals 2–1. Thereafter victories over St Mirren and Dundee led to a final against Raith Rovers, then in the Second Division, on 12 March.

In the league, their form stuttered a little, the highlight being a resounding 4–0 win over Celtic at Ibrox on New Year's Day 1949. A disappointing defeat at the hands of Third Lanark was then followed by a run of 11 consecutive undefeated matches up to the highly dramatic round of final games of the season.

The League Cup Final took place on 12 March in front of a slightly disappointing crowd of 57,450. Rangers, although clear favourites, struggled against the Second Division men and had Brown to thank for being level at half-time. Two saves in particular were outstanding, the first from a Frank Joyner header in the seventh minute, which he had to stretch to put over the bar. Five minutes later he had to dive full length to save a rocket shot from Willie Penman from 20 yards. In the second half, Willie Thornton set up goals from Torry Gillick and Willie Paton to win Rangers the trophy, despite it not having been a gilded performance. This was the second cause for celebration that month in the Brown household, as his wife Ruth had earlier given birth to their first daughter, Carolyn, in Bridge of Allan.

In the Scottish Cup, Rangers enjoyed a reasonably easy passage to the final. Wins against Highland League side Elgin City, Motherwell, Partick Thistle and East Fife took them through to meet Clyde on 23 April in front of 120,162. The cup then was considered a hugely important competition and attracted enormous interest. An emphatic 4–1 scoreline meant the cup was headed to Ibrox for the second year in succession. Two George Young penalties, another diving Williamson header, in his only cup game that season, and a Duncanson goal saw them home. Brown now had two medals, and the question was whether he and his team-mates could clinch the Treble by adding the league title.

The final league games were played a week after the cup final, on 30 April, and the odds seemed set against Rangers. Dundee were leading them by one point and needed to defeat Falkirk at Brockville to guarantee them the title. Rangers were away to Albion Rovers at Cliftonhill and had to win to keep their hopes alive. Falkirk, although sitting in sixth in the table, had lost their previous four games and had lost earlier in the season to Dundee at Dens Park. The Dark Blues were favourites, but on the day they folded and lost 4–1 to the Bairns. At Cliftonhill,

Rangers won by the same margin: the title was theirs, as was the Treble. Brown was thrilled to have taken part in such a historic feat, especially so as an ever-present, and an integral part of the 'Iron Curtain'. Of the maximum 180 league appearances available to them in the 30-game season, the 'Curtain' in total missed only seven.

After the Cliftonhill match, the Rangers party made its way to the St Enoch Hotel in Glasgow city centre for a celebratory dinner, which went on late into the night.

Brown's good form in both the previous and the current season prompted several commentators to call for him to be restored to the national team, but these calls fell on deaf ears until he was selected for the home international match against Northern Ireland on 17 November at Hampden. A home team which included his centre-half clubmate George Young as captain, the only other member of the 'Iron Curtain' selected, and old schoolmate Billy Steel at inside-forward, soon fell behind to a bustling opposition that included Manchester United's Johnny Carey, future manager of Everton among others, and the inimitable Peter Doherty in its line-up. After five minutes, Scotland were two down thanks to Walsh. However, new cap Billy Houliston of Queen of the South pulled one back before the interval, and Jimmy Mason of Third Lanark squared the game with 17 minutes remaining. In the final minute, Houliston sealed a dream debut by notching the winner to secure the points to send the 93,000 crowd home happy.

Selection policy then was somewhat erratic, being in the hands of the international selection committee, most of whom were club directors but few of whom – if any – had experience of playing professional football. Players found favour and sometimes, as soon as they did so, lost it for no logically apparent reason. Brown's last cap had been in the corresponding fixture two years previously, when he had enjoyed a decent match. In more recent internationals, the selectors had opted for three keepers, Miller of Celtic, Black of Southampton and Cowan of Morton, while Brown's claims were overlooked despite him playing consistently well. He is unsure why that was so, but is of the opinion that the erratic nature of selection simply reflected the essentially amateur and short-sighted nature of the set-up within the SFA then.

Eleven days after Rangers' 1949 League Cup win over Raith Rovers, Brown's sterling performance was rewarded with selection for the Scottish league XI against the English league XI at Hampden. League internationals were prestigious games, particularly the ones against the 'Auld Enemy', but because of increasing fixture lists and the importance of European competition, they lost their lustre, the last Scottish league international taking place in 1976. Although the gulf in quality between the two leagues then was not so pronounced as now, the English league tended to come out on top. This match continued the trend, with England recording a 3–0 win at Ibrox before a crowd of 90,000. Frank Swift, the visitors' famous keeper, was their 'personality' of the day. Other stars in a strong team included Mannion, Mortensen, Milburn and Finney, those last three each scoring. Brown was blameless for all the goals, and he, half-back Tommy Gallagher of Dundee and George Young were considered the successes of the home team and favourites for selection for the full international at Wembley the next month. It came as no surprise to Brown that despite that prediction, Jimmy Cowan was named in goals. Indeed, he went on to distinguish himself in the Scots' win in what was sometimes referred to as 'Cowan's match'.

After the historic Treble, there was always a risk that season 1949/50 might be an anti-climax for Brown and his Light Blues team-mates. However, those fears were quelled, with success in the league and Scottish Cup and a semi-final place in the

League Cup. Again Brown had a perfect record of appearances in all competitions, an accolade shared by three other members of the 'Iron Curtain': Young, McColl and Cox. The others, Woodburn and Shaw, missed, respectively, one league game, and one league and one Scottish Cup game. The important role played by the 'Iron Curtain' in securing trophies for Rangers at this time cannot be overstated. Hibs again were their strongest challengers in the league, finishing only a point behind them.

In their first encounter of the season, the Edinburgh side deprived them of their 100 per cent record, beating the Ibrox outfit 1–0 in front of 51,500 at Easter Road. At the halfway stage, Hibs were leading by three points. On 21 January, Rangers won a crucial match 1–0 against a strong-going Hearts team at a sold-out Tynecastle (a 49,000 attendance), in which Brown distinguished himself with a string of fine saves. Two stood out: a thumping shot from Jimmy Wardhaugh that he palmed over the bar and an Alfie Conn 'thunderbolt' from 20 yards that had 'goal' stamped all over it until Brown sprang 'like a panther at full stretch' from one side of the goal to the other to put it round the post for a corner.

Exemplifying the selectors' vagaries at this time, Brown earned selection for the Scottish league side against their English counterparts at Middlesbrough on 22 March 1950. Despite Cowan having played what many considered 'the game of his life' at Wembley the previous year, Brown, who was by all accounts enjoying an excellent season, replaced him for this inter-league match. Fellow 'Iron Curtain' colleagues Young, Woodburn and Cox were also selected, but, despite their presence, the English prevailed once again in front of a crowd of 40,000 at Ayresome Park, this time by a score of 3–1. Match reports gave plaudits to Brown and Cox, the former being described as a 'crack' keeper who had 'an excellent match'. Mannion and Mortensen excelled for the hosts.

A month later, the league was reaching an exciting climax. In Rangers' penultimate fixture, against Hibs at Ibrox, Brown and opposite number Tommy Younger, future Liverpool keeper and Scottish international, both kept clean sheets to keep the title chase alive to the last game of the season. An astonishing attendance of 101,000 witnessed the match. Rangers needed a point at Cathkin Park against Third Lanark to be sure of the crown. With Rangers two up and apparently cruising, Thirds struck back twice to equalise, but the Ibrox side held on in a nail-biting finish to claim the necessary point for the title and for Brown to win his third league medal.

In the League Cup, after surprisingly being taken to extra time by Cowdenbeath in the quarter-final, Rangers succumbed to another Fife side in the semi-final, East Fife, who won 2–1 after extra time – the first victory over Rangers in their history. Sweet revenge was gained, however, in the Scottish Cup Final, watched by 120,000, where Rangers ran out emphatic 3–0 winners over the Fife men – enabling Brown not only to keep a clean sheet but also to collect his third cup medal in successive years. Although he was not to know it at the time, that would be the final domestic honour he won as a Rangers player.

At the end of the season in May, Brown went on tour with the club for two weeks to Denmark and Sweden to play some friendlies in what should have been a relaxing break from the rigours of competitive football and a welcome reward for a successful season. However, as this took place during school term time, there appears to have been a misunderstanding over whether he had been given permission from the Stirlingshire Education Committee to travel. Reports suggested the issue had gone to a vote, with the majority against Brown, leading him to resign. To reassure his wife, he telephoned her from Copenhagen to confirm he had not resigned and the reports were inaccurate. What had happened was that his leave of absence had not attracted unanimous approval from the Committee but there was no question of his resigning. In fact, a member of the Committee, Miss Harvie Anderson, thoughtfully wrote to his wife to confirm this in his absence abroad, explaining that 'the value of Mr Brown's services to the children ... of this county is considerable ...'.

A light-hearted incident at Prestwick Airport saw the tour off to an amusing start. As the customs official in departures marked the players' luggage with green chalk, George Young inquired, tongue in cheek, if Jimmy McGrory (Celtic manager) had provided him with it. Rather unusually, the Rangers party shared their flight to Copenhagen with a group of 18 farmers from the Lossiemouth area en route to Scandinavia on an agricultural studies course. Brown remembers a highly enjoyable trip, apart from the initial uncertainty concerning his education authority. Various leisure activities were organised for them, including race meetings and tickets to watch Sheffield Wednesday, who were touring at the same time, play against local opposition. Rangers were unbeaten throughout in low-key friendlies including games against Danish team Staevnet and Swedish side Malmo, and the last game of the trip was against the strongest opposition, a Copenhagen Select, in that city. At this time Rangers were unbeaten in matches against European opposition. In front of 20,000 fans, they unfortunately relinquished that record due to a mistake by Brown. He explained, 'The match took place on a boiling hot day, more suitable for a day on the beach than playing football. With a minute to go, we were drawing 1–1 and were content to see the game out on that basis. A doctor who was playing for the select, I think his name was Lindstrom or similar, swung over a high ball towards my goal at a kind of oblique angle that seemed to me to be going past, which I thought suited us as it would give the team a breather as I took up time collecting the ball for a goal kick. But, to my surprise and disappointment, it took an odd turn and hit the inside of the post before going into the net to give them the win. I must say that spoiled my weekend. Apart from that incident it was a successful and enjoyable tour.'

Over the next two seasons, Rangers failed to win a trophy, Hibs being their principal nemesis, now with the 'Famous Five' in full flow: Gordon Smith, Bobby Johnstone, Lawrie Reilly, Eddie Turnbull and Willie Ormond. In 1950/51, the Edinburgh side won the league in a canter, ten points ahead of the Ibrox men. The Easter Road team, watched by 102,000 fans, knocked them out of the Scottish Cup in the second round at Ibrox, while in the League Cup, Rangers failed to qualify from their section. This was effectively the last season of the 'Iron Curtain' in its original format, as Jock Shaw wound down his career. Although he remained a Rangers player for a few more seasons, his appearances from now on were sporadic.

The following season, Hibs again beat them to the league flag, and the League Cup Final was lost to Dundee, for whom Johnny Pattillo scored. He would later become St Johnstone manager and would be replaced by Brown when he took over at Muirton Park. They also were knocked out of the Scottish Cup in the fourth round in a replay at Fir Park, the first game at Ibrox having attracted 82,000 fans. In both seasons, Brown recorded the highest number of appearances, playing in the full programme of league fixtures apart from the final one of the 1951/52 season against Aberdeen, as well as in all cup ties.

Although these seasons had been trophyless for Brown with his club, he found himself back in favour with the Scottish league XI selectors in particular. In addition to the league internationals previously mentioned, he played in another six, the final one being against the League of Ireland on 17 March 1952 at Dalymount Park in Dublin, a 2–0 win for the Scots. The others were against the Irish league on 27 September 1950 at Windsor

Park, Belfast, a 4–0 victory; against the English league again at Ibrox two months later, a 1–0 win thanks to a goal from Celtic's John McPhail; against the League of Ireland on 17 January 1951 at Parkhead, a resounding 7–0 triumph; against the Irish league at Ibrox on 26 September 1951, a 3–0 success; and a month afterwards, against the English league at Hillsborough in front of a crowd of more than 49,000, a narrow 2–1 defeat.

Brown played well in all these games, particularly the latter one. In a Scottish side that included fellow 'Iron Curtain' members Young, Woodburn and Cox, along with Billy Steel and future Rangers manager Willie Waddell, Brown excelled in what was hailed as 'a brilliant display' during which he effected several magnificent saves. At right-back for the opposition was Spurs' Alf Ramsey, who, in the build-up to the match was rated 'an ice cool' defender, a description that would resonate later in his managerial career. A strong home team's goals were scored by Nat Lofthouse and Tom Finney, with Aberdeen's George Hamilton netting the Scottish response.

A fortnight before the Hillsborough game, Brown played for Rangers in a special challenge match under the lights against Arsenal at Highbury. This was a resumption of the famous fixture initiated by Struth and legendary Arsenal manager Herbert Chapman in the 1930s, when the two top British clubs met six times alternately home and away between 1933 and 1938. An Arsenal historian researched further to find the roots of the challenge went deeper, with a match between the clubs having taken place in 1892 in Plumstead, a 3–2 win for the Glasgow men, followed by a 1–1 draw in Glasgow in 1908.

On this occasion, Rangers flew south from Renfrew Airport near Glasgow to Northolt in west London, then a two-and-a-half-hour flight, before lunching in their hotel, the Charing Cross. Afternoon tea followed later, and their coach to Highbury left at 6.15pm in time for the 7.30pm kick-off. An exciting game in front of a crowd of 62,000 saw the Gunners edge it by 3–2, with the success of the evening encouraging both clubs to pledge to play a 'return' game in the future in Glasgow. Rangers officials were particularly interested in the technical aspects of the floodlights and received much useful information from Arsenal to help with the installation of their own at Ibrox. This was the first time Brown had played competitively under lights, and he had enjoyed the atmosphere.

His continuing good form in club and representative matches had again provoked a clamour for his recall to the national side for the annual English international on 5 April 1952. Pundits placed him ahead of main rivals George Farm and Jimmy Cowan, although nobody could predict with confidence whom the selectors, in their infinite wisdom, would pick. But, on this occasion, the pundits called it correctly and Brown was given the nod for the game. 'Iron Curtain' colleagues Young and Woodburn were also nominated, as were Hibs' talented trio of Gordon Smith, Lawrie Reilly and Bobby Johnstone, later to become the first player to score in two successive FA Cup finals, with Manchester City in 1955 and 1956. Ian McMillan of Airdrieonians, 'The Wee Prime Minister' as he was known, made his international debut and would become an influential player for Rangers just after Brown left the club.

England fielded a number of well-known names including Alf Ramsey, captain Billy Wright, keeper Gil Merrick, Nat Lofthouse and Tom Finney. After a closely fought encounter in front of 134,000 fans, England won 2–1, with both their goals scored in the first half by Manchester United's prolific centre-forward Stan Pearson, and Lawrie Reilly scoring Scotland's goal 15 minutes before full time. Although Brown played well, this rang the curtain down on his international career. And, a few months later, his club career was to receive a setback from which it never fully recovered.

Chapter 7

Final Years as a Player

O N 5 August 1952, Brown prepared to take up his customary place in Rangers' goal for their opening game of the season, a League Cup tie against Hearts at Tynecastle. He had enjoyed the customary family summer break in Devon with his wife's family, and pre-season training had gone well. His football and teaching careers had been combining well, and he was enjoying his duties, by now in Alloa.

Rangers stuck to their usual pre-match routine, meeting at the St Enoch Hotel for a light lunch and brief tactical discussion before boarding their coach to Edinburgh. They were virtually at full strength, with Young, McColl, Woodburn, Cox, Thornton and Waddell all present. Hearts too fielded a strong team, with experienced players such as full-back Bobby Parker, wing-half Freddie Glidden and their dynamic front three of Alfie Conn, Willie Bauld and Jimmy Wardhaugh, known as 'The Terrible Trio'. The game was a sell-out, with nearly 50,000 packed into Tynecastle eagerly anticipating a close-fought 90 minutes.

In the week leading up to the game, the weather had been exceptionally hot. An hour before kick-off, the heavens opened and a deluge of rain cascaded down on the bone-hard pitch, parched because of the hot weather. Hearts took the lead in the 11th minute and ran out 5–0 winners. Brown takes up the story: 'I was devastated with this result, it had never happened to me before. Because of the amount of rain on the hard pitch, it could not drain away properly and we were caught unprepared. It meant that when the ball was hit, it skidded on the surface, and that made it difficult for me to handle. Hearts adapted much better to the conditions than we did – we seemed to be caught cold. Conn put them ahead then added another after the half-hour mark. At half-time, the team was downcast and I wasn't particularly popular. Mr Struth had some strong words with us. In the second half, Wardhaugh got two and Bauld the other – they certainly lived up to their nickname right enough! I took the rap for the defeat, but on reflection I don't now think it was all down to me. Certainly I could have done better with some of the goals, but some of my team-mates could also have done better. I don't think I got the protection I should have from my defence. Anyway, as far as Rangers were concerned this was a disaster, something completely unheard of! The atmosphere in the dressing room after the game was funereal, like a death in the family. The Glasgow evening papers' billboards proclaimed "Disaster in Edinburgh!" People flocked to buy them to find out what had happened, thinking there had been a terrible accident of some sort in the capital, only to find out it was about a heavy Rangers defeat! Although Mr Struth was clearly unhappy, he did not give anyone a public rollicking – that was not his style – instead, he'd speak individually to players on the Monday after. As I was part-time, he spoke to me at training on the Tuesday evening. He had already previously raised with me once or twice the question of my part-time status, but it had not caused a difficulty between us. But this time he said to me straight that if I remained part-time I could not expect to keep my first-team place. It was all very cordial – there was no animosity at all. It may be that one or two players had said something to him about my position after Tynecastle; that's possible, but I just don't know. I explained to him that I did not want to give up my teaching work, as I had to think about life after football, particularly as I was entering the final stage of my career. It was difficult as at this time I was an internationalist, playing for probably the biggest club in Britain, and I was reluctant to give up playing for the first team. But the bottom line was I had to look to the future after football, and that meant I had to keep my teaching going. So I knew that I'd lose my virtually automatic first-team place, but that was the way it was. The team was due to play Motherwell the next night in another League Cup tie, and George Niven, who had been at Ibrox a couple of years, replaced me. That caused no problem at all between me and George, who was a friend of mine, and he did well when he came in.'

* * * * *

The press did not wholly blame Brown for the Tynecastle defeat. W.M. Gall wrote, 'Brown was not responsible. For the first goal the ball came off Woodburn's boot, was passed instantly to Conn who sent in a deceptive long lob. For the second, Young failed to intercept Conn's shot. Rangers' forwards showed ineptitude. Dropping Brown is a puzzle!'

However, that would be the only first-team game Brown played all season, Niven proving a capable deputy. Indeed, the team went on to win the league and Scottish Cup with Niven in goals. He was philosophical about it. He appreciated that

At Dunipace Primary School – Bobby is fourth from right in the back row. Billy Steel is next to the teacher

Bobby as goalkeeper at Larbert Village School, c.1935

A young Bobby in goalie strip, c.1936

Falkirk High School sports champion, second from right, 1940

Bobby's first season at Queen's Park, 1940/41, with Joe Kyle on his left

Bobby and friend Adam Veitch on their tandem tour of the Highlands, c.1941

Bobby in his Queen's Park tracksuit top, c.1941

Bobby in Fleet Air Arm uniform, c. 1943

Bobby [in numberless top] on a cross-country run near Plymouth, c.1943

Bobby's first Scotland international v. the RAF. Captain Matt Busby is in front

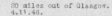

Wedding to Ruth, 6 July 1946

The anonymous letter sent to Bobby in his first season at Rangers

With Rangers team-mates Thornton, Duncanson and Young and wives at a club function, c.1948

Bobby safely collects the ball in a game v. Hibs at a packed Ibrox. Shaw is facing him and Young is on the ground

Rangers line up with Benfica prior to kick-off in Lisbon, 1948

Bobby in goalmouth action at Ibrox. Woodburn is looking on

Bobby Brown runs out for Rangers behind skipper Jock Shaw

Bobby in Rangers' Treble-winning squad, 1949. Manager Struth far left and trainer Smith far right

Bobby in Scotland team with Young in centre front and Cox on Bobby's left

Bobby diving to save in a Rangers v. Celtic game

As a PE teacher in charge of cup-winning Denny High School team, c.1950

Bobby in action for Scottish league v. English league. Cox and Nat Lofthouse are on the right

Bobby leaps to clutch the ball for Scotland v. Ireland at a packed Hampden

Bobby diving full length – Dundee v. Rangers, 1949

Bobby fishing in the River Tay with ex-team-mate Torry Gillick, c.1960

Bobby as St Johnstone manager, 1964/65

Bobby with family, wife Ruth, daughters Carolyn, Alison and, in front, Gilllian, mid-1960s

Bobby in his room at the SFA office while Scotland manager

With the Scotland squad at Hendon before Wembley 1967. Wallace is absent

Bobby with members of the Scotland 'World Tour' party 1967, including Alex Ferguson, back, third from right, Alan Anderson of Hearts is next to Bobby

Bobby in conversation with Sir Alf Ramsey at Wembley, 1967

With Jock Stein, Celtic manager and a successor as Scotland manager

With Willie Johnston and Bobby Lennox at Largs prior to a Scotland fixture

Bobby and Sir Alf Ramsey walk out together at Hampden Park in 1970 prior to Scotland v. England

Bobby as Scotland manager with Helmut Schoen, West German manager

Bobby's wife Ruth

Bobby out rambling in the Scottish Highlands, c.2000

Bobby with 'Iron Curtain' colleagues during an Ibrox reunion, Shaw and Cox at rear, Brown, Young and McColl at front

With ramblers' group heading to the hills, c.2010

*In Blue Room,
Ibrox in centre of
ex-Rangers players
at the club's 140th
anniversary 2013,
flanked on his
left by Johnny
Hubbard and Jim
Forrest on his right*

*Bobby holding
the League Cup
after performing
the cup draw at
Hampden Park,
2012*

*Recently at home
in his study
in front of a
backdrop of career
photos*

economically he was not losing out, as he continued on first-team terms, sharing the same bonuses they did. Reserve-team football was not the same, of course, playing in front of sparse crowds as opposed to the enormous ones he had been used to. There was nothing like the atmosphere at first-team games. He was sorry his incredible run of 255 consecutive league and cup games had come to an end. He felt the quality of his goalkeeping suffered a little, given he was playing at a lower level. But there was no pressure on him to move on; he continued to feel appreciated and knew that he was liable to be called on in the event of Niven being injured or losing form. He always felt well treated by the club. Nor did the prospect of moving elsewhere strongly appeal to him. He was settled happily teaching, and was happy living with his family in their comfortable house at Cambuskenneth, as were they.

Despite the constant diet of reserve-team football, Brown found himself back in favour for part of the following season. This would be Struth's final one as manager after 34 years at the helm, a record which will surely never be surpassed. Brought into the team for the away fixture against Raith Rovers, he played in all the remaining league matches bar one, the game against Hamilton Academical on 6 March 1954, 21 games altogether. Niven took the jersey for the other nine. Despite no longer having first claim on the position, Brown still made headlines. Observers thought he was their best player in both the 3–3 draw with Hearts and the 2–2 draw with Hibs. He also played in the return challenge match against Arsenal at Ibrox, hanselling the new floodlights, in December 1953, and featured in four Scottish Cup ties, a total of 25 appearances. Unfortunately, it was not a vintage season. They finished fourth in the league behind winners Celtic and only reached the semi-finals of both cups. Struth had been in increasingly poor health and stepped down as manager at the end of the season while remaining a director. His place was taken by Scot Symon, a former team-mate of Brown's at Ibrox, who had played at left-half when Brown made his debut against Airdrie.

Symon was a double Scottish international at football and cricket. Both caps were won in 1938, against Hungary at football and against Australia at cricket, a game in which he took five wickets for 33 runs at Forthill, Dundee. Unfortunately the advent of war hampered his career, although he played regularly for Rangers throughout it. He was considered a tough-tackling wing-half and a gifted passer of the ball. Brown thought a lot of him as a player, and he and their respective wives were good friends off the pitch, frequently socialising in each other's houses. Symon first managed East Fife, winning the League Cup with them in 1949 and reaching the Scottish Cup Final the same year, an outstanding achievement for a small club. Brown remembered, 'The area round Methil where East Fife played was still very much a mining community then, and it was through the local miners that Scot first took an interest in pigeon racing, which was their main hobby. He caught the bug in a big way, and it was soon his main interest away from football and his family. Scot was an exceptionally decent bloke, a great player, and he and I always got on well.' After East Fife, he took over at Preston North End, leading them to the FA Cup Final in 1953 before returning to Ibrox.

Symon would go on to achieve a lot of success as Rangers manager, but his first season was not particularly notable: third in the league, quarter-finalists in the League Cup and a last-16 place in the Scottish Cup. Brown's good personal relationship with him did not compromise the manager's team selection, as he was chosen for only eight league games and a handful of friendlies during that season. One of them was a match against The Army at Ibrox in October 1954, which Rangers lost 2–1, Brown and Woodburn the pick of a poor Light Blues team. This was, of course, in the days of National Service, and The Army could select a team of top players, including former soldiers. That evening, players including Tom Finney, Albert Quixall, John Charles, Frank Blunstone and Ronnie Clayton donned their colours. Another match in which he played was in the ongoing series between Arsenal and Rangers, this time at Highbury, on 15 March 1955, which ended in a 3–3 draw. The hosts included famous Welsh keeper Jack Kelsey and Tommy Lawton, against whom Brown was credited with two very good saves. A young Rangers outside-right, Alex Scott, later of Everton, was highly praised for his two goals.

Otherwise, the norm had been playing with the reserves, who were 'looked after' by legendary ex-Ranger Bob McPhail, a club icon from the 1930s who held their appearances and goalscoring records. Brown thoroughly enjoyed his contact with McPhail: 'Bob was a lovely man – he used to look after the reserves for Mr Struth in a part-time capacity, and then Scot when he took over. By this time he had his own electrical business near Ibrox, but enjoyed his continued involvement in the club. He was really Mr Struth's "eyes and ears" in the reserve team, not in a bad way, but he would report back to him on how players were progressing or otherwise. There was not much in the way of tactical input from him – he'd have a quiet word here and there with players. He was quietly spoken but had the players' respect because of who he was. We shared many an enjoyable chat on coach trips together to games up and down the country. In a way he was nearer my generation than the young guys in the reserves, and we probably had more in common.'

Away from football, life was busy for Brown and his family. He had continued teaching in Alloa, initially at Grange Junior Secondary School and later at Alloa Academy. He enjoyed his time at both schools, particularly at Grange, where he ran the football team and counted future Scottish international Willie Morgan and future St Johnstone player Ron McKinven among his pupils. The school team was well supported by the enthusiastic headmaster, Mr Elton Crichton, every Saturday. In the summer term, Brown was in charge of school athletics, entering boys for the Scottish Schools' Championships. As Alloa Academy was a rugby school, he was not involved in that but played a full part in other school sports including outdoors activities. He remembers on one occasion leading a group of six final-year boys on an expedition to the Cairngorms, where, in the course of a day, they covered 26 miles, including climbing four 4,000-feet-plus peaks – Cairn Gorm, Cairn Toul, Ben Macdhui and Braeriach – and crossing part of the famous Lairig Ghru pass.

At home at Cambuskenneth, he and his wife were bringing up a young family and enjoyed life in the country to the full. They owned hens, were keen gardeners – growing a variety of vegetables and plants in their greenhouse – and loved walking their two dogs, one called 'Ranger'! Brown was also a handyman who built his own garage and dabbled in carpentry. While being out of the first team was not ideal, there was plenty going on in his life to occupy him. He would admit that his interest in the game at the top level had begun to wane a little through effectively being displaced, although he was always ready to step in when required. As time wore on, he began to think more about life after football, and family interests were at the top of his list. And, although not figuring regularly in the first team, he was not forgotten. Questions were asked in the press as to how long his 'exile' from top-team football was to last. Articles appeared mitigating his role in the emphatic defeat by Hearts, and at the same time being critical of Young and Woodburn.

His situation aroused much speculation, as well as serious interest from other clubs. He was officially available for transfer, but Rangers appeared reluctant to name a price, which probably revealed their uncertainty over his leaving. The figure of £6,000 was quoted at times, but commentators considered it excessive for a keeper of his age playing mostly second-team football. A number of clubs from both sides of the border tried to secure his services. Hearts pursued him for a while, but Rangers delayed dealing with them. Fulham, Notts County, Sheffield Wednesday and Portsmouth also wanted to buy him, but neither Brown nor the club were persuaded. The closest he came to being transferred was to Huddersfield Town, whose Scottish manager, Andy Beattie, a predecessor as Scottish team manager, was keen to acquire him. Terms were agreed, including Brown's placement at a nearby college to continue teaching, but the deal foundered on the accommodation being offered by Huddersfield. The club could only provide a two-bedroomed house, whereas Brown insisted on a three-bedroomed one as his family was used to a large house. No compromise was possible, and the transfer did not proceed. Although nearly everything was in place for the move, Brown commented, 'It didn't go ahead because of the house. I didn't see why I should accept something less than my family was living in up in Scotland. On reflection, I'm not truly sure my heart was in the move in any event, and in hindsight I'm glad I didn't go south. As it turned out, everything worked out well for me up here.'

Symon's second season in charge would be Brown's final one. He was used sparingly, being fielded in only three league games, all around New Year 1956. The first was the traditional New Year Old Firm match at Parkhead, which Rangers won thanks to a goal from South African forward Don Kitchenbrand. At centre-half for the home team was Jock Stein, and at inside-forward, Bobby Collins, later to become well known at Everton and Leeds United. Five days later, he was in goal against Dundee at Ibrox in a 3–1 win, and a fortnight after that he played his final game for the Rangers first team, against East Fife at Ibrox, a 3–0 win. By now, the only survivors of the Iron Curtain were Brown himself, Ian McColl and George Young. Niven was well established as regular first-team keeper, and a youngster, Billy Ritchie, who would later claim the position, was also on the books. In May 1956, after more than 300 games and 100 shut-outs for Rangers, Brown was sold to Falkirk for £2,200.

Leaving Ibrox was a wrench, but Brown had foreseen it for some time. 'It was a great club to have been at, even though the beginning and the end were not maybe ideal. I soon got over the initial difficulties and am pleased and proud to be able to say I played in a fantastic team with some outstanding players. We enjoyed a lot of success, and much of that was down to Mr Struth and the high standards he set and the team spirit he created. We were a pretty close bunch really, like a band of brothers I always think. In a way, at Rangers you were spoiled as a player because everything was the best, the stadium was superb, crowds were huge, the training facilities excellent, and the club looked after you extremely well if you played your part. When you travelled, you did so in comfort and were accommodated in the best hotels – everything was geared to the philosophy of "Rangers are best", and that applied off the park as well as on it. Naturally, high standards were expected of the players, but everything was in place to enable players to excel. The last few years were at times a little disappointing, but that was largely because of my circumstances, being a part-timer, and there was never any bitterness or hostility on either side. I could completely understand their viewpoint, and I think they respected my wish to continue teaching. Overall I consider myself hugely fortunate and privileged to have spent ten years at Ibrox.'

Brown was a team-mate of many top players at Rangers, and is the last surviving member of the famous Iron Curtain defence. It is fitting, perhaps, that his reminiscences start with his fellow defenders.

'George Young was a pillar of a player, a giant for Rangers in defence, mostly at right-back. His nickname was "Corky" or "Big Cork", as he always carried a champagne cork in his shorts for luck, which a waiter had given him during the celebrations after the 1948 Scottish Cup win. Although we knew each other from schools football, we didn't immediately hit it off at Ibrox. Like others in the team, he knew of my financial arrangements, which caused a bit of division, and on the pitch we used to get in each other's way sometimes at first. "Big Cork" could be quite voluble and wasn't slow to let me know if he thought I could have done better. By the same token, I would respond in kind, but before long we had a good understanding and mutual respect. Mr Struth always had a high regard for him and paid a lot of attention to his opinions. As I say, he was a giant in defence, a good captain for a while and an excellent kicker of a dead ball. If we got a free kick in our half, for example, he could launch it upfield to find the head of Willie Thornton, who would either put it in the net or knock it down to somebody else to do so. Although a big, strongly built bloke, he never gave referees any trouble, was never sent off and, remarkably, only booked once. He ran a successful hotel for a while at Tillietudlem in Lanarkshire when he retired from the game.

'Jock "Tiger" Shaw at left-back was a great Rangers skipper, and we had a good understanding. If you made a mistake, he was supportive, and we communicated well on the pitch. I suppose you could describe Jock as "couthy", a very down-to-earth guy who, appropriately for an ex-miner, "called a spade a spade". As his "Tiger" nickname suggests, he was a ferocious tackler, what you might call an "old style" full-back, an "up and at 'em" type player who once he won his tackle would clear the ball upfield. As captain mostly during my time, he led by example and got those round him playing. He was very dependable, never negative, and was one of the club's longest-serving players. When he was still playing, he had a newsagent's shop near Ibrox, and once he retired he was groundsman at the club for years.

'Ian McColl at right-half had been at Queen's Park at the same time as me and was one of my predecessors as Scottish manager. Before that, he managed Sunderland. As a player, Ian was a stalwart Ranger, a strong tackler and good header of the ball. He was defensively minded, unlike Cox on the other flank, and in a way was almost a dual centre-half with Woodburn. An extremely useful player, he could be quite an intense chap and was very much his own man. At team meetings, he was never afraid to voice his thoughts, although he could be a bit sensitive to criticism. An assiduous trainer, I remember he would practise on his own to improve his weaker foot by standing on the track at Ibrox and kicking the ball back and forward off the perimeter wall. His moods were a bit changeable, and he tended to hold fairly strong views. Latterly he thought entry to the club's Hall of Fame was being made too easy for some, and that as a result it was being devalued a little. Away from football, he was a qualified civil engineer, and latterly he and his wife operated a very successful guest house in Bearsden.

'Willie Woodburn, "Big Ben", was an absolutely brilliant centre-half, the best I ever saw. He really was a superb player, athletic, ferocious and fearless in the tackle – he'd go through a brick wall for you – and excellent in the air. He truly had all the qualities of a top international player, but, as is well known, his temperament let him down at times. I still think what happened to him, being banned *sine die* by the SFA, was well over the top, but opponents knew they could rile him and he would react. He was well warned about controlling his temper, but ultimately it was to no avail. A Stirling Albion player did just that, and "Ben" reacted violently and was sent off. The SFA adjudged that to be one too many and banned him *sine die*, although nowadays that would never happen. I think in all he was sent off four or five times. You could tell when his anger was building, as he would start to tug at his jersey with his left hand about chest height, and that was the warning sign. The trouble was, once it started, he seemed unable to control it. And it wasn't just provocation to him that got him angry – the same would happen if he felt team-mates were being unfairly treated. I remember one game where Billy Williamson was upended unceremoniously in the first half, and at the interval in the dressing room "Ben" was saying, "I'll have him!" He was a Ranger through and through. On the other hand, off the pitch he was completely different – he was charm personified. My wife and his wife, Jean, were very good friends, and we were too. We used to socialise together, and, as I say, he was completely different away from the pitch. When his playing career finished, he became a well-known football journalist and had an interest in a garage in Edinburgh.

'The last member of the "Curtain" was left-half Sammy Cox. He and I had been team-mates at Queen's Park and made our Rangers debuts the same day against Airdrie. Although he was a lithely built fellow, Sammy could certainly tackle and make them count! He was very fast, always kept himself very fit and was a more attack-minded player than McColl on the other side. At times he played almost like an inside-forward and could snatch the occasional goal. He was a real 90-minute man and had a good temperament, always cheery and open – he was easy company to be with. A good team-mate, he never moaned and never held grudges. After he stopped playing, he emigrated to Canada, where he lived until his death in 2015.

'Among the forwards, the two top men were Willie Waddell and Willie Thornton. Waddell, or "Deedle", was an exceptional outside-right with real pace and two great feet. He was very direct, a great crosser of the ball, and combined particularly well with centre-forward Thornton. I always thought of them as a twosome. "Deedle's" pinpoint crosses would be expertly met by the skilful head of Thornton. But Waddell at times was moody and, if not happy with himself or others, would retreat into his shell. Latterly he enjoyed a cigarette and a drink and could be very single-minded. After he stopped playing, he was a successful manager at Kilmarnock and Rangers, while between these jobs he was a football journalist when I was Scotland manager. He was one of my fiercest critics, and I used to think he didn't fully appreciate the difficulties I worked under, with players frequently calling off. I used to say to him that we can all be experts at quarter to five, i.e. with hindsight. However, he was a truly outstanding Ranger, there is no doubt about that.

'As was Willie Thornton: he was a different sort of bloke, although him and Waddell were great friends off the pitch. My wife and I were good friends with Thornton and his wife, and we all once spent a holiday together in Devon. At centre-forward, he very much complemented Waddell and, as I've said, was a deadly header of the ball. From Winchburgh in West Lothian, he joined Rangers from school in about 1936 and was another player whose career was interrupted by the war. He had an exemplary war record, winning the Military Medal for Gallantry in 1943, as a gunner in the Royal Artillery, part of the Eighth Army campaign in North Africa and then Sicily. The Medal was awarded to non-commissioned officers and was the equivalent of the Military Cross for commissioned officers. Willie was a very personable chap, very unassuming and a great friend. After he stopped playing, he went into management with Dundee and Partick Thistle and then returned to Ibrox as assistant to Waddell.

'Other figures included inside-forward Torry Gillick, a real character and extremely talented footballer but an equally lazy trainer! Again the war interrupted his career. In the 1930s, he went from Ibrox to Everton and then returned, but by the end of the war his best days were largely behind him. Jimmy Duncanson was a versatile forward who was much underrated but a valuable player. He would run miles during a game and was always good for a goal. Johnny Hubbard, the South African outside-left, was a slightly built skilful winger who could carry the ball well and send over lovely crosses. He, of course, was a famed penalty taker, very seldom missing from the spot. Eddie Rutherford, another winger, was more of a runner who would take on the full-back. He was a two-footed player who could play on either wing and, if not in Waddell's class, was still pretty useful. Billy Williamson was another PE teacher, a versatile and talented forward who perhaps lacked consistency. He was not an ever-present but could come into the team and score vital goals. And my path just crossed briefly with Jerry Dawson, my famous predecessor between the posts at Ibrox, shortly before he moved to Falkirk. He was a great character and a bit of a joker – very popular with everyone at Ibrox, which added to the pressure on me! Clearly he was an excellent keeper, although maybe not the best kicker of a ball. Finally, George Niven who effectively replaced me in Rangers' first team was a really good bloke, and the two of us had a good rapport. He was not the tallest for a keeper but was courageous and effective and fitted in well. Originally he was from Blairhall in Fife and was signed from Coupar Angus Juniors.'

Being in effect a Falkirk 'Bairn' himself, when Brown signed for the Brockville club it meant the wheel had turned full circle, back to where it had all started. His friend, the house builder Duncan Ogilvie, was a member of the Falkirk board, and he acted as a go-between for Brown and the club. Their manager, Bob Shankly, was persuaded to make a bid for him, and when Scot Symon accepted the offer of £2,200, Brown decided to cut his ties with Ibrox. By now he was 33 and near the end of his career, and it suited him to join his 'local' club to see out his playing days. Falkirk were in the top tier and had just finished 14th of 18 in the 1955/56 season. They played in a notoriously tight ground at Brockville and by today's standards were fairly well supported, with average crowds about the 8,000–9,000 mark.

Shankly was brother of Bill of Liverpool fame and a well-regarded manager in his own right, his greatest achievement coming in 1962 when he won the top league with Dundee and led them to the European Cup semi-final. According to Brown, 'I thought Shankly quite a good manager, but nothing special. Managers then seldom came out on to the training ground, and Shankly, although always a friendly guy, didn't strike me as particularly knowledgeable tactically. The trainer was Ernie Godfrey, and I really had more to do with him. In my first season, I played 16 out of 34 league games and half a dozen in the League Cup. We again finished 14th in the league, and what became clear to me, as I knew it would, was that this "wasn't Rangers". I say that without any disrespect to Falkirk, but they were just on a different level to Rangers in all sorts of ways. I have to accept also that, at this time, my appetite for playing was diminishing – I had had a full career by this stage, including some memorable highlights, and I felt I was only going in one direction. A few injuries were also coming my way, and I didn't want to jeopardise my future. On one occasion, when I was suffering from a groin strain, I was persuaded to take a cortisone injection to let me play, but I remember how uncomfortable I felt when the effects of the injection wore off and how long that feeling lasted. That was not something I wanted to repeat. It's only fair to point out there were some good players around Brockville at the time: guys like full-back Alec Parker, who later starred for Everton; the other full-back, Ian Rae; Jim McIntosh; fellow ex-Rangers Derek Grierson and John

Prentice (my predecessor as Scottish manager); fellow keeper Bert Slater, later of Liverpool; and centre-forward Doug Moran.'

Brown stayed on for a final season, playing only six league games and a handful of cup games, before hanging up his boots in April 1958 aged 35. It had been a long and fulfilling career. As at Rangers, he had been a part-time player at Falkirk while a PE teacher at Alloa Academy. He now began to consider whether there may be another niche in the game for him.

Chapter 8

St Johnstone Manager

WHILE running down his playing career at Falkirk, Brown had been thinking about giving management a try. As a PE teacher he had coached school teams with a degree of success, and the idea of management in senior football became more appealing as time passed. He had always been interested in improving his knowledge of the game, and, as we have already seen, he had attended an SFA coaching course at Ibrox just after the end of the war.

With an eye on his future, in 1953 he attended a residential two-week FA coaching course at St Luke's PE College, Exeter, organised by Walter Winterbottom, the FA's director of coaching. This was a wide-ranging, comprehensive course attended by about a hundred potential coaches, which combined practical work on the pitch with classroom lectures. Brown's section leader was Bill Nicholson, an ex-international and future highly successful Spurs manager whose name became synonymous with the club after leading it to the century's first double win of league and cup in 1961. According to Brown, 'I was very impressed by Bill Nicholson and learned a lot from him. He was extremely knowledgeable, had an appealing, down-to-earth manner and an excellent sense of humour. All his sessions were well organised and very enjoyable. He made it all worthwhile. And Walter Winterbottom was also impressive. He gave several lectures, and it was apparent he was a master of his subject and very well educated. The whole course was a great experience, and I was pleased to gain my coaching badge at the end, which, of course, was good for my CV.'

When an advertisement appeared at the end of the 1957/58 season for a manager of the Perth club St Johnstone, Brown decided to apply for it. A week or so later, he attended the lawyer's office of chairman Mr Alex Lamond in Perth for an interview. Other directors were present including James Clarke, Fred Voigt, Willie Dewar and Jack McKinlay. All of them were aware of Brown's successful playing career and were impressed by his immaculate appearance, his articulate communication skills and his ideas on management. Brown felt confident about the outcome, and the next day his confidence was justified when Mr Lamond phoned to offer him the job, which he accepted, at the princely wage of £5 per week plus expenses. It was a part-time club, and he would be a part-time manager, continuing to teach at Alloa Academy.

The club was not in rude health either on or off the pitch. It was saddled with debt around the £20,000 mark, a considerable amount for a small provincial club, while the previous season it had finished 11th in the old 19-team Second Division. Crowds had fallen, and the board had decided to dispense with the services of player/manager Johnny Pattillo, formerly a well-known Dundee forward, in an effort to revitalise the club. At the interview, the directors told Brown their aim was for him to take them into the 'upper half' of the division and reduce the debt. For his part, Brown thought St Johnstone was a good club at which to cut his managerial teeth. It was not in a very good place, he was beginning with 'a clean sheet' and, in his opinion, the 'only way was up'. He also had confidence in his own ability to improve the situation.

A fruitful association with the Saints therefore began, which would last almost nine years, during which time he would stabilise them financially, increase crowds, lead them to two second-tier titles, facilitate improvements to their Muirton Park ground through the installation of floodlights, the construction of a new covered enclosure and the provision of a gym, and establish them as a top-tier club. Along the way he wheeled and dealed extensively in the transfer market, mostly very astutely, to provide the economic base for the club to grow on and off the pitch. Critics may point to the success enjoyed by the manager who followed him, Willie Ormond (also a successor as national team manager) – but, without demeaning his achievements, he did so with a squad of players who had mostly been recruited latterly by Brown. And, of course, as a result of his excellent work at Perth, Brown secured the national team manager's post in 1967.

Since their admission to the Scottish Football League in 1911, the Saints had flitted between the top two divisions, with their best spell coming in the 1930s, when they twice finished in fifth place in the old First Division. At that time, they were managed by another former Ranger and Scottish international, Tommy Muirhead. When Brown took over, they had last featured in the top league in 1939, having been consigned to the lower division in the course of reorganisation after the war.

Brown began in purposeful fashion, deciding to have a 'clear-out' of players except three whom he retained: winger Joe Carr, full-back Charlie McFadyen and keeper Billy Taylor. He then embarked on frequent scouting missions at junior games in the west of Scotland, and scanned the transfer lists of top league teams to secure worthwhile free transfers. His philosophy was to combine youth with experience. He also decided he would keep some distance between the players and himself, in contrast to the previous managerial regime. He recognised that at times he would have to make difficult decisions to drop players, and wanted to avoid the risk of being perceived to have 'favourites'. To avoid the inconvenience and expense of players travelling twice per week to Perth for training, most being based in the west of the country, he arranged the hire of a training ground two nights per week from Glasgow cricket club Cartha. Apart from the practical benefits of having all the players training together, it also helped in the development of good team spirit. Among the players recruited who would play significant roles in future were John Liddell, a prolific scorer in the juniors from Greenock; his brother Dan, an outside-right; Willie Haughey, another striker signed from Falkirk; and ex-Rangers and Queen's Park centre-half John Valentine.

At first it seemed Brown's methods were not paying off, as at Christmas the team were fourth from bottom, before setting off on a strong run to finish in sixth position. Their defensive record was much improved, conceding 44 goals in 36 games compared with the previous year's 85. It was the lowest in the division, four better than champions Ayr United. Crowds were also up by about a third, to an average of just under 4,000, a figure that would surely be welcomed today, when Saints games often fail to attract 3,000 fans. Total debt had been halved, much to the satisfaction of the board, who rewarded Brown with a wage increase to £10 per week plus expenses. He was thoroughly enjoying the challenge, particularly as improvement was evident, which he aimed to build on in his second season.

That started well with a 7–3 home win over Cowdenbeath, with ace marksmen Haughey and Liddell both notching hat-tricks. Apart from a period of two weeks, the team would maintain top position until the end of the season, when they were crowned champions of the old Second Division – the first time they had won it since 1924. Other additions to the squad included skipper Ron McKinven, signed from Queen's Park – an ex-pupil of Brown's at Grange school in Alloa, whose progress he had monitored. McKinven, an architect, was still an amateur at this stage and in September 1960 represented Great Britain in three games in the Rome Olympics before turning professional and enjoying a lengthy career with Saints. Norrie Innes, a former Scottish under-23 cap, was another useful signing, from Stirling Albion; and Jim Lachlan, a solid full-back, was acquired from Falkirk. Matt McVittie, a purposeful half-back, was signed from Celtic to shore up the midfield. Brown was quietly optimistic, with the level of experience he had introduced to the team. As the season unfolded, Dundee United were proving to be their biggest rivals, with a 16,000 crowd at Muirton Park attesting to this at New Year as Saints and United fought out a 1–1 draw. Meanwhile, Taylor's consistently reliable displays in goal were attracting attention, and Leeds United tabled a £7,000 bid for him, which Brown rejected.

With eight games remaining, Saints lost their hitherto unbeaten home record to Hamilton Accies 3–2, a match from which only keeper Taylor and full-back Lachlan emerged with any credit. That was followed by a defeat away to Albion Rovers, and some fans began to doubt whether promotion was feasible. However, they were soon back on track, with a good away win at East Fife and a home success over Stenhousemuir to steady their position at the top of the table with four matches left.

A break from league football enabled the club to undertake a mini-tour of the Highlands, where they recorded wins against Inverness Caledonian and Ross County, 6–1 and 2–1 respectively, keeping team morale high – as did wing-half John Docherty's selection for a Second Division Select to play in a match against Scotland under-23s. Meanwhile, the squad had been reinforced by Brown's judicious signing from East Fife of Ian Gardiner, an ex-Scottish international.

With three games to go, Saints required three points out of six for the title. A nervy 3–2 home win against East Stirlingshire in front of a crowd of 7,000, with a brace from Joe Carr and a first goal from Gardiner, put Saints on the right track. On 27 April, the title was secured in England, a 2–0 defeat of Berwick Rangers at their Shielfield Park being sufficient to edge them over the line. Three days later, they completed their programme with an away draw at Morton to finish three points in front of Dundee United.

The season had been a great success for Brown, and a vindication of his approach to the task as a 'rookie' manager. Not only had he led them to the title after years in the doldrums, but average attendances had almost doubled to 7,500.

'That was a great season in what was only my second as manager. Although not a particularly big "football town", there was nevertheless a real feel-good factor throughout Perth thanks to this success. It undoubtedly added to the town's sense of its identity, and civic leaders were very conscious and appreciative of that. The town had been starved of top football for years, and there was genuine excitement it was coming back. And we had achieved it within our means, through sensible dealings in the transfer market. The club was treated to a memorable civic reception in Perth Town Hall by Lord Provost Buchan, which was very enjoyable and much appreciated. Some old players and officials who had been involved in the previous win in 1924 and promotion in 1932 were tracked down and were generous with their praise, which added to the sense of achievement felt by the team.'

The campaign was a particular success for strikers John Liddell and Willie Haughey, who each weighed in with 27 league goals. The club generously provided a week's holiday in Blackpool as a 'thank you' for the winning squad, including manager Brown, and a good time was had by all.

Brown was excited about competing in the top tier, but apprehensive about the strength of his squad. By now he had appointed a trainer – John Mathers, an ex-St Johnstone player before and after the war. Consideration had been given to going full-time, but the board were reluctant to take that step at this juncture although Brown had been sounded out about the possibility of doing so in future. As anticipated, their first season in the top league proved difficult.

One player whom he had recruited to bring experience and contribute with a few goals, but who, as Brown candidly admits, was a failure, was Jimmy Gauld, bought from Swindon Town for £3,000. 'Gauld had played for a few clubs including Charlton and Everton in the old English First Division and did quite well. He was a particularly successful goalscorer at a lower level with my old club Plymouth Argyle, where I still had contacts, and then Swindon Town. I have to admit I bought him largely on his reputation at Plymouth, but it was clear when he appeared that he was overweight. Later I learned from one of my players, Doug Newlands, that Gauld, who was struggling to keep up at training, had asked him to run alongside him to make his lack of condition look less obvious! Another player also later reported that the first time he met Gauld he had tried to sell him a watch! He used to go betting every day and really was a bit of a disaster. After four games and no goals scored, I had seen enough and realised I'd made a mistake, and sent him packing on the train south after personally delivering his boots to him and driving him to the station. Thankfully we recouped some of the fee by selling him to Mansfield Town. He later became the central figure in a football betting scandal in England, which led to a number of players being prosecuted and imprisoned. As the ringleader, Gauld himself was sentenced to four years' imprisonment in January 1965 and banned for life from football. Thankfully he wasn't with us long enough to get mixed up in anything like that, but I have to confess he was not my best buy.'

With weeks of their season remaining, Saints looked relegation candidates, but a good home win against Motherwell in front of 10,000 fans and an away win over Raith Rovers in the final game of the season steered them clear. Brown had to settle for 15th position in an 18-team division, although it was scant consolation that only four points separated them from Dundee United in ninth place. On the positive side, average attendances were the highest ever at 10,500, an increase of almost 50 per cent from the previous year.

A significant signing by Brown during the 1960/61 season was one Alex Ferguson from Queen's Park, later of course to acquire a knighthood and managerial fame and fortune with Aberdeen and Manchester United. Brown kept in contact with his old club, Queen's Park, alert to its potential as a source of promising young players. He had received good reports of Ferguson, including one from his skipper, McKinven, who had been a team-mate of Ferguson's at Hampden, and another from Saints' part-time scout in Glasgow, Willie Neill. Neill was an electrician with his own business, which Brown invested in when it became 'Brown and Neill'. His own observations confirmed these reports, and he arranged to meet Ferguson in Glasgow to sign him. As an amateur, as Brown was before joining Rangers, Ferguson could negotiate his own signing-on fee and accepted the £300 offered. Brown laughs, 'He never forgave me for that, as he thought he should have been given more, but that was the going rate at the time. In fact, he was not difficult to deal with – I think it was only later he thought he should have received more. When I watched him, I could see he had an eye for goal and was awkward to play against. He wasn't what you would call a free-running player but was good in the penalty box and good with his head. He was enthusiastic and always appeared to be "up for it". I felt he could come up and do a job for me, and, although not always in the first team, he did well at Perth. From an early stage you could tell he had something about him. In team talks the day before a game, he always had plenty to say, mostly in a positive way, but sometimes his opinions could be annoying. He had a lot of influence on others in the team and was a bit of a spokesman for the dressing room. The financial side of things interested him, and he always wanted to know in advance details of bonus payments for the more important games. In all he played some 45 games for us over four seasons and scored 22 goals, a good return. He moved to Dunfermline Athletic in 1964 in exchange for Dan McIlindon. Perhaps his best game for us was against Rangers at Ibrox in December 1963, when, in tricky underfoot conditions, he scored a hat-trick in a 3–1 win, the only St Johnstone player, I think, ever to do so against Rangers. No doubt Rangers took note of that, as he later signed for them. And I selected him for the Scotland XI 'World Tour' in 1967, as I felt he could get me goals, which he did. I have to say I have nothing but respect and admiration for what he went on to achieve in his managerial career.'

Another signing that season, which led to an interesting contact with West Ham United, was goalkeeper Ian Ower from well-known junior side Kirkintilloch Rob Roy. Brown signed him principally as back-up to first-choice keeper Billy Taylor, but soon other clubs were expressing an interest in him after good performances in the reserves and occasionally the first team. Ron Greenwood, West Ham manager and, of course, later England manager, was one who showed interest and came up to Perth to speak to Brown about a possible transfer. 'Ron was a great guy, a real gent and a pleasure to be with. We had a pleasant chat about his interest in Ower, and, as he was due to play for us the next day at Stranraer, I suggested to Ron he could travel down there with us on the coach to see the player in action, which he did. As it turned out, he didn't take his interest any further, but we enjoyed each other's company.

'A couple of years or so later, we were looking for attractive opposition for our first game under the new floodlights at Muirton Park, which was also to be a benefit match for former player Ernie Ewen. I decided to contact Ron at West Ham to see if he would bring his team up to play us. They had won the FA Cup earlier that year, and, with some top players in their team, I thought they would be a good draw. Ron was appreciative of how we had treated him previously and agreed to play us. Unfortunately, on the night concerned, 16 December 1964, the weather could hardly have been worse – there was horrendous rain, sleet and wind, which cut down the anticipated attendance drastically to only 5,000. Before kick-off, their captain, Bobby Moore, who was injured and unable to play, nevertheless led the team out carrying the FA Cup, which was taken on a tour of the ground. The conditions spoiled the match as a spectacle, but we did well to hold them to a 4–3 win. Johnny Byrne scored a hat-trick for the Hammers, and Geoff Hurst scored the winner. Another future World Cup hero, Martin Peters, also played that night, and afterwards we had an enjoyable get-together in the boardroom before they headed off south.'

That 15th-place finish persuaded St Johnstone's board that if they were to progress, they had to convert to full-time status for the next season. Brown was also finally persuaded to give up his teaching career to become the club's full-time manager. This was not an easy decision to reach, but he felt this was too good an opportunity to pass up. He was very happy at the club, he enjoyed working with its very supportive board, and both he and his wife, Ruth, were in favour of moving house to be nearer Perth, as had been suggested by the club. His measure of success to this point had not gone unnoticed, and he received an approach from Hibs to take the helm at Easter Road. This was a serious approach, with Brown meeting chairman Harry Swan and his director brother at the Hawes Inn in South Queensferry to discuss the proposal. However, St Johnstone offered their manager a five-year contract to secure his continued services at Muirton Park, which he was happy to accept. In the meantime, Brown and his family had moved to the village of Stanley, near Perth, where they settled in well and soon began enjoying life there.

While changes for the better were taking place off the pitch, that progress was not reflected on the pitch in the league, although the League Cup was more profitable. Despite being drawn in a tough qualifying section with Celtic, Hibs and Partick Thistle, Saints topped the group and, in the quarter-final, defeated Motherwell to reach the semi-final of a national cup competition for the first time in their history. The home leg in that tie attracted a crowd of 14,500. Their opponents in the semi at Parkhead were Rangers, who edged them 3–2 despite Taylor having an outstanding game in goals. As far as the league was concerned, the Saints could only finish second bottom, in one of the relegation spots. Their fate came down to the last game of the season at home against Dundee, their Tayside rivals, who at the time had perhaps the best team in their history. A point for them would secure their first and only top-league title, while a point for the Saints would ensure First Division survival. Suggestions in advance that both teams would compromise and settle for a draw serving both their interests were swatted aside by Brown, who firmly declared there would be 'no fix' in this game. Adding spice to the occasion was the fact that Dundee were managed by Bob Shankly, Brown's old manager at Falkirk. In the event, Dundee ran out comfortable 3–0 winners and the following season would reach the semi-final of the European

Cup, scarcely believable now. Brown was slightly surprised and disappointed that Shankly did not come to speak to him after the game, but appreciated that his team's celebrations may have distracted him. During the season, trainer John Mathers left to join Falkirk, as Brown was concerned he was too close to some players. He was replaced by Frank Christie from East Fife, who was an excellent acquisition. Christie had been a good wing-half for the Fifers, for whom he had scored the opening goal in their 1953 League Cup win.

Saints' anguish was not lessened by sharing the same points total as Airdrie and St Mirren, whose superior goal averages placed them above the Saints. Had goal difference applied as it now does, St Mirren would have been relegated, not St Johnstone.

In Brown's opinion, 'This did not come as a complete surprise. I think we probably had been promoted too quickly, without the necessary strength in depth, and without an established reserve team for players to gain experience in before going into the first team.'

His disappointment was tempered by the club chairman's reaction to this setback, as Mr Lamond invited him and his wife out for dinner that evening to Dunkeld House Hotel as a 'thank you' for his efforts and to discuss plans for the coming season. Brown's support from his chairman and board during his spell with the Saints was consistently good and a big factor in his continuing enthusiasm at Muirton Park.

That next season, 1962/63, Brown led the Saints to the Second Division title for the second time in four seasons, winning by a comfortable six points from runners-up East Stirlingshire. And, for the second consecutive year they enjoyed a run to the semi-finals of the League Cup. First in their section, featuring Clyde, Stranraer and Cowdenbeath, they qualified for a quarter-final tie against Queen of the South, whom they defeated to reach the semi against Hearts. But they were no match for the Tynecastle men, who won comfortably 4–0 at Easter Road. Players whom Brown brought in that season included Bobby Kemp, an exciting winger from Montrose who was later sold on at a profit to Hearts; long-serving full-back Willie Coburn, bought from Perthshire junior side Crieff Earngrove; and a skilful half-back, Willie Renton, from the Fife junior team Lochore Welfare.

However, central to their league success was a young midfield player, Jim Townsend, who represented one of Brown's shrewdest pieces of transfer business. He had bought him the previous season largely by chance. Returning from a scouting trip to Greenock, he stopped to watch the last half hour of a game involving junior team Port Glasgow Rangers, for whom Townsend was playing. He did so solely out of interest and to pass the time while he ate a snack. He had no idea who was playing or whether they had any pedigree. The fair-haired midfielder caught Brown's eye immediately, and by the end of the game he had decided to sign him. At this stage, unknown to Brown, a number of clubs, including Manchester United, Manchester City and Celtic, were interested in the player, who had been a Scottish Youth international. He spoke to the club secretary and Townsend himself, who, there and then, agreed to join St Johnstone. The transfer fee was £80 and two footballs for Port Glasgow Rangers.

Brown takes up the story, 'Townsend was a great buy for me – he was a revelation. After some reserve games, he was in the first team, and during our promotion season he was the player who made the team tick, no doubt about that. Once we were back in the First Division, bigger clubs began to take an interest, and Raich Carter, Middlesbrough's manager, the famous former English international, offered £27,500 for him, which we were very happy to accept. Unfortunately, Carter was later sacked, Townsend's form dropped and the opportunity arose for me to buy him back, which I did for the knock-down price of £5,000. He regained his form after a spell back in Perth, which led to other clubs once more taking an interest in him. Just when I was leaving Perth to take the Scotland job, Tommy Walker, the Hearts manager, came in for him and paid £19,000 to take him to Tynecastle. This was undoubtedly the best piece of business I did at St Johnstone, for, although nowadays these fees may sound paltry, then they amounted to a lot of money for provincial clubs like ours. Those dealings financed the new floodlights and other ground improvements at Muirton, as well as reducing our overdraft. I thought highly of Townsend's ability, which is why, as with Ferguson, I selected him for the Scotland XI "World Tour".'

Saints were top throughout most of the season, but towards the end stumbled to defeats by Ayr United and Albion Rovers. They redeemed themselves with a good 2–1 win against near rivals Morton in front of a crowd of 11,500 at Muirton, before clinching the title by beating Montrose 1–0.

In their first season back in the top league, 1963/64, Brown led them to a respectable 13th place, with home and away victories over champions Rangers among the highlights. Winning their League Cup section was followed by a disappointing loss to Berwick Rangers in the play-off for a quarter-final place. Average attendances had jumped about 25 per cent from their year in the Second Division to about 7,300. Other important players had been added during the season: Bill 'Buck' McCarry from Falkirk, who would become a St Johnstone icon; Jim Harrower, ex-Liverpool and Scotland under-23 inside-forward, also signed from Falkirk; and full-back Jim Richmond, former Kilmarnock skipper.

The following season Brown's team consolidated their position in the top league by again finishing 13th, and he again strengthened his squad by acquiring midfielder Neil Duffy from Partick Thistle and striker Gordon Whitelaw from Airdrie. Both had played together at Partick previously and enjoyed a good understanding. Whitelaw was a former Scottish amateur international and had also represented Scotland at basketball. He had a long career at Perth, during which he was a prolific goalscorer. At the end of the season, Brown went on a scouting trip with a club director to Scandinavia, which at the time was a good source of players for Scottish teams, particularly Morton and Dundee United, but returned without signing anyone.

One very influential signing he did make about this time was tenacious midfielder Alex MacDonald, later to become a mainstay of a successful Rangers team that won the European Cup Winners' Cup in 1972 and a Scottish international. At that time, MacDonald was a 17-year-old playing for juvenile side Glasgow United, about whom Brown had received good reports, and he invited him to play trials for the reserves. In games against Third Lanark and Dundee, MacDonald did well, scoring a couple of goals, and Brown decided to go to Glasgow to sign him. He called at MacDonald's grandmother's house in the Tradeston district, where he was living, and she told him that Alex was out in the street nearby playing football. Brown tracked him down and took him to a nearby café, Pollok Snacks, for 'signing talks'. MacDonald recalls, 'I'd played a couple of trials for them but had heard nothing about signing. I was out with my mates in the street, kicking a ball about between buildings that were then in the process of being demolished, and I remember I was wearing my elephant cords and sannies [sports shoes]. Bobby Brown approached me out of the blue about signing for St Johnstone, which came as a complete surprise. We went to the local café, me at 17 on my own, no agents or parents with me, discussing terms with Bobby! We agreed I would get £125 for signing on, and I was absolutely delighted.

Half of that went to my granny. It was a great breakthrough for me, and, of course, a few years later I got my big move to Ibrox. Going to St Johnstone was really good for me and helped my development tremendously. After a first season mostly in the reserves, I became a first-team regular. For me, Brown was a great manager, I had the utmost respect for him – he was a real gent. My main asset was my energy, and Brown gave me a free role in the team to express myself. I knew he had a great reputation as a player, and I listened to all the advice he gave me. I could be a bit boisterous as a youngster, and there's no doubt he was a good calming influence on me.' As it transpired, Brown found MacDonald in Tradeston just in time, because, as he left the area, he saw a large black car in the vicinity containing Joe Harvey and Stan Seymour of Newcastle United, who were also there to try to sign MacDonald. This was another excellent piece of business for the club by Brown, because just over a year after he left for the Scotland job, MacDonald was transferred to Rangers for £65,000.

In his penultimate year with the club, 1965/66, the team finished in 14th position to maintain their top-tier status, and reached the quarter-finals of the Scottish Cup for the first time since 1935, losing 1–0 to eventual winners Rangers at Ibrox. One novelty was a challenge match against European opposition, the Czechoslovak team, Slovan Bratislava, under the floodlights at Muirton in November 1965 – a 2–0 win for the Perth men. Brown's wheelings and dealings in the transfer market brought in important players John Kilgannon from Dunfermline Athletic, Benny Rooney from Dundee United and Fred Aitken from the Fife Juniors.

Brown's final season at Muirton came to an end in February 1967 when he was appointed Scotland manager. The team went on to finish that season under new manager Willie Ormond in 15th place, although comfortably clear of the relegation spots, managing to keep their top-flight status for the fourth year in a row. Two years later, Ormond secured them a sixth-place finish, and two years after that he led them to the club's best-ever finish of third in the top division. Many of the players involved then were Brown's signings, including goalkeeper Jim Donaldson, Willie Coburn, 'Buck' McCarry, winger Ian McPhee, Gordon Whitelaw, Benny Rooney and Fred Aitken; and Brown can properly claim credit for laying the foundations for Ormond's successful team.

During his time at Muirton Park, Brown had dealings with a number of his fellow managers, among them Tommy Walker of Hearts, Bobby Ancell of Motherwell, Jock Stein of Celtic, Tommy Pearson of Aberdeen, Jerry Kerr of Dundee United, Jimmy McKinnell of Queen of the South and, of course, Scot Symon of Rangers. 'Tommy Walker was an absolute gent, an outstanding player, of course, with Hearts, Chelsea and Scotland who was never booked or sent off. He was my dad's idol. We had a good relationship and I remember the two of us both did readings at Dunfermline Abbey in a special Sportsmen's Service just after the war. Ancell was a football purist ahead of his time. He was well known for wanting to play the game the right way and encouraged his outstanding young team, known as the "Ancell Babes", to do so. He brought on a number of young, talented players including Billy Hunter, Pat Quinn, Ian St John and others. Jock Stein was a superb manager. We always got on well and he was helpful to me. Pearson did well at Aberdeen – he was a very quiet chap who was always courteous. His successor at Aberdeen, Eddie Turnbull, whom I knew, of course, from school days, was a different kettle of fish – very forthright, he called a spade a spade. Kerr was in charge of our near rivals; he was affable and approachable, it was always a pleasure doing business with him. Shaw was a splendid bloke, quiet and disciplined, a former Scottish team trainer when I played in 1946. And McKinnell at Queen's always extended a great welcome to you!'

He looks back with a degree of pride and many happy memories at his time at St Johnstone: 'In many ways, they were the happiest days of my life. I had a great set-up there and worked with a fantastic board who were very supportive and trusted me to do the job and left me to get on with it. When I joined, they really were in a poor state and I like to think I did well by them in improving their finances through my transfer dealings and bringing them a measure of success on the park. I thoroughly enjoyed my time there, and it was a big decision to leave. As a family, we very much enjoyed living in the village of Stanley near Perth, where we had a nice house in Duchess Street, about 400 yards from the River Tay. Being a country boy at heart, I really liked the lifestyle there, being able to walk my dogs in the surrounding countryside and fishing in the Tay. A neighbour was a ghillie and he taught me how to fish, which I got very keen on. On one unforgettable occasion, after a struggle lasting about an hour, I landed a 32lb salmon. I sold it to the local fishmonger, who put it on display in his window, where one of my daughters recognised it and proudly pointed it out to her schoolmates. Often I would be finished work and back home by about half past two and able to be fishing by three. Sometimes, of course, I had to be out in the evenings at training sessions or board meetings, but it really was a great life and Stanley was a very friendly place to live. In those days, the media were not so intrusive as now, and, although I got occasional criticism in the local newspaper, I was left by and large in peace to do my job and get on with my life. My wife, Ruth, thoroughly enjoyed our time there too. She became involved in the community in Stanley and ran the local Brownies troop. I did begin to feel, as time went on, that the job – although highly enjoyable – was becoming less of a challenge, and that's why when the Scotland job came up I decided to take it. St Johnstone, however, was a great learning curve, and I always have the fondest memories of my time there.'

St Johnstone acknowledged their appreciation of Brown's services in a formal company minute of 7 February 1967, in which they also extended their congratulations to him on being appointed Scotland manager. Chairman Mr A. Lamond hosted a farewell dinner in Brown's honour at the Royal George Hotel in Perth on 15 February, where, during a very convivial evening, he was complimented in a number of speeches for his excellent work on behalf of the club and several handsome leaving gifts were presented to him. Now he had to face up to his biggest challenge so far – managing Scotland!

Chapter 9

Scotland Manager – Early Days and World Tour

W HEN Brown's appointment as Scotland manager was announced on 6 February 1967, it would be fair to say it came as a surprise to most people with an interest in the Scottish game. Although he had enjoyed an excellent playing career with Rangers and Scotland, his only managerial experience had been with St Johnstone. There he had done very well on limited resources, but the club was not one of the big names in Scotland. Clearly, however, note had been taken of his work in Perth, where he was the second longest-serving club manager in the First Division after Rangers' Scot Symon. He also enjoyed an appealing image, cut a debonair figure, was in his early 40s, had a charming personality, and was intelligent and articulate. In short, he had many of the required attributes for managerial success, except, perhaps, experience at the very top level. One of the first hurdles he had to overcome was to convince all concerned that he was the right man for the job, and the Wembley win helped considerably in that regard.

From his perspective, this was the sort of challenge he had been looking for, as he recalled. 'While I was extremely happy at St Johnstone and thoroughly enjoyed a good quality of life that went with the job, there was something missing. I was almost in too much of a "comfort zone" and needed a more demanding challenge. My remit with the Saints – to do as well as possible in the top division – was always going to be limited by financial considerations: that was the reality of it. I felt it was time to take on something bigger, and the Scotland job fitted the bill. As it happened, the approach from the SFA came right out of the blue. I never applied for the job. One evening in early February 1967, after I had been out walking the dogs by the River Tay near my home in Stanley, I was told by my wife that Willie Allan of the SFA had phoned and I was to call him back. When I did, he invited me to an interview for the job in Glasgow with the SFA president, Tom Reid, the chairman of Partick Thistle, and members of the international selection committee. As far as I recall, the interview was not particularly long. I felt it went well and said after to my wife I thought they would offer me it. Later on that same evening, Willie phoned me again at home and said the job was mine if I wanted it.

'When I was actually offered it I did undergo some soul searching, even though I knew the limitations of the St Johnstone job. My family was happily settled in Stanley; my daughters were happy with their schooling in the area; my wife liked it very much and was involved in various community activities. I was also happy there but realised I could not be at St Johnstone all my days. This was the top job in Scottish football and a once-in-a-lifetime opportunity. When I discussed it at length with my wife, she agreed that it was a great opportunity to further my career and supported my decision to accept it, even though she understood it would mean having to move nearer Glasgow. Things were different back then in terms of ease of communication, and, while it is possible today to undertake the job without being based near Glasgow, then it was considered necessary to live in the area.'

Considering the history of the role, he might be considered a brave man taking it on. Most of the previous managers' tenures had ended in tears. Aberdeenshire-born Andy Beattie, a former Scottish international himself, was the first holder of the post and was in charge during the country's ill-fated debut in the World Cup in 1954 in Switzerland. It was a part-time appointment, but he and the SFA had a difficult relationship – leading to his resignation during the World Cup, citing a lack of support and direction. At that time, the international selection committee was all-powerful and picked the team with some input from the manager, which was hardly an ideal arrangement. Matt Busby was the next appointee, also part-time, for the World Cup finals in 1958 in Sweden, but tragically the Manchester United Munich air disaster in February of that year ruled him out. Instead the team went to Sweden under the supervision of Dawson Walker, the Clyde FC trainer, and were the only team at the finals without a manager. After that, Andy Beattie was surprisingly reappointed, but the relationship continued to be difficult.

He was relieved of his post after going to watch his new club, Nottingham Forest, play Blackpool instead of attending Scotland's match against Wales in Cardiff. Ian McColl, former team-mate of Brown's and then Sunderland manager, was the next occupant of the 'hot seat'. He was unlucky not to have taken Scotland to the World Cup finals in Chile in 1962, losing out to Czechoslovakia in a play-off, but that did not prevent the SFA dismissing him during the qualification series for the 1966 finals.

Next man up was Celtic's Jock Stein on a temporary basis, but he narrowly failed to qualify for 1966, leaving Scotland looking on as England achieved their greatest success. Stein, as happened to his predecessors and as would happen to Brown, suffered from a lack of co-operation from some clubs in making players available. He was quoted after he left the post as saying, 'Most roads are paved with good intentions but this was littered with obstacles.' Portentous words, given how Brown's experience would evolve.

The job was then advertised as being suitable for 'those with other business interests', reaffirming the perception that the SFA considered the job was not full-time. Up until this point, the team was still being picked by the international selection committee along with the manager. That committee was formed by club directors and officials – willing and enthusiastic individuals, but very few with hands-on experience of the professional game. Many of those officials enjoyed the position of power they occupied in the Scottish game and were loath to loosen their grip on it. Sometimes referred to as 'the blazers and flannels men', they did not want to forego the privileges that went with their position. This credo was being persisted with despite the obvious success enjoyed by England under Sir Alf Ramsey, who had had total control of all England international football matters since being appointed in 1963.

It was rumoured that the SFA hoped to appoint Willie Waddell, another former team-mate of Brown's at Rangers, who had successfully managed Kilmarnock; or Eddie Turnbull, a schoolboy team-mate of Brown's and highly thought-of manager of Aberdeen – but if so, neither took the bait. Instead, yet another old team-mate of Brown's was appointed – John Prentice, then a promising manager of Clyde who Brown had played with occasionally at Rangers and Falkirk. His appointment was significant, as it was the first full-time one. However, it was to prove short-lived because of difficulties over contract details, and Prentice was sacked after only a few months in October 1966, when he went on an unauthorised trip to Canada for a job interview. In the fallout from his dismissal, Prentice reportedly commented, 'The SFA don't want a team manager, they want someone to carry the can.' Due to the brevity of his tenure, the effectiveness of a full-time appointment could not be said to have been tested.

Malcolm Macdonald, Kilmarnock manager and noted ex-Celtic player, occupied the position on a temporary basis for a period pending Brown's appointment.

That was the backdrop against which Brown, in practical terms, became the country's first full-time manager with complete control over team selection – something he wisely insisted on and which the SFA finally accepted. The history of his predecessors' difficulties did not dissuade Brown from accepting the appointment. He did so with a strong, positive attitude that he could change the national football fortunes for the better. He had a number of strategies that he wished to employ and was prepared to work all the hours necessary to succeed.

Accolades and good wishes rang in his ears as he eased into the managerial chair. Jock Stein was quoted as saying, 'Bobby Brown is a good man who has done very well with limited resources at St Johnstone.' The chairman of the international selection committee, Hugh Nelson of Arbroath, stated, 'Bobby Brown will get every chance and all the backing of the SFA.' Mr Alex Lamond, long-serving St Johnstone chairman, remarked, 'Bobby Brown is a young man of excellent character. While we are sorry to see him go, we're delighted for him. Bobby Brown was a credit to St Johnstone and will be to Scotland.'

For his part, on his appointment Brown stated, 'I feel particularly happy to be given this opportunity at the top level in football. This is a tremendous step forward for me. I have my ideas about the job, but I'd prefer to say nothing about my plans till I get my commitments with St Johnstone cleared up. St Johnstone are preparing for a Scottish Cup tie at Aberdeen on 18 February, and I have to focus my full attention on this. I shall start my duties as Scotland manager on 20 February.'

His contract was for four years at an annual salary of £4,000, roughly equivalent to £65,000 today, which represented a significant increase on his income at St Johnstone. In addition, all expenses incurred on SFA duty would be met.

He was provided with his own room on the second floor of the Association's offices in Park Gardens, Glasgow, and secretarial back-up. Before Brown's appointment, Willie Allan, who had initially joined the SFA in 1938 as junior clerk before rising through the ranks to become the secretary and a powerful figure in the Association, had opened all mail in the office irrespective of to whom it was addressed. Brown did not consider it appropriate that mail addressed to him be opened by anyone other than him, and informed Allan that in future he would be opening his own mail, which initially caused minor tension between them, but that soon evaporated. Although Allan's views on the subject changed once Brown had established himself in the position, Brown had the clear impression that initially Allan was not in favour of a full-time manager.

While his insistence on being solely responsible for team selection was accepted, he still had to operate with the selection committee. That involved liaison in a number of areas, such as providing them with match reports, sharing his thoughts on individual players and team progress, giving explanations if sought on aspects of selection, arrangement of scouting trips and friendlies, and securing availability of players for matches and training sessions. Once he had selected a team, he was expected to inform the selectors first, then the players and the press.

As alluded to, one of the major difficulties faced by previous Scottish managers was securing the availability of players, particularly from English clubs, which were under no obligation to release them. One of Brown's immediate aims was to try to improve that situation by establishing goodwill and worthwhile rapport with as many managers as possible, especially those in England. Within weeks of starting the job, he had held meetings with Bill Shankly of Liverpool, Ian McColl of Sunderland, Tommy Docherty of Chelsea, Bertie Mee of Arsenal, Ronnie Allen of Wolves and Stan Cullis of Birmingham City. Although he already knew a lot of the Scottish-based managers, he cultivated as many of them as he could to 'buy into' his plans for the team. He intended to spread the net as widely as possible to identify all talent available to him, and to succeed in that aim he needed as much co-operation as possible from club managers. What he looked for in a player in order of importance, he made clear, were skill, fitness and tactical awareness.

Brown did not have much time to wallow in the delight of the Wembley win, as the next fixture for him was against the USSR – the first time the countries had met. The game was arranged for exactly a month later, Wednesday 10 May, at Hampden Park. This was a demanding test, as the Soviets had been semi-finalists at the previous year's World Cup. The difficulty of the task was made greater as it came so soon after Wembley – it was a friendly with nothing at stake, and it was the end of the season. On top of that, Brown could field only seven of his Wembley heroes: Simpson, Gemmell, McCreadie, Baxter (capt.), McCalliog, Law and Lennox. Leeds United and Rangers players were denied him because of their European club commitments. Replacing Greig and McKinnon were the Celtic duo of McNeill and Clark, while Jimmy Johnstone returned and Arsenal's Frank McLintock came in for the injured Bremner.

The Soviets were clearly taking this seriously, given the intensity of their three-hour training session at Hampden on the Sunday beforehand, followed by a one-hour session the next day. They lowered the tempo on the day before the game by taking their squad to the cinema in Glasgow. The press thought, tongue in cheek, they were indulging in a bit of one-upmanship by fielding their famous goalkeeper Lev Yashin, who at 37 was a year older than home custodian Ronnie Simpson.

The Scots assembled in a Glasgow hotel on the Monday before going down the coast to their favoured venue at Largs to prepare. Much of the talk around the camp centred on a proposed £80,000 bid from Manchester United for Jim McCalliog, no doubt partly on the strength of his superb Wembley display. Injury worries over Johnstone, McLintock, Law and McCalliog himself were also in the public arena and causing concern. Brown declared to the press, 'I have maintained the pattern, and the changes I have made will tell me something. There is no question of experimenting, as we want to win all our games.'

In front of a 53,000 crowd under the floodlights, Scotland failed to capitalise on the success of Wembley and lost 2–0 to a proficient and well-organised Russian side. Despite home pressure from the kick-off, the visitors took the lead after 16 minutes when an ill-judged Gemmell passback beat his own keeper and clubmate Simpson. That resulted in the Scots pushing forward at every opportunity, leaving them vulnerable to the counter-attack, and four minutes before half-time the Russians took advantage as Medvid scored from 25 yards to double their lead. Willie Wallace, unfortunate not to be on from the start, replaced the injured Law at half-time, becoming the seventh Celt on the pitch and adding threat to the attack. Despite the home team being camped in the opposition's half, they were unable to penetrate a sound defence, with Baxter, captain for the night, being disappointingly ineffective. One newspaper headline the next day read, 'Russians survive second half pounding' All the Scots' second-half efforts were in vain as the Russians ran out 2–0 winners to some booing and slow handclapping from the home fans.

Afterwards Brown commented, 'There were individual failures but the main fault was slowness in the build-up.' Privately he thought it a bit of a setback, although he was not unduly disheartened, particularly given the calibre of the opposition and his slightly under-strength team. He also appreciated the difficulty implicit in following the Wembley 'high'.

His commitments as national manager were coming thick and fast in the first months following his appointment. Five days after the Russian game, he was due to set off on a 'World Tour' with a Scotland squad. When he took on the job in February, one question the SFA posed him was whether he had any particular ideas as to how he would tackle it. He responded by suggesting that, as a new manager, he would like to take a squad of mainly young, up-and-coming players on an extensive tour to give him the opportunity to work with them, live with them and get to know them. By coincidence, the SFA had been contemplating organising a tour along these lines. Brown and the Association then began planning a 'World Tour' to begin on 15 May for about a month. Unfortunately, many senior players were unavailable due to club commitments and injuries. This was something of a golden era for Scottish clubs in Europe, with Celtic preparing to play the European Cup Final of 'Lisbon Lions' fame, Rangers about to play Bayern Munich in Germany in the Cup Winners' Cup Final, which they would lose to an extra-time goal, and Kilmarnock playing Leeds United in a semi-final of the Fairs Cup (predecessor of the UEFA Cup), a 4–2 aggregate win for the English team. In addition, Dundee United had earlier in the season, in their European debut, beaten Barcelona home and away in the Fairs Cup. As a result, these clubs' players were ruled out; and McCreadie and McLintock were injured, the former in the FA Cup Final and the latter in the game against Russia. However, Brown was not unduly upset, as he considered the exercise to be part of his long-term aim to qualify for the World Cup finals in Mexico in 1970, and the opportunity to weigh up some younger players was welcome. It was accepted that this would not be a full-strength touring party, nor would the opposition represent the top level in the international game. As a result, the fixtures would not be considered full internationals, nor would caps be awarded by Scotland. But he also regarded the tour partly as a goodwill mission, as there were many Scottish expatriates in most of the countries they would visit. With that in mind, the tourists took with them 150 quaichs as gifts for opponents and their officials.

In undertaking a foreign tour, Scotland were continuing a tradition begun in 1929 when they travelled to play Norway in Bergen, Germany in Berlin and Holland in Amsterdam. This was followed two years later by another continental tour involving games against Austria, Italy and Switzerland in Geneva. Further similar tours followed – but all were short, featuring a handful of games in each, and these were full internationals. Brown's 'World Tour' was different, and would nowadays be described as a 'Development XI Tour'. It was to last almost five weeks, with nine games in Israel, Hong Kong, Australia, New Zealand and Canada. Originally another game against China had been planned, but political upheaval there ruled it out. The only real precedent for such a tour was in 1949, when the Scots played nine games on a tour of the USA and Canada, but the tourists then were mostly full internationals.

The squad selected by Brown was as follows:

Goalkeepers – Jim Cruickshank (Hearts), Harry Thomson (Burnley).

Defence – Alan Anderson (Hearts), Eddie Colquhoun (Sheffield United), Willie Callaghan (Dunfermline Athletic), Hugh Tinney (Bury), Ian Ure (Arsenal), John Woodward (Arsenal).

Midfield – Bobby Hope (West Bromwich Albion), Doug Fraser (West Bromwich Albion), Andy Penman (Rangers), Jim Townsend (Hearts), Harry Hood (Clyde), Willie Morgan (Burnley/Manchester United).

Forwards – Joe Harper (Huddersfield Town), Alex Ferguson (Dunfermline Athletic), Jim McCalliog (Sheffield Wednesday).

Defender Jackie McGrory and forward Tommy McLean joined the party in Australia once their club Kilmarnock had been eliminated from the Fairs Cup.

The only full caps among them were Cruickshank, Ure, Penman, McGrory and McCalliog. Jim Cruickshank, like manager Brown, started his career with Queen's Park before moving on to Hearts, where he earned his first of six caps against West Germany in 1964. Ayrshireman and centre-half Ure, a member of Dundee's outstanding league champions in 1962, won the first of his 11 caps that year against West Germany. Later he went on to star with Arsenal and Manchester United. Midfield schemer Andy Penman had also been a member of that successful Dundee team and won his only cap in 1966 against Holland. Just before the tour began, he joined Rangers from Dundee, but he had not yet played for them. Centre-half Jackie McGrory played almost 400 games for Kilmarnock and was a member of their team which won their only league title in 1965, the year he won the first of his three caps, against Northern Ireland. And McCalliog, the 20-year-old from Glasgow's

Gorbals, made his Scottish debut at Wembley as we have seen.

In the future, Callaghan, Colquhoun, Fraser, Harper, Hope, McLean and Morgan would also go on to win full caps. Full-back Callaghan, a Dunfermline Athletic stalwart, earned the first of his two caps against the Republic of Ireland in 1970. Central defender Eddie Colquhoun, from Prestonpans, near Edinburgh, began his career with Bury before joining West Bromwich Albion and then Sheffield United. He was first capped in 1971 while with them, and went on to win eight more caps. Doug Fraser, originally from Eaglesham, near East Kilbride, was a midfielder who captained the team after Ure's injury in the opening game against Israel. He received his first cap in 1968 against Holland, but only earned one more. A junior player with Blantyre Celtic, he was spotted by the famous Aberdeen scout Bobby Calder and began his career with the Dons before going on to West Bromwich Albion and Nottingham Forest. Striker Joe Harper, from Greenock, won four caps, the first coming in 1972 against Denmark. He enjoyed a lengthy and successful career for a number of clubs including Morton, Aberdeen, Hibs and Everton. Winger Tommy McLean, who was born in Ashgill, Larkhall, was one of three well-known footballing brothers, Willie and Jim being the others. A member of Kilmarnock's league-winning team of 1965, he later joined Rangers. He won six caps, the first being against Denmark in 1969, and later was a successful manager with Motherwell, Hearts and Dundee United. Sauchie-born winger Willie Morgan earned 21 caps, the first against Northern Ireland later in 1967. During a long career, he represented Burnley, Manchester United and Bolton Wanderers with distinction.

The remaining players all enjoyed excellent club careers, and some had minor international honours. Goalkeeper Thomson, who was brought up in Penicuik near Edinburgh, started off at junior side Bo'ness United before going firstly to Burnley and then Blackpool. Edinburgh's Alan Anderson made his name with home-town team Hearts as a commanding centre-half, playing over 400 games, many as captain. Prior to that, he played for Millwall and Scunthorpe United. Full back Hugh Tinney started off with Partick Thistle, where he earned two under-23 caps for Scotland, before transferring to Bury where he played the rest of his career. Central defender John Woodward, from Possilpark in Glasgow, earned Scotland youth caps and was at Arsenal for about four years without making the hoped-for breakthrough. After Highbury, he joined York City. Harry Hood, a clever attacking midfielder and useful marksman, won an under-23 cap against England and was picked for the Scottish league XI. Clubs he played for included Clyde, Sunderland and Celtic. And there was a striker called Alex Ferguson, who needs little introduction. He also began his career with Queen's Park, thereafter moving to St Johnstone, Dunfermline Athletic and Rangers among others. Although he never won a full cap, he did represent the Scottish league.

In the circumstances, Brown felt the squad contained a good balance of potential and experience.

Making up the party were SFA president Tom Reid of Partick Thistle; vice president Hugh Nelson; W.P. Allan, SFA secretary; Dr Downie, the medical officer; and Walter McCrae, trainer.

The captain for the tour was Ian Ure, who recalled it had a delicate start. 'It was the end of a long, hard season, and some players frankly wanted to be away on holiday and recharge their batteries. However, we had committed ourselves and did approach it in the right spirit. One difficulty that arose at the beginning was the daily spending allowance for the players. If I remember correctly, it was fixed at about £2 per day. We were going to be away for almost five weeks, and many of us thought that wasn't enough. As captain, I was the spokesman, and raised it with Bobby Brown, who listened sympathetically. As this type of financial issue was not in his remit, he had to raise it with Tom Reid, the president. He, by the way, was a real character, a very gregarious fellow. Thankfully he saw sense and agreed to increase the amount to, I think, double the original figure, and so a potentially embarrassing issue was avoided.'

The home-based members of the party assembled at the North British Hotel in Glasgow before travelling to London to meet up with those based in England. After a night in the White Hart Hotel in Windsor, they flew out to Tel Aviv on the first leg of their tour. Their arrival there coincided with celebrations for the country's Independence Day, but there was also widespread tension due to deteriorating relations with neighbours Egypt, who had mobilised forces along the border in the Sinai Peninsula. The Scottish party settled into the Ramat Aviv Garden hotel, conscious of a visible security presence. Because of the situation, Dunfermline Athletic's planned forthcoming tour of Egypt was cancelled. Shortly afterwards, matters were exacerbated by Egypt's leader Nasser closing the Tiran Straits to Israeli shipping, thereby denying access to the Red Sea. This and other provocations led to the Six Day War between the countries in early June.

Although Israel was not a world power in the game, the sport had gained hugely in popularity there since its national association was formed in 1928. They could not be considered pushovers, as, six months earlier, friendly matches against Poland and Romania had resulted in a draw and a single-goal defeat respectively.

The match took place on 16 May at the Ramat Gan national stadium in the city of that name, east of Tel Aviv. The Scots' preparations were not ideal, as they only arrived at the ground about a quarter of an hour before the start.

A healthy attendance of 27,000 was present to see Morgan shoot the visitors ahead, before Spiegel equalised just before half-time. Six minutes from full time, Ferguson scored the winner with a header from a Morgan cross. It was not the most entertaining of games, but, as Brown said later, 'I was happy with our performance. This was the first time the boys had been together, and they had to play on a hard, bumpy pitch.' When questioned about his football philosophy, he went on to add, 'I'm looking for the dedicated craftsmen and not the temperamental prima donna players.'

The result lost some of its sparkle when it was later discovered that captain Ure had broken his jaw in a challenge, which signalled the end of his tour, as he had to return to England for treatment. He commented, 'It was an awful injury, I can clearly recall their dirty wee squat centre-forward deliberately elbowing me in the face. It was incredibly sore and I spent a very uncomfortable night before flying back the next day. My recollection is that the medical facilities in Tel Aviv were not the best and the fracture diagnosis was not confirmed till I arrived back home. It was one of the worst injuries I ever had. Unbelievably, six months later in training at Arsenal, Terry Neill accidentally broke my jaw again in virtually the same place! So my tour was fairly brief, but I thought Bobby was a really nice guy – maybe too nice for a football manager – but we certainly had a harmonious group thanks to him. He was always courteous and very polished and articulate.'

At one stage, the players were allowed a night out. McCalliog remembers their being chaperoned by security wherever they went, and at one point that evening they visited a nightclub run by Mandy Rice-Davies, one of the leading figures embroiled in the Profumo–Christine Keeler scandal in the early 1960s, when the then Minister of War was brought down amid allegations of consorting with prostitutes. Rice-Davies then married an

Israeli businessman, Rafi Shauli, with whom she set up home in Tel Aviv and opened a nightclub, Mandy's. There they spent an enjoyable evening, with Ure describing her as being 'charming with the players'. They then spent the next two days in the city doing some sightseeing and light training before flying out on the evening of the 19th on the next leg of their trip.

Air travel not being what it is now, this meant flying first to Phnom Penh in Cambodia, arriving there the following day at midday. After a four-hour stopover, the party then caught a flight to Hong Kong, which they reached five hours later, and settled into the Ascot House hotel in Happy Valley. They soon realised they had gone from a gently simmering hotspot to a full-blown one, as street disturbances were breaking out all over Hong Kong. Because of that, they were to spend a lot of time under curfew, closeted in their comfortable hotel.

The day following their arrival saw 167 people arrested as a result of riots. The unrest had begun earlier that year because of labour disputes instigated by communist-led trades unions, fomented by strong anti-British sentiments – Hong Kong was then still a British colony. The trouble was also associated with events in the ongoing Cultural Revolution in neighbouring China, which had brought about the cancellation of the proposed match there. In Hong Kong, clashes in the streets between rioters waving their 'Little Red Books' and police with their batons and tear gas were an everyday occurrence. The commercial area had become virtually paralysed. Brown recollects the atmosphere being 'rather concerning', particularly when the decision was taken to call off the game supposed to take place on 22 May because of security fears. There were also fears the second game might have to be cancelled, but it did go ahead on 25 May, the same day that Celtic were creating football history in becoming the first British team to win the European Cup.

It was played at the Government Stadium in front of 7,000 fans, on a damp night under the floodlights. The local team took an early lead when a poor Anderson passback resulted in a goal. But two goals by Ferguson and one apiece from Hood and Callaghan gave the Scotland XI the win. An excellent display by the Hong Kong keeper prevented a bigger win.

The local press described it as 'an easy win' but pointed out the home team were at a disadvantage as four of their best players, all police officers, had had to withdraw to assist in dealing with the civil disturbances. The sport was still relatively young there, their national association having been formed just over 50 years previously. It was also reported that the Scottish team had exposed weaknesses in the Colony players, particularly in positional play, while 'McCalliog covered virtually every blade of grass, Ferguson and Hope showed great ball control and Fraser was a very good captain'.

Fraser had never represented Scotland in any guise before the Israeli match, and remembered, 'I felt very proud to be wearing the Scotland shirt for the first time. The situation in Hong Kong was not good because of the riots and trouble. During our game I remember there were lots of Chinese on top of the hill above the stadium with megaphones, constantly chanting some sort of slogans throughout the match. I don't know what they were saying, which was probably just as well, but it didn't sound too friendly! In the end it was a fairly comfortable win. Despite the difficulties, I liked Hong Kong – it was a very vibrant place. We managed to go shopping one day, and I had a suit made up in 24 hours. After our flight to Australia, I left it behind on the plane, and so never had a chance to wear it! I had a lot of time for Bobby – he was good at getting your attention and putting things over clearly. There was an excellent mix of players, and everything went well as far as I was concerned, apart from the fatigue because of the amount of travel.'

Before the tour, Alex Ferguson had been described by the home press as 'having a reputation for taking half chances, probably the best snapper upper of goals in Scotland today'. While nowadays a candidate for being considered one of the sport's greatest all-time managers, his playing career has tended to be undervalued, partly perhaps because of comparison with his managerial exploits and also because he never gained a full cap. Brown, who managed him while at St Johnstone before his move to Dunfermline, rated him quite highly. 'He was a very useful player for us at St Johnstone – he always played well, and, though never in the very top bracket, he was very good in the penalty box, a reliable goalscorer. He was difficult to dispossess and always played to win. That's why I took him on tour. It's been suggested that he and I did not get on but that's not true – we may not be on each other's Christmas cards list, but we got on OK. Alex was fine on tour, he mixed in well with the other lads and was well thought of.'

After another day in Hong Kong – which, despite the local difficulties, Brown liked very much – the tourists left on the next leg to Australia, arriving in Sydney on 27 May after a 12-hour flight and making for their base at the Manhattan Hotel at Potts Point, a suburb of the city. Football had been played in Australia at the end of the previous century, but only became organised in the early 20th century.

One of the central figures in its formalisation in the state of Victoria was an expatriate Scot, Harry John Dockerty. In 1909, he donated a beautiful cup for a competition, named in his honour, which was referred to as 'Victoria's FA Cup', and by 1967 was competed for by almost 200 clubs. Despite the progress of the game, however, it still ranked below Aussie Rules football and the two rugby codes in importance. In their previous three internationals, Australia had beaten Malaysia twice and Taiwan.

The first tour game, which, according to the local press, was the home nation's first full international, took place in Sydney on 28 May, the second anniversary of Dockerty's death, with his widow Mary Jane present as guest of honour. In front of 35,000 people at the Showground, the Scots won 1–0 thanks to a first-half Ferguson goal, when he netted a rebound. By now, the hosts were affectionately labelling their visitors as 'Haggis Bashers'. After the match, Brown was critical of the pitch, claiming it was 'impossible to play good football on such a bumpy surface, which made the game untidy'. He did have a point because, only a short time before, as its name suggests, it had been the venue for the country's annual prime livestock parade during the Royal Easter Show, which in its wake had left a rough surface.

Tommy McLean had been selected in the original squad for the tour, subject to Kilmarnock's commitments in the Fairs Cup. After their elimination by Leeds United, he travelled to join the party in Sydney along with clubmate Jackie McGrory, a replacement for the injured Ure. McLean recalled, 'The travel was a killer – it took Jackie and me 36 hours to get out there. We had six stopovers for flight changes, including Rome, Zurich, Karachi, Calcutta and Singapore. I always remember we were met at Sydney Airport by Walter McCrae, who was also our club trainer. He told us the squad was going out that night to a Cliff Richard concert and to grab a few hours' sleep. Well, Jackie and I were totally exhausted and slept round the clock, including through the concert! I really enjoyed the tour apart from the punishing travel. We met a lot of Scots living out there, who would come to our hotels to speak to us, and also some Scottish players based there. The Australian games were the most competitive – they were a good standard – but the New Zealand and Canadian ones were a lower level. Bobby Brown was very good – his man-management was first class, and, although not big on tactics, he spoke individually to players to ensure each knew his role. He and McCrae were a good combination: McCrae was more of a military disciplinarian type. I had a lot of respect for Bobby – he was a great ambassador for Scotland.'

Two days later, the tourists flew from Sydney to Adelaide, where they based themselves at the Parkroyal Motel. The Australian press, while not exuding optimism for the forthcoming game, did not feel their side had been outclassed in Sydney. Certainly the Scots were taking nothing for granted, putting in a hard 90-minute training session at the local Hindmarsh stadium shortly after arrival. Meanwhile, their opponents contented themselves with a light workout at the match venue, the Norwood Oval. In contrast to the Sydney Showground, Brown declared himself happy with the well-turfed Oval and predicted a 'big win' for his team.

The next day at the Oval, in front of a 20,000 crowd, the Scots won 2–1. Townsend notched the first with a shot from 30 yards, and then, against the run of play, Baartz equalised. Both teams then exchanged some meaty tackles before Morgan headed home the winner from a Fraser cross. Brown stated afterwards, 'This was a good standard of international football and served to emphasise that Australia has made amazing strides in a few years. We tried to win by as many goals as we could, but Australia had other ideas.' The Australia coach, Jo Venglos, commented, 'I'm happy our team played well. It would have been something of an upset if we had beaten the tough and skilful Scottish side.' Venglos, of course, went on to have a distinguished career in management, including a spell as Celtic manager in season 1998/99. The Czechoslovak, who had played for Slovan Bratislava in his homeland, had gone out to Australia the previous year to manage FC Prague in Sydney before becoming coach of the national team, a job he continued in until 1969.

After a couple of days in Adelaide, the tourists flew to Melbourne, where the third and final match was to take place. Once installed in their hotel, they did a light training session before the match the next day. That took place at Olympic Park, and, in front of 25,000 fans, the Scottish XI won 2–0 to achieve a clean sweep over the home nation. Ferguson scored both goals in the second half, with the Scots being quicker on the ball and McLean a menace to the opposition defence.

Australia treated these games as full internationals and awarded caps for them. Initially, in some quarters, there was criticism of the Scots for sending what they perceived as a second-rate squad and accusations from Australians that they had been patronised. However, as the tour unfolded, they appreciated the difficulties the Scots were faced with in bringing their 'name' players, and relations improved. Several exiled Scots featured in the Aussies' line-ups, including Alan Westwater, originally from Bridge of Allan, who had played for Stirling Albion and whose father, Willie, played for Morton; Billy Cook, formerly of junior team Ardrossan Winton Rovers and Kilmarnock; Hammy McMeechan, formerly of Carlisle United and Exeter; and Archie Blue, previously with Hearts, Carlisle United and Exeter.

This segment of the trip had been very successful, not only on the pitch but also off it, where Brown and his players were popular ambassadors for their country at the various functions they attended, some organised by expatriates. Brown recalled with much amusement how at one function he was asked whether 'that one-legged newspaper seller at the bottom of Buchanan Street in Glasgow still had his stance there?!'

Following the Melbourne match, the party left to fly firstly to Sydney and thereafter to Wellington in New Zealand, where they stayed in the Hotel St George. Organised football had been played there since 1891, and although popular recreationally it was lower down the pecking order than the national sport of rugby. However, it did have a reasonable following, especially among expatriates, many of whom were of Scottish descent. This was the first football tour there by a British national team. The next day, at Lower Hutt Recreation Ground, in front of 5,000 spectators, they played the New Zealand under-23 team. This proved a bit of a mismatch, as they won 7–2 after leading 1–0 at half-time due to an own goal. In the second half, Harper claimed a hat-trick, McCalliog two and McLean a penalty. In reports on the match, the three goalscorers received the most plaudits.

The next day they were on the move again – this time to Auckland, an hour and a half's flight away. The Royal International Hotel was the squad's base before their fixture against an Auckland Provincial XI. Brown reported six players were on the injuries list, but in the event most were fit to play. The game took place two days after their arrival at Newmarket Park, under the floodlights before a crowd of 15,000, and resulted in a 4–0 victory for the Scots. Ferguson this time notched a first-half hat-trick, with Penman netting the fourth. Several exiled Scots appeared for the home team – goalkeeper Arthur Stroud, an Aberdonian who had played for Arbroath; Glaswegian Tom McNab, a centre-half formerly of Partick Thistle, East Stirlingshire and Nottingham Forest; George Lamont, a winger originally from Alexandria, Dunbartonshire who was playing for Mount Wellington; and Bert Ormond, a striker who had previously turned out for Falkirk and Airdrie, then playing for Blockhouse Bay. He was a brother of future St Johnstone and Scotland manager Willie. With the exception of Stroud, all were full Kiwi internationals.

The tourists had little time to savour this latest success before undertaking the tiring trip to Vancouver the following day. Three lengthy flights later, via Los Angeles and Seattle, they reached their destination, where they were taken to their plush hotel, The Devonshire, in the Hornby area of the city, now unfortunately demolished. The national football association in Canada had been formed in 1912, and, although the game was widely played there, it did not have the profile of ice hockey and gridiron football. The game against Vancouver All Stars had been brought forward 24 hours and was due to kick off only 12 hours after the Scots' arrival in Canada. Despite the unsatisfactory scheduling, they defeated their opponents 4–1 in the city's Empire Stadium, scene of the 1954 Empire Games and the unforgettable mile race between Roger Bannister and his great Australian rival John Landy. They led 3–0 at half-time thanks to a McCalliog double and one by Ferguson, with McLean scoring in the second half. A match report stated that despite the Scots' lack of rest after their long journey, 'they had too much skill for Vancouver and Cruickshank in goal was rarely troubled'.

Their relentless schedule was nearing its conclusion, with one match remaining, in Winnipeg. The day after the Vancouver game, they embarked on a five-hour flight to their final venue, where they were accommodated in the airport hotel. A poorly attended fixture in front of about 3,000 at Alexander Park on 13 June wrapped up the tour. The opposition was called a 'Canada Olympic XI', a team due to represent the country in the forthcoming Pan American Games in Winnipeg. Despite their fatigue, the Scots won easily 7–2, again in something of a mismatch. Harper demonstrated his goalscoring talents by claiming five, with Hope and Morgan scoring the others.

There remained the lengthy trip home, firstly a three-hour flight to Toronto followed by an eight-hour one to Prestwick where they arrived shortly after 6am. Unsurprisingly, they were exhausted after a punishing travelling schedule covering about 30,000 miles in a month, passing through many time zones, playing nine games, eating many dinners and shaking countless hands at the various functions organised for them.

Brown recollected, 'It was a very successful trip, particularly from the football perspective. We won all nine games we played, despite over the month having to combat many changes in venue, climate, food and local customs. At times it almost seemed as if we were living in airports. All things considered, 33 goals for and eight against was a very good return. All the players did well, but I thought Townsend, Hope, skipper Fraser, Hood and McLean were the pick of the bunch. And Cruickshank in goals did well. Of course it will be pointed out that our opposition was not top rank, but make no mistake, they all wanted to do their best against us and try to get a result. It also has to be kept in mind that this was not a full-strength squad we had, because of club commitments and injuries, which was a bit disappointing from the point of view of future planning. However, a number of the lads with us did go on to win full caps in the years to come, and blooding them in this way, I think, proved invaluable. Apart from the football, the trip was also a big success. I like to think we made friends everywhere we went, particularly with the expatriate communities, and we received great welcomes and hospitality from our various hosts. Hong Kong in particular was slightly concerning at times with the civil unrest, but we emerged unscathed, thankfully. I think I can safely say that everyone on the trip really enjoyed it.'

There is no doubt that statistically and socially the tour was very successful, but, although it was not appreciated at the time, the call-offs by top players beforehand foreshadowed what would ultimately bedevil and effectively derail Brown's career as national team manager.

Chapter 10

The Quest for Mexico 1970

A S NATIONAL manager, Bobby's immediate objective
was to secure qualification for the country to the
European Nations' Cup finals in 1968, to be played
in Italy. The overriding objective, however, was to secure
qualification for the World Cup finals in Mexico in 1970.
Scotland were still smarting after their 1966 failure, a feeling
merely exacerbated by England's success. Illustrative of the
importance Brown attached to Mexico was a meeting he held
in London in August 1967 with officials of the British Olympic
Committee to discuss their findings on the effects of altitude
and heat on athletes, after they had sent experts there on a fact-
finding mission with regard to the upcoming Olympics there in
1968. Acclimatisation was considered very important, and he
also had a meeting on the same topic with Sheffield Wednesday
officials about their close-season club tour to Mexico. This
was typical of Brown's painstaking approach to preparation:
nothing was to be left to chance.

The Home International Championship was doubling as a qualifying group for the European Nations' Cup, and, as has been seen, the Wembley success in April had provided a great fillip to Scotland's hopes. Although that win was followed by a defeat to Russia, that could be seen as an end-of-season friendly with little at stake. The subsequent undefeated World Tour, albeit not against front-rank opposition and featuring an under-strength Scottish squad, boosted hopes of continued success in the remaining qualifying matches, the first of which was against Northern Ireland in October in Belfast.

Selection problems loomed for Brown, as Billy Bremner and Jim Baxter were both suspended; Jimmy Johnstone was likely to be suspended, as he had an appearance before the Referees' Committee a week before the game; and Willie Henderson and Bobby Lennox were injured. Although Ian Ure and Denis Law had been sent off for a spat while playing against each other in an Arsenal v. Manchester United game on 6 October, they at least were free to play, as there was no disciplinary committee meeting before the Northern Ireland game.

Scotland, as is their wont, made life difficult for themselves by losing 1–0 as a result of a defensive error. Centre-half Ron McKinnon failed to cut out a George Best cross, which fell to Dave Clements for the only goal. Brown was disappointed with the result, criticising his players for a lack of 'grit and determination'. However, Ian Ure, who played alongside McKinnon, thought, 'Our defeat was really all down to one man and that was George Best. He beat us virtually single-handed, he had a tremendous game.' Backing Ure's opinion, many consider this was Best's finest ever international appearance. It could have been worse, as Simpson saved a penalty. But the result meant that, to qualify, Scotland had to win both remaining fixtures against Wales and England, the first of which was against Wales in a month's time at Hampden.

Brown's preparations for the game included a full-scale practice match at Largs' Inverclyde centre against a Kilmarnock XI facilitated by their manager, Malcolm Macdonald, to whom Brown extended his gratitude. On a fairly unpleasant Wednesday evening, Scotland edged the game 3-2 in front of some 55,000 fans, thanks to a late McKinnon goal added to Gilzean's earlier double, in what was to be Jim Baxter's final international appearance. Brown was particularly pleased with his side's fighting qualities. With England beating Northern Ireland, that meant England were a point ahead in the section before the final tie against the Scots in February 1968. To qualify, Scotland therefore had to win to secure the prize of a place in the Nations' Cup finals, while a draw would suffice for England.

At the beginning of November 1967, the draw for the qualifying games for the Mexico World Cup was made in Casablanca, placing Scotland in the same group as West Germany, Austria and Cyprus. At that time, surprising as it appears now, Scotland had never lost to Germany in five fixtures since 1929. Brown was optimistic about qualifying for Mexico, believing we produced some of the best players in the world and that we had no reason to be pessimistic. He gave the quest for World Cup qualification priority, stating, 'This is the most important thing! I want to qualify more than anything.'

In the months before the England game, he travelled thousands of miles scouting players all over England and Scotland. Not only was his practice to watch a player in action, but he also made a point of speaking to his club manager and officials about him – partly for goodwill purposes, but also to find out more information about his character to help him assess his likely compatibility with the team. He was particularly keen on discovering younger players whom he could, over time, seek to mould into a team and to try to create a 'club spirit' in the national team.

To this end, he considered the under-23 team, for which he was also responsible, as an important potential source of players and sought to encourage these youngsters to aim for a place in the full team. As a virtual dress rehearsal for the England game, an under-23 international between the two countries took place two weeks beforehand at Hampden. Although a 'friendly' with nothing at stake, it set the tone for the intensity of the build-up to the full international. A crowd of only 15,000 saw Scotland lose 2–1 in a hotly contested and controversial game. A goalkeeping blunder by Bobby Ferguson led to England's opening goal by Martin Chivers, with Harry Hood equalising just after half-time before Rodney Marsh netted the winner. The controversy arose through what was considered by Brown and the home press as the crude play of their opponents, much of which went unpunished by the referee. In the second half, Peter Osgood and Emlyn Hughes were booked for apparently violent fouls, and afterwards Brown was quoted as saying that 'some of the English tackling was nauseating'. The press reserved particular condemnation for Brian Kidd for his alleged 'two-fingered salute' to the crowd after Marsh's goal. Sir Alf was unrepentant, however, stating he would not discipline any of his players, as any petulance on their part was only due to overenthusiasm.

In the intervening two weeks, anticipation mounted over the clash. A Scotland–England game at any time, especially then, was big box office – but this one carried extra weight. The reward for the winner was highly prized, and the quarter-final opponent – Spain – was already identified, with dates fixed for the home and away encounters in April and May. That quarter-final spot seemed within grasping distance. Scotland had not previously participated in the Nations' Cup, then a comparatively young tournament, and although England had done so in 1964, they lost to France in the preliminary round. Now, both were keen to make their mark. Apart from the occasion being enhanced by that incentive, Scotland continued to nurse a grievance over their non-participation in the 1966 World Cup and England's success. England, for their part, did not harbour fond memories of Scotland being the first team to defeat them after their famous win – and that on their home pitch and more convincingly than suggested by the scoreline. The recent under-23 game had aroused strong feelings, particularly on the part of the Scots. It was all adding up to a cliffhanger of a game. Naturally the press was playing its part in the build-up, with headlines such as 'Make Or Break Day For Scotland And England', and 'Hampden Showdown'.

As usual, ahead of the game, Bobby Brown had worries about the make-up of his team. There was a fitness issue with talisman Denis Law, who had a knee injury; Jim Baxter was suffering a loss of form with new club Nottingham Forest – should he replace him with the in-form but less experienced Charlie Cooke? Ian Ure, who would have been first pick in the centre of defence, was out injured – should he play Celtic's Billy McNeill, whose last cap was in 1965? What about the mesmeric Jimmy Johnstone, Celtic's winger, who on his day was virtually unplayable? All these questions and others were swirling around in the manager's head in the lead-up to the game.

In contrast, England appeared to have a relatively untroubled build-up. Sir Alf had his players together from the Tuesday onwards, initially at Lilleshall before coming north to their base at Troon on the Ayrshire coast, some 30 miles south of Glasgow. Further up the Ayrshire coast, Scotland had their usual training camp at Largs, where they could access the facilities at the National Inverclyde Centre. Thanks to the co-operation of Jock Stein, Brown arranged a 'warm-up' match there against a Celtic XI set up to play in the way England were expected to do. Even that was not without its problems, as reportedly Jimmy Johnstone refused to run the line during the game, leading to Brown declaring him to be 'not mentally attuned' to play at Hampden.

Brown announced the following team: Simpson; Gemmell, McNeill, McKinnon, McCreadie; Greig, Bremner, Cooke; Lennox, W. Johnston, Gilzean. Shortly after, he had to contend with Gilzean's withdrawal because of injury and called in Celtic's John Hughes, himself not long recovered from injury. Sir Alf selected: Banks; Newton, Labone, Moore, Wilson; Mullery, Ball, Peters; Hurst, Summerbee, R. Charlton – a team containing seven of his World Cup winners. Adding some spice, and with a glance back to the recent under-23 game, Ramsey suggested the Scots' line-up was reliant on 'brawn', adding he had a slight fitness concern over Peters, whom he described as the 'best midfielder in the world'.

Bobby Brown was positive, stating that Scotland had 'a wonderful chance'. He accepted that nothing less than a win would suffice and thought his team had the necessary skill, strength and running power, emphasising his preference for what he described as 'all-purpose players'. He also expressed regret that he seemed unable to have available all the players he wanted, through injury or suspensions, during his year or so in the job, apart from the 1967 Wembley match. Always considered a 'gentleman' of the game, when questioned by the press whether he could be ruthless, he responded that he was a strict disciplinarian and that if players did not conform to what was laid down by him, then they were out of the reckoning.

Interest in the match was reaching fever level, and all 134,000 tickets had been sold well in advance. English fans were present in numbers, and ticket touts were doing brisk business. 'Spies' representing the seven countries who had already qualified for the Nations' Cup quarter-finals – namely Spain, France, Yugoslavia, Bulgaria, Hungary, Russia and Italy – were all present with a watching brief. Brazilian manager Aymoré Moreira and Helmut Schoen, manager of Scotland's forthcoming World Cup qualification opponents West Germany, were also present.

The pitch was not in good condition due to recent adverse weather and had been protected by tons of straw in the days beforehand. The condition of the surrounding track was so poor that the pre-match entertainment programme of athletics and cycling had to be cancelled. After the pipe band performances and presentation of the teams to Princess Alexandra, the match got under way at a raucous Hampden that appeared to be bursting at the seams. An early 'goal' by Lennox was chalked off for an infringement, and shortly after, against the run of play, Peters scored from distance. Shortly before half-time, Lennox crossed for Hughes to place an excellent header past Banks to tie the game, which was how it ended despite Scotland having more of the play. After the match, Brown commented that he thought Lennox's goal was valid and that the Scots could hold their heads high given how they played. Cooke had an outstanding game and vindicated Brown's selection of him ahead of Baxter. It was frustrating for him to come so close to qualifying for a major finals only to miss out. He maintained he was upset at losing the Northern Irish game, but reflected that three points out of four from the world champions was acceptable. It meant he could now concentrate all his energies on trying to take the country to Mexico. As for Sir Alf, he rather provocatively suggested his team had 'outclassed' Scotland, which seemed very much a minority view.

Brown found himself in the next dugout to Ramsey yet again just over a month later, for the Scottish league match against their English counterparts at Ayresome Park, Middlesbrough, where goals from Hunt and Newton secured the home win. Brown had little luck with his debutant keeper Peter McLoy of Motherwell, who some observers considered at fault for both goals. On a brighter note, Willie Callaghan made an excellent debut at full-back, with Brown rating him the best defender on the field. Callaghan himself attributed his good form to the confidence Brown and senior players instilled in him, enabling him to feel 'quite relaxed'. Other players who impressed Brown that evening with an eye on the World Cup games were Hughes, Colin Stein and Dave Smith.

The manager was trying to arrange an end-of-season 'mini-tour' to further World Cup preparation, with games against Russia and Holland in May. He was also planning to travel to Austria to watch their tie against Cyprus, and had already seen West Germany against Switzerland and Wales. After the 'mini-tour', he was going to Hanover to watch West Germany play England on 1 June. He could not be accused of not doing his homework. At the same time, he was continually frustrated over the difficulties he faced getting the players he wanted together, whether for friendly or competitive fixtures or for training sessions. He would also have liked to have more warm-up games arranged before World Cup qualification began. Looking over his shoulder, figuratively speaking, in the direction of his counterpart, Helmut Schoen, in charge of West Germany, did not help, as he had arranged an eight-day get-together for his pool of players in June. Another example to aspire to emulate was Brazil, who were undertaking a 16-game build-up to Mexico – 'a dream to manager Brown' as one observer put it.

Even Brown's hopes for a two-game 'mini-tour' were dashed when Russia pulled out of the proposed game, leaving in place only the match against Holland in Amsterdam at the end of May. The timing of the fixture meant a number of Brown's first choices were unavailable through apparent injuries, club tours, holidays and other commitments. Illustrative of Brown's difficulties was Spurs' withdrawal of their players Gilzean and Robertson within half an hour of the announcement of his squad. Matters were made worse when Billy Bremner failed to appear at the airport to travel with the squad, and news of injury ruling him out was only received by Brown once in Amsterdam. Apparently he was injured in a testimonial game for Welsh international Ivor Allchurch and sent a telegram to the SFA informing them, but this was never received. Adding salt to the wounds, Neil Martin of Coventry was injured in training at the Olympic stadium in Amsterdam and had to withdraw. Brown fielded four new caps: Doug Fraser and Bobby Hope of West Bromwich, Bobby Moncur of Newcastle United and George McLean of Dundee.

In the circumstances, he was generally happy with the no-score draw given the team he was able to field. He thought Scotland could have won, as they had three good chances that they were unable to convert, and was pleased with the performances of keeper Clark and debutant Moncur. Twenty thousand fans watched the game, which featured in the home team future Celtic manager Wim Jansen, and famous Dutch names of the 1970s Rob Rensenbrink and Wim van Hanegem. The Scottish press was critical of aspects of the team's play and of the timing of the game. Brown responded, 'We must have more competitive internationals next season and more under-23 games. I would like to call about 35 players to Largs for training to play full-scale practice games including under-23 players.' Ever keen to improve his education as a coach, in the days following the Holland match he attended a UEFA coaches' course in Zeist along with another 25 leading European coaches.

The reality was that Brown was struggling to obtain co-operation from the English Football League and their FA to release Anglo-Scots for the Scotland team. There was no obligation on English clubs to do so, which led to some demands north of the border for an 'all-tartan' home-based team. This Brown always steadfastly refused to countenance, as he knew that many of his best players were English-based, and that to pursue such a policy would amount to shooting himself in the foot. Nevertheless, there arose a perception among many Scottish fans that their national team's woes could be placed at the feet of the 'Anglos', as either they did not appear or, when they did, gave the impression of being less committed to the cause, an impression strongly refuted by Brown. 'I knew very well what side my bread was buttered on as they say. It was a fact of life then, as now, that many of the best Scottish players moved down south to play in stronger leagues and to improve their own earning potential. While it often frustrated the life out of me not being able to assemble the players I really wanted, I have to say that I never thought for a moment that once on the pitch the Anglos gave less than their home-based team-mates.' Tommy Docherty, Brown's successor as Scotland manager, who was at the game in Amsterdam, sympathised with his difficulties and suggested that any player transferred from Scotland to England should have a clause in his contract guaranteeing his release for Scotland team games and training. In the course of this debate, it was pointed out that West Germany had no difficulty in securing the services of two of their top players, Schnellinger and Haller, from AC Milan and Bologna respectively.

Despite his problems, Brown remained unwavering in his aim and optimism to see Scotland qualify for Mexico. By June 1968 he had already watched all three of Scotland's opponents in action, five months before their first tie. He expressed the wish to take a squad to play games in Mexico or South America in the summer of 1969, to undergo practical experience of acclimatisation and to learn more first-hand about conditions there. With the first qualifier against Austria looming in

November at Hampden, and then Cyprus away a month later, he was anxious to arrange warm-up games. A minor personal issue had to be dealt with first: surgery for varicose veins. He had been booked some time ahead into the Nuffield Nursing Home in London in July, where, by coincidence, a fellow patient was the actress Liz Taylor – not for varicose veins treatment! Despite his family's good-natured ribbing, he commented that it was a pure coincidence he was there at the same time. When she found out he was there, she sent him a message wishing him good luck for his operation and saying that she hoped to meet him before they left the clinic. He maintains he cannot recall if they did meet!

Once he was fit again, he drew up his preparations for the qualifying matches. He intended to announce a pool of 24 players in September, a priority being to locate a third keeper as back-up to Simpson and Cruickshank. In the course of his search for one, he had looked at more than 20 goalkeepers in Scotland and England, including Lawrence of Liverpool, Martin of Southampton, Ferguson of West Ham and Whigham of Middlesbrough. He wanted to continue spreading the net as widely as possible for players, particularly in England, and intended to increase his level of contact with English managers to assist with this. A warm-up international was looked on as a must on the date allocated for it – 16 October – with East Germany a possibility. There was to be an improved financial incentive for the players to qualify for Mexico, with a potential £15,000 pot to be shared among them, loose change by today's standards but not so then. And, perhaps most radically of all, he intended to hold weekly Monday get-togethers for all his international squad members, including English-based players, in the lead-up to the Austrian match at Hampden on 6 November. Self-evidently, this was to improve team-building, facilitate Brown's assessment of players, create better understanding among them, heighten tactical awareness and aspire to a club atmosphere in the squad. No stone was being left unturned by Brown in his quest. In the 18 months since his appointment, he reckoned he had travelled 50,000 miles in the course of his duties, many of which were on scouting missions.

His first minor setback was that East Germany could only offer Scotland a home fixture, and, as it was felt there was too much travel involved, Brown and his officials began looking elsewhere. An opportunity for him to assess some of his players came with the league international against Ireland in Dublin in early September. Again Brown's preparations were foiled by player withdrawals – three within 12 hours. Celtic's Tommy Gemmell and Jimmy Johnstone were the first to drop out, due to 'flu. The former had been drenched in heavy rainfall while playing charity cricket for Celtic on the Sunday afternoon four days before the match, something almost impossible to imagine happening nowadays. Johnstone had apparently also developed symptoms overnight on the Sunday, this being the third time in a year he had missed an international. The third casualty was Willie Callaghan, who had trained with the squad at Firhill on Monday but, on return to his home in Fife, had developed a temperature, after which he was ruled out on medical advice. Willie Henderson and Celtic's Willie O'Neill replaced Gemmell and Johnstone, while Pat Stanton was called in for Callaghan. As his club manager at Hibs, Bob Shankly, was only notified of that mid-evening, he had to ask local police to instruct Stanton, who lived outside Edinburgh, to report the next day to the Scottish party, as he had been unable to contact him – something else very difficult to imagine nowadays.

Brown recalled, 'These regular withdrawals were quite disheartening, but one had to be philosophical and keep pursuing the ultimate objective of qualifying. The game ended in a scoreless draw, which was not wholly satisfactory, but in the circumstances not bad. It was an untidy, physical game and at times it looked like Gaelic football was being played. I remember the conditions in the dressing room were shocking – there were no basins or hot water to deal with injuries. It was like a battlefield in there, and I also remember John Greig saying it was one of the toughest matches he had played in.'

However, better news awaited Brown with confirmation of a game against Denmark in Copenhagen on 16 October. He issued his initial pool for the World Cup games, featuring Herriot of Birmingham City as his third goalkeeper and Colin Stein, Willie Callaghan and, for the first time, Eddie Gray. There was no place for Jim Baxter, still out of form in Nottingham. This pool would form the core of his regular Monday squad sessions before the first game against Austria. He had also enlisted the help of three trainers with the national squad: John Cumming of Hearts, Harold Davis of Queen's Park and Tom McNiven. At the beginning of September, Brown went to Berne to see Austria take on Switzerland, in a match that the Swiss won 1–0. The Austrians fielded a much-changed team, but Brown remarked he was not despondent over what he saw, although he thought it would be foolish to underestimate them.

Predictably, the Monday sessions were also beset by non-appearances in September, with nine players missing on one occasion and 11 on another, leading to press criticism. Brown, however, maintained they were of value, particularly in regard to improved player communication and team spirit. At the beginning of October, he named his squad for the Denmark game, knowing before he did so that he would not have available Ure, Gilzean, Law, Morgan, Gray, Cooke or Blackpool's Tony Green because of club commitments. Henderson was injured, and there was no place for Jimmy Johnstone, whose omission drew a 'no comment' response from Brown in answer to questions. A few days later, Jock Stein suspended Johnstone for a week for disciplinary reasons arising from his reaction to being substituted in a recent league game.

A week before going to Copenhagen, Brown held his final Hampden get-together, which included a full game against a young Celtic team, again facilitated by the co-operation of Jock Stein, with whom Brown enjoyed a good relationship. Among the young Celts were future assistant England manager John Gorman, the enigmatic but supremely talented sweeper George Connelly and future iconic full-back Danny McGrain.

In poor conditions on a muddy ground at Idraetspark Stadium, the Scots beat the Danes thanks to a second-half Bobby Lennox goal in a match watched by 12,000 fans. There was criticism of the Scottish performance, but Brown deflected that, making it clear that criticism made no difference to him. He defended his team, maintaining the game served its purpose before the important Austrian game and that conditions had been a leveller. The Austrian coach, Leopold Stastny, watched it and, doubtless seeking a psychological advantage, told the press that they were afraid of meeting Scotland, with their famous fighting spirit, at Hampden. Another observer was Herr Schoen, who diplomatically referred to the many good players Scotland had in reserve who did not play in Copenhagen. One curious footnote was a suggestion that some SFA officials were unhappy that, near the end of the game, Brown had substituted Cormack for McCalliog, the reason for their alleged discontent being that Cormack's match fee would increase from £30 as an unused substitute to £60 for playing! To make matters worse, Cormack had apparently not even kicked the ball. However, Brown was having no truck with that, as he had no alternative but to put him on as McCalliog was unfit to continue.

A few days prior to the Danish game, Jimmy Johnstone hit the headlines again by declaring to the press that he did not wish to play for Scotland again, without disclosing any substantial reason. There was a suggestion that the last time he appeared for the team against Wales, about a year previously, he had been upset when fans started chanting the name of his Rangers rival Willie Henderson. Although, as has been seen, Brown had had occasion not to play the red-haired maestro, there was never any personal difficulty between them. Indeed, in addition to appreciating his immense value to his team if in the right frame of mind, Brown found Johnstone an endearing character, as so many did. Despite Johnstone's position, Brown decided to choose him for the Austrian game.

Now the focus was fully on that, and, as ever, Brown had been assiduous in his homework. When recently in Vienna to watch the Austrians play West Germany, he had spoken to German television officials to ask that he be provided with a film of the match, to which they agreed. He then arranged with the BBC in Glasgow to access a studio for screening it, so his squad was then able to watch it. Austria's coach Stastny, indulging in more psychological ploys, was quoted ahead of the match that Scotland would win 5–1, which did not fool Brown for a minute. 'I knew this was going to be a tough match even if in the build-up to it Austria had not been particularly impressive. When I saw them recently lose narrowly to West Germany they played better than the previous time I'd watched them. I thought we would win if players played to their capabilities but I certainly did not think we would win by four goals or anything like it,' he commented. On this occasion at least, Brown had been fortunate regarding withdrawals and was able to select almost his strongest side.

This was a fixture with a backstory. In 1963, the teams had met in a friendly at Hampden, a game that would earn itself a place in football's hall of shame. The Austrians appeared to try to kick Scotland off the park, which led to their having two players sent off. As matters threatened to deteriorate further,

English referee Jim Finney took the unusual but probably correct decision to abandon the game with 11 minutes left. Unsurprisingly, that caused rancour between the respective associations, and it would be naïve to suggest that the bad feeling had completely evaporated by the time of this game.

Once the game was under way before an 80,000-plus crowd, it was immediately evident that all had not been forgiven and forgotten, as a feisty physical match unfolded, with the home team, on this occasion, giving as good as they got. In what was described as 'a bruising game with a lot of kicking and hacking', the Scots secured a vital 2–1 win to secure a positive start to their campaign, just reward for manager Brown's hard work and the players for buying into his aims and vision. The margin of victory could have been greater, but the crossbar denied them three times and the Austrians went unpunished for several handling offences in the penalty box. A Denis Law header and a close-range Bremner goal gave Scotland the win. Brown was perturbed by the physicality of the opposition and relieved to have avoided serious injury. He was also delighted to have a winning start.

The press gave the hosts a mixed reception. There was praise for the victory, with Brown being applauded for his Monday squad sessions and the team spirit he had fostered. There were demands to keep this team intact for future games to let it develop, much as Sir Alf had been perceived to do with his English team. On the other hand, Scots players were slated for their physicality, giving rise to calls that some should forfeit their winning bonus and some should never be selected again for Scotland – a suggestion roundly rejected by Brown, who considered his team had played robustly as required but within the laws of the game.

The second tie, against Cyprus, in the capital, Nicosia, was only a month ahead, and Brown's attentions turned to that.

Late in November, he went to the island to watch the game between Cyprus and West Germany, which the latter only won 1–0, courtesy of a last-minute Muller goal. It also gave him an opportunity to familiarise himself with the location and likely conditions. He was glad he did so, as he was shocked by the state of the pitch, which he described as 'being like concrete with small stones scattered all over it'. He did not think the result was a fluke, as it seemed to him that the Cypriots had improved since Austria had beaten them 7–1 in Vienna, and it was possible the Germans could have lost.

For this game, Brown was less fortunate regarding player availability, having to make six changes from the Austrian match, bringing in Herriot, Fraser, T. McLean, Murdoch, Stein and Gilzean for Simpson, Gemmell, Johnstone, Lennox, Law and Hughes. He had to deal with other difficulties, too, over travel arrangements and hotel accommodation. The SFA, in the face of much media criticism, had elected to travel by scheduled flights, which involved stopovers at London, Rome and Athens, resulting in the journey taking 14 hours. There was a two-hour delay at Athens while their aircraft was thoroughly checked over for possible damage due to extreme turbulence on the leg from Rome. Critics compared this with a charter flight for fans that took just over five hours to reach Cyprus and accused the Association of penny pinching. There was not much Brown could do about that, as the logistics were not within his remit. Criticism also came his way for locating the team's hotel in Famagusta, a 40-mile trip from Nicosia, when a quality hotel in the capital was available. But Brown knew that a lot of Scottish fans were booked in at it and wisely thought it better his squad were not subject to any distractions in that regard.

When interviewed ahead of the game, he reiterated his concern over the state of the pitch, which at least now his team had seen for themselves, having trained there. He acknowledged that it would not be conducive to free-flowing football, but remained optimistic. When asked about his difficulties as Scottish manager, he repeated that there were big problems in getting players together and arranging more games. He pointed out that it was going to be difficult to fit in a game before the next game against West Germany, in April 1969, and that four or five months without one was unsatisfactory. He aimed to create a club-type spirit in his squad, and his ideal was to emulate the outstanding Hungarians of 1953, his favourite team, who exemplified great teamwork allied to a flair for the unexpected. He repeated that Scotland produced talented players and had the country reached the 1966 finals it would have done well. Finally, he explained that critics did not bother him very much – criticism came with the job, and it was necessary to follow your own convictions and strategy.

Heavy rain preceded kick-off, turning the pitch into a mud bath and drenching the 7,000 spectators, many of whom were British servicemen waving 'Scotland' banners. After entertainment by an RAF pipe band, Scotland were soon into their stride and led 5–0 by half-time, which was how it ended. Gilzean and Murdoch each scored doubles, and an own goal by a Cypriot defender completed the nap. Brown was delighted with the outcome particularly given the earlier criticism and expressed optimism about Mexico. He was especially pleased with the play of McLean, Cooke, Gilzean and Murdoch. The press heralded 'A Great Win In Cyprus' and congratulated Brown, highlighting the effectiveness of him persisting with Monday training sessions despite the difficulties. Meanwhile, the Cypriots were unstinting in their praise of Scotland, describing them as the best team to have played there. Their coach, Pambos Avraamides, remarked, 'Scotland have better players than West Germany. I think Scotland for Mexico, a very good side indeed.'

Brown could not have made a better start, gathering full points from the first two games. But the biggest challenge, West Germany, was next on his radar. They had been ever-presents at all the World Cups, were winners in 1954 and, in the eyes of at least some, were unfortunate to be only runners up to England in 1966. But, in the five games they had played against Scotland going back to 1929, they had never won: a tally of three losses and two draws. Could Brown maintain that fine record?

His hopes of fitting in a warm-up game were dashed, largely because a backlog of domestic fixtures made it impossible. Instead he had to settle for two under-23 matches against England and Wales and a league international against England. In the latter, a 3–1 defeat to the English league at Hampden did little to boost confidence, although remarkably Murdoch and Greig each missed penalties, both their kicks striking the same post before rebounding. He continued, where possible, with his Monday sessions, but again they were often of limited value through players' non-attendance, one of the worst examples being in early February, when, of the 28 players called up to train, only 14 appeared. Injuries, cup ties and club policy were offered as explanations for this disappointment. Meanwhile, West Germany had been able to complete a 12-match tour of South America and had two games lined up against club sides, along with a friendly against Wales in Frankfurt.

After announcing a 17-man pool on 10 April, six days ahead of the Hampden fixture, Brown suffered two withdrawals within a couple of days: keeper Herriot and winger Hughes. Adding to his worries, Bremner was receiving treatment for injury at Leeds, Gilzean and Cooke were to join the squad late because of club commitments and Law had an ongoing eye problem. At least the Old Firm's league matches the weekend before the German fixture had been cancelled to avoid risk of injury to their players in Brown's squad. This was a minor step in the right direction for the manager in terms of national support. As expected, the Germans brought a strong squad including Haller, Muller, Overath, Held, Schnellinger, Vogts (a successor of Brown as Scotland's national manager), Beckenbauer and Schulz, and held their training camp at Kilmarnock's Rugby Park. Prior to the game, Brown's problems cleared up, but captain Bremner was criticised for only appearing at Scotland's Largs training camp 24 hours before kick-off.

During an interview, Brown expressed satisfaction with preparation, making it clear that his emphasis on developing a club spirit transcended any Old Firm rivalries in his squad. He added that the Celtic and Rangers players in his pools always mixed well, and to prevent the possibility of cliques being formed, he would split up players from the same club – for example, Lennox and Johnstone of Celtic used to room together, but he now paired Johnstone with McCreadie and made other similar pairings. He also stressed that while he wanted method in his team, he also wanted flair. Another factor he was keen to emphasise regarding consistency of selection was making it clear to players that one bad game did not warrant loss of their place in the squad.

The game was played in front of 115,000 and resulted in a 1–1 draw. A defensive mistake led to a first-half Muller goal, equalised late in the second half by Murdoch. It was clear to all that West Germany were a very capable and well-drilled side. Brown regretted dropping a point and the defensive mistake that led to it. He recalled, 'It was frustrating to lose such an avoidable goal. The Germans were a very good side – we mustn't forget that at the time they were ranked number two in Europe, and we were number eight. On the plus side, we had good performances from Gilzean, Greig, McCreadie and Murdoch, who scored a fantastic goal. Although some of the fans criticised Law, he played well to my instructions, which were to lie deep to bring Beckenbauer out of defence and leave a gap there. We also missed some good chances, especially in the first half. I thought overall it was a wonderful game.'

His former Rangers team-mate Willie Woodburn, now a football journalist, was of a similar opinion. He wrote that it looked as if the Germans had been playing together for years, with great teamwork and understanding. He noted Scotland's previous game had been four months earlier, whereas in that time the Germans had played several times. The result meant Scotland and West Germany were tied on five points, each having played three games with three more to come, with two of Scotland's being away.

* * * * *

There was no doubt this was a minor setback for Brown in his Mexico campaign, making it doubly important to win the next match, against Cyprus in Glasgow a month later, with the Home Internationals sandwiched in between. Brown realised this would be a very demanding period, coming as it did at the end of a long, hard season. It entailed in the space of ten days travelling to Wales for the game against them, then back to Largs to prepare for the Northern Irish match at Hampden and after that down to Wembley for the English game. There then followed a few days' break for the players before facing Cyprus at home. While the Home Internationals were prestigious, Brown recognised his ultimate priority was a win over Cyprus and knew he would have to shuffle his pack of players as well as he could to ensure that.

At Wrexham, in a high-scoring match, Brown led his team to a 5–3 win over a strong Welsh team featuring the likes of Sprake, Toshack, Durban, and Ron and Wyn Davies. For Brown, his best performers were Gemmell, McNeill, Gilzean and especially Cooke. Despite Bremner arriving a day late for the Scots' training camp at Chester and Law's non-availability, all had gone well for them in the Principality. There was concern expressed before the start of the Championship, as the Home Associations had, for the first time, agreed to allow live screening of matches for a fee of £30,000 each – leading to dire warnings about the adverse influence of television on the game and how 'football was selling its soul', which has some resonance today. At Wrexham, a camera gantry had been constructed in front of the stand, partially obscuring the view of some spectators and causing complaints. Brown was happy with the result, but a little concerned about the Welsh comeback to within two goals of his team.

Against a Northern Ireland side managed by Billy Bingham and featuring Jennings, Best, Neill and Dougan, Brown's men managed a 1–1 draw on a filthy night at Hampden in front of a meagre 7,843 crowd, the lowest ever for a Hampden Home International. The weather and live television coverage were blamed. Brown blamed the lack of atmosphere for a sub-par display, but was content to extend his record to nine games unbeaten.

In the lead-up to Wembley, Jimmy Johnstone was again a figure of controversy, as, instead of travelling to London with the squad, he returned to his home in Uddingston – prompting Jock Stein to summon him to Parkhead. After their meeting, Stein issued a withering statement critical of the winger, adding that Bobby Brown was better without him at Wembley. When asked by journalists in London about the issue, Brown was fairly tight-lipped, merely stating that he had withdrawn Johnstone from the squad. At this remove, he can only recall that there were personal issues involved preventing Johnstone's participation.

Wembley brought a 4–1 defeat for the Scots, which Brown found hugely disappointing, as he remembered, 'I thought we were well in the game at 2–1 down, then John Greig was penalised for a tackle on Peters, which I must say I thought was legitimate. That made it 3–1, and after that England pulled away. I have to say they played very well on the day, but for me it was a hard defeat to take; I knew it would be a difficult game but didn't think we would lose by three goals. That said, I really don't think the score fairly reflected the play, but it was a sore one.' Because of live TV coverage, the kick-off was at 7.30pm, which was far from universally popular, particularly with the Scottish fans. Despite it being a 100,000 sell-out, 'only' 90,000 turned up, reflecting disapproval of the kick-off time.

As a result of that defeat, there was a lot of pressure on Brown to lift his team for the forthcoming Cyprus meeting. His recollection is that it was not difficult to do so, as the players themselves appreciated the importance of the match in regard to their Mexico quest. As none had ever played in a World Cup finals, they were desperate to do so, particularly the 'Anglos' who had had to live with England's 1966 success since then. Without being complacent, they appreciated that their opposition was not the strongest and were amateurs whose day jobs ranged from bank clerks to garage attendants and barmen, which added its own pressure. Their coach, Eli Fuchs, was an engaging fellow who two years previously had been South Africa's manager of the year with Port Elizabeth FC, one of whose mainstays was Matt Gray, formerly of Third Lanark. He professed to entertain no hope of winning. Although the odds were firmly in Scotland's favour, Brown was quite rightly wary of a potential banana skin. He commented, 'There's no such thing as a surefire win in football and I was certainly taking nothing for granted. I drummed into my players not to think this was going to be easy and that they would have to be at their best to win. They were well aware of the game's importance.'

As it transpired, it was an easy 8–0 win for the Scots in front of 39,000 fans, with Stein notching four goals and Eddie Gray, McNeill, Henderson and Gemmell also on the scoresheet. But for some fine saves by the Cypriot keeper, the score would have been higher. Home hopes for Mexico were being kept well and truly alive.

In the wake of this win, there were increased calls for Brown to receive more support in his efforts to bring players together for regular training sessions prior to the next vital fixtures, against West Germany on 22 October and Austria on 5 November. A feeling of optimism about Scotland's chances was developing, with the realisation that in their past ten matches they had lost only once, to reigning world champions England. Brown was anxious to arrange two friendlies in the coming months, with Belgium, who had already qualified for Mexico, being one opponent in his sights. But first he had to deal with an ear problem that required minor surgery. Because of the amount of flying he had been doing, the pressure had caused small bones in his ear to fuse, and an operation to separate them was necessary.

Disappointingly, despite the SFA's best efforts, Belgium withdrew from the planned game and Brown was left with only a match against the Republic of Ireland in Dublin as a warm-up. The close season had also hindered his efforts to bring players together. This contrasted starkly with West Germany's preparations – they had friendlies organised against Austria and Bulgaria as well as regular squad training sessions. Neighbours England had even organised a summer tour. The Irish game resulted in a 1–1 draw and did not reveal much new to Brown. Its value was limited, as it had to be played only 24 hours after a round of league games in Scotland. One positive aspect for the manager was the play of Bobby Moncur, the Newcastle United captain.

Reflecting the importance of the tie, on the weekend beforehand all league matches in Scotland involving the 11 home-based players in Brown's pool were cancelled to assist him. In West Germany, all league matches on the same date had been cancelled. In the days leading up to the game, he had to deal with his usual disappointments. McCreadie, Hughes and Lennox all pulled out because of injury. Brown went to Parkhead himself to supervise the fitness tests undergone by the Celtic duo and reluctantly had to accept they were unfit. Stanton, Hugh Curran of Wolves and Tommy McLean were brought in as replacements. The game was to be played on a Wednesday evening in Hamburg's 72,000-capacity Volkspark Stadium, and was attracting enormous interest. It had been sold out for three months, with the Scots' allocation of 3,000 tickets having been sold out well in advance. Because of the way the group results had gone, Scotland needed a win for a chance to qualify – nothing less would do. A win for the hosts would guarantee them their place in Mexico. It was effectively 'winner take all'.

The Germans featured their usual all-star cast including Beckenbauer, Seeler, Schulz, Vogts, Haller, Maier and Libuda, and confident noises were emanating from their training camp at Malente, 30 miles outside Hamburg, where they were assembled for the ten days prior to the match. Brown had insisted that Scotland fly out on the Sunday before, to allow more time to prepare. On their chartered flight, 23 members of the press accompanied the Scottish party, which also included 11 SFA officials; this did not escape the notice of the press, particularly as the squad of players had been reduced from the original 22 to 18.

On arrival at Hamburg Airport, the Germans, meticulously prepared as ever, presented bouquets of red and white carnations to each member of the Scottish party, presumably, as Brown and the press at least hoped, unaware of the significance of that floral colour scheme's connotation here (with death).

The Scots settled into their luxurious accommodation in the city's Atlantic Hotel, where debutant Hugh Curran, formerly a free-transfer player with Third Lanark and Shamrock Rovers, was the centre of press attention, even eclipsing the presence of French actress and singer Juliette Greco, also a guest in the hotel. In West Germany, the tie had been labelled the 'Match of the Year' and had grossed their FA its biggest ever single gate of £80,000. Tickets were fetching up to £60 on the black market, equivalent to about £850 today. Several famous managers had flown in to watch the game, including the legendary Brazilian Didi, now manager of Peru, and Joao Saldanha, of Brazil. The bookmakers fixed Scotland's odds at 4/1, while the Germans were at 8/11, comfortable favourites. Despite that, Brown felt he had the players to pull off a win provided they were not overawed by a passionate home support. It was no exaggeration to say that the eyes of European football, if not world football, were on Hamburg that week.

* * * * *

But the football gods had not finished with Brown yet: he suffered another blow in the early hours of the eve of the game. Striker Curran was unwell and had to be ruled out. Brown and the team doctor were called to his room at 2am, when he was found to have a temperature of 104 degrees. He had complained of feeling unwell after a training session the previous evening at the Volkspark Stadium. Room-mate Charlie Cooke was moved as a precaution, and Brown crossed his fingers that no further calamities befell his team. Stein was called on to replace Curran.

On the night, Brown's team played well and with total commitment, but lost 3–2. It was enormously disappointing, as it ended Scotland's hopes of Mexico, but the manner of defeat made it even worse. All observers bar perhaps the most one-eyed German fan were agreed that the Scots were the better team and did not deserve to lose. Even well-known English journalist Desmond Hackett, no great lover of the Scots putting it neutrally, thought that if the game had been decided on points, Scotland would have been clear winners. Many thought it was the best Scottish performance seen in years, spoiled by the inept refereeing of Herr Droz of Switzerland.

Jimmy Johnstone, so often a controversial figure with his country, scored the first goal within three minutes after Maier could only palm out an Eddie Gray shot into his path. Fichtel equalised from a corner that keeper Herriot might have reached first. On 59 minutes, Muller clearly punched his marker McNeill and, as the Celt lay prostrate on the ground, scored to put his team ahead, prompting a pitch invasion by some home fans. After that, Gilzean scored a well-taken headed goal from a long high ball from McKinnon to draw Scotland level. Then, with about ten minutes to go, and Scotland upfield pushing for the winner, German winger Libuda, nicknamed 'Stan' because of his tricky Stanley Matthews-type play, broke past Gemmell and continued his run before slotting it past Herriot to send the vociferous German support into raptures. With minutes remaining, Gemmell lost his temper with Haller for a foul on him and was sent off for retaliation, to cap a miserable end to the evening for Scotland.

One newspaper headline screamed 'Robbery With Violence', an opinion with which Brown agreed. The Germans were guilty of a lot of foul play, most of which went unpunished, the worst example being seconds before Muller's goal. Brown thought the players were victims of a grossly weak referee, and that the second German goal was a 'diabolical decision'. Although he had expected a robust, physical game, he considered it an injustice that Scotland lost. He had clearly seen that McNeill was punched on the face by Muller and left lying on the ground as the German scored their second goal. Gemmell's ordering off was wrong, he felt, as the referee had completely ignored Haller's initial foul on him. Despite the outcome, he thought his team could hold their heads high. He also thought that if Herriot had come further off his line to cut the angle as Libuda headed in towards goal, the keeper might have been able to prevent the score. He was very frustrated that, after such a positive and wholehearted showing, his team should be denied by poor refereeing and elements of misfortune.

Although of little consolation ultimately, it was reassuring to hear that others thought similarly about his team's display. Joao Saldanha stated, 'Scotland outplayed the Germans. I am happier from Brazil's point of view that West Germany are going to Mexico rather than the Scots.' Popular German newspaper *Bild Zeitung* commented that 'it was great drama and outdid every other football match ever played in Germany'. A number of other German newspapers thought it a 'tragedy' that Scotland, the losers, were not to be going to Mexico. There was no doubt that Scotland were hugely unfortunate to lose the game and thus a berth in the World Cup finals. Normally such an outcome would result in the home press criticising the manager, but not on this occasion. Instead the reaction was one of universal support for Brown to continue in charge, with more calls for him to be given increased backing. His initial contract was now entering its final year, and hopes were expressed that it would be renewed. There remained the 'dead rubber' game of the World Cup group against Austria in Vienna.

Whether it was because of the game's status is not known, but Brown suffered yet again a number of withdrawals from his squad. Jimmy Johnstone, Willie Johnston, Tommy McLean, McCreadie, Cormack and Peter Marinello were all unavailable for different reasons. Among those called in as replacements were Leeds United's Peter Lorimer and John Connolly, a promising winger from Brown's previous club St Johnstone who would later become well known at Everton. Aware of recent history between the two countries, the Austrian FA secretary, Herr Liegel, made a point of apologising for 'events in recent games between the countries' and expressing hope that the 'bitterness would disappear'.

The game was played in the famous old Prater Stadium, ending in a 2–0 win for the Austrians. It was a poor Scottish performance, with Brown commenting that he felt let down by experienced players. He felt it was a game that should not have been lost, as his team controlled the midfield but gave away two goals and missed a number of 'sitters'. There was little interest in the match: although a crowd of 45,000 had been predicted, only 10,000 attended. Herr Liegel's conciliatory remarks did not prevent sections of the Austrian press condemning the Scots for rough play, particularly John Greig, a charge refuted by Brown. On a positive note, Brown had managed to blood two new players: centre-back Francis Burns of Manchester United and Hugh Curran, both of whom fitted in well and were identified as 'ones for the future'.

Chapter 11

Final Years as Scotland Manager

WITH World Cup hopes now extinguished, the manager's next focus was on the Home International Championship in April 1970. Before then, agreement was reached on a new four-year contract for Brown, with a six-month notice clause which either side could invoke. This suited Brown and appeared to satisfy the media. There had also been continuing speculation over whether Brown would go to Mexico as an observer courtesy of the SFA. He had already been invited to spend time at Brazil's, West Germany's and England's training camps in Mexico by their respective managers, a reflection of the high regard in which he was held. Prior to the start of the Championship, the SFA confirmed he would be going to Mexico with their blessing, a trip he thoroughly enjoyed, as will be seen.

After Vienna, the only intervening fixtures Brown had were league internationals against the Irish league in November 1969, a 5–2 win for the Scots at Ibrox, and against the English league, a 3–2 reverse. Despite the poor showing in Vienna, the Scots confounded their critics by playing well in the Championship and sharing the title. A narrow 1–0 away win at Windsor Park in Belfast, by a team skippered by Arsenal's Frank McLintock, saw them off to a good start. The Scot who really stood out in the opinion of Brown and others was Moncur at sweeper, who nullified the Northern Irish attacks time after time. After colliding with him, Best was sent off for dissent, compounding matters by throwing mud in the referee's direction. With a refreshing candour seldom evident today, his manager, Billy Bingham, said that he deserved to be sent off. A goalless draw at home against Wales set the scene for the 'big one', the match against England at Hampden. A crowd of 137,438 crammed into the old stadium, their enthusiasm for the cause clearly little diminished by World Cup disappointment.

In front of that tremendous support, Scotland could only manage a 0–0 draw, but had good cause to feel aggrieved about the referee's failure to award them a penalty. Everyone inside the ground apart from the referee could see that Labone clearly fouled Stein in the penalty box in the 20th minute, but play was waved on. Again Moncur had an outstanding game, and Celtic's David Hay, Willie Carr of Coventry and John O'Hare of Derby County did well throughout the series.

Brown commented that he was very pleased with the outcome of the Championship. He added, 'A new era for young players on the verge of international honours has arrived, for example David Hay of Celtic has proved himself one of the most mature players in Scotland. And there is no doubt in anyone's mind that Bobby Moncur has made the week his own.' Underlining Moncur's fine performances, another press headline announced, 'Moncur ended the week as the discovery of them all'. For his part, the player paid tribute to the immense spirit and confidence engendered in him and the squad by Brown. He recollected, 'I was concussed near the end at Hampden and had to go to hospital to be checked over. I then had to catch a train to Linlithgow to visit my parents in Kirkliston. As I had never played club football in Scotland, I wasn't very well known and nobody recognised me, but I was relieved to hear a number of fans on the train say that "that guy from Newcastle" had played OK!'

Going to the World Cup finals that summer in Mexico was one of the highlights of his time as Scotland manager. Although it would have been even better had he been there in charge of the Scottish team, he considered it a 'real privilege' to have been able to attend what is often considered the greatest World Cup of all. 'I went in a small group with Bobby Robson, then manager of Ipswich Town, Don Howe, then Arsenal coach, and Dave Sexton, the Chelsea manager at that time and later Manchester United boss. The SFA secretary, Willie Allan, and I had discussed my going to the finals, and he and the international selection committee sanctioned the trip. I went with these three, as far as I remember, after I had been speaking to Bertie Mee, the Arsenal manager, with whom I had an excellent relationship. He mentioned that his coach, Don Howe, was going with the others, and as I was also intending to go, he suggested making contact to link up with them, which is what happened. We had a wonderful time based in Guadalajara, and we all enjoyed each other's company. After going to the various matches, we would meet up in the evenings for dinner and socialise together. In a sense, it was like a dream come true, being there watching the best teams and players in the world. As we were all engrossed in football, we would discuss it constantly and exchange our opinions and thoughts on what we had seen. It really was a fantastic opportunity and one I shall always be grateful for having had. The final itself, of course, was special, and who can ever forget the wonder goal of Carlos Alberto?

Magnificent, absolutely magnificent. His team-mates Gerson and Rivelino also stood out in my mind, and of course Pele, just an absolutely magnificent team.'

Later that summer, away from the serious business of international football, Brown organised a special charity match between an 'International All Stars XI' and his local team, Rhu Amateurs, an excellent club who had won the Scottish Amateur Cup three years previously. The match was sponsored by the local Rotary Club, of which Brown was now a member, and its purpose was to raise funds to acquire a minibus for mentally handicapped people in the area. Using his contacts, Brown persuaded former players to 'come out of retirement' to provide high-profile opposition for his local team and to attract as big a crowd as possible. Jock Stein was the 'impartial referee', entertaining the 3,000-strong crowd with some amusing decisions, and occasionally crucial interventions involving jersey pulling and tackles at crucial moments. Brown pulled on his goalie's jersey once again, and thanks to his persuasive powers his team-mates included ex-Rangers Willie Woodburn and Billy Williamson; Harry Haddock and Davie White, ex-Clyde; Jim Kennedy, ex-Celtic; Dave McParland, ex-Partick Thistle; Tommy Preston, ex-Hibs; and Jimmy Murray, ex-Hearts. Thanks to Stein's 'judicious' refereeing, the 'All Stars' won 2–1, but, more importantly, and very satisfyingly from Brown's perspective, a large sum was raised for an extremely worthwhile cause while an absorbed crowd thoroughly enjoyed themselves.

The next major tournament on Brown's schedule was the European Nations' Cup, whose finals were scheduled for 1972 in Belgium, and qualification for which began in November 1970 with a home game against Denmark. The other teams in Scotland's group were Belgium and Portugal. On paper, the draw gave Scotland a decent prospect of progressing, but disappointing results in the group, followed by a poor Home International Championship, would spell the end of his time as Scotland manager.

For the Danish encounter, Brown selected an experienced pool and then endured the usual anxious wait to find out how many of his players he would have available. On the back of his successful Home Internationals, Bobby Moncur was appointed by Brown as captain for the first time, prompting him to comment, 'I'm thrilled to be skipper. I've captained Newcastle United for the last three years and back in 1960 captained Scottish Schoolboys against England at Pittodrie.' The evening Moncur's appointment was announced, Brown gave the squad permission for a night out in Largs on the understanding that it was to be 'sensible' and that they would observe a 10pm curfew. Moncur recalled, 'Well, we were in a bar and it started getting towards ten o'clock and no one was moving, so I thought I'd better suggest we should be getting back to the hotel. You have to remember that there were a number of older and more experienced pros in the squad. As I got gingerly to my feet to say this, I was met by some industrial language to the effect we were going nowhere. At this point I felt my captaincy was not off to the best of starts, to put it mildly. However, I decided I had to set an example and said I was being professional and was going back. When I reached the door of the bar, I was on my own and feeling a bit down. But as I was about to leave, I felt an arm on my shoulder and a voice saying, "skipper I'm with you", and Denis Law appeared alongside me. The others soon followed, and I'll never forget Denis for what he did then.'

A team-mate at Newcastle, Preben Arentoft, formerly of Morton, was Danish, and Moncur had obtained information from him on some of the Scots' opponents. As always, Brown's preparation was faultless and included taking his squad to the BBC studios in Glasgow to watch film of the recent matches against West Germany and Cyprus. Expectation was high for a Scottish win, as the Danes then only selected amateur players, on this occasion a number of students, teachers, a soldier, a machinist and a banker.

Predicted comfortable wins in football often fail to materialise, and Brown was not falling into the trap of thinking this would be easy. After a hard-fought game his team squeezed a 1–0 win, with almost 25,000 in attendance for the Wednesday evening match. Although he knew Scotland did not play well, he was pleased to have the points in the bag and to have made a successful start to the campaign. As it was the team's first game in almost six months, he felt allowances had to be made, but called for another game to be arranged before the next tie, against Belgium in three months' time. Afterwards, he was criticised by Jock Stein for replacing his player David Hay with Rangers' Sandy Jardine 12 minutes before the end after fans began chanting Jardine's name. The implication was clear, but Brown was having none of it, addressing a sharp response to Stein, 'I've always had reasonable cooperation from Jock Stein and hope to continue doing so; I emphasise though I am looking for cooperation and not direction.'

The tenor of that comment, however, masked what was in private a very good relationship between the two. Stein was a big horse-racing fan, and Brown remembered accompanying him to Ayr races, driven there by Sean Fallon, his assistant at Celtic. 'Jock was having an unsuccessful day until near the end, when a jockey walked by, saying in a low voice, "Hey big man, 'Glenkiln' in the last race, penalty kick", meaning a certainty. Jock put his remaining cash on the tip and was delighted to see it romp home and win him some decent money.'

Attempts to arrange a warm-up international before playing Belgium frustratingly came to naught. However, a week prior to the date in Liege, a special game was held at Hampden in aid of the Ibrox Disaster Fund between a Rangers/Celtic Select and a Scotland XI. On 2 January 1971, Scotland suffered its worst football tragedy when, during the traditional New Year's Old Firm derby at Ibrox, a stairway collapsed, leading to the deaths of 66 people with hundreds injured. Colin Stein scored a last-minute equaliser as fans were beginning to descend the stairway to leave the ground. They turned back up it to celebrate, but, in doing so, collided with others leaving, leading to a fatal crush with bodies piled on top of each other. In the wake of the tragedy, the Old Firm laid aside their customary antipathy to pull together, particularly for the benefit of the families of the deceased and injured; this game was one example of that co-operation. Although this was secondary in the circumstances, it also served Brown's purposes well, given the upcoming Belgian fixture.

On a night when the result was unimportant, Scotland beat the Select 2–1, watched by an 81,000 crowd. The Select included guest players Peter Bonetti, the Chelsea goalkeeper later to finish his career at Dundee United, and Manchester United stars George Best and Bobby Charlton. Archie Gemmill made his first appearance in a Scotland shirt that evening, doing well enough for Brown to draft him into his squad for Belgium. Overall, Brown was very pleased with how his team played and thought it augured well for the European tie. On top of that, it was reckoned the game had raised £37,500 for the fund, swelling the total to £250,000. With what was by now an almost monotonous regularity, Brown's squad suffered call-offs on the eve of travelling to Liege: McLintock, Cormack and Harper were all out. He reminisced, 'I had no choice but to be philosophical and put on a brave face. From the players' perspective, I had to be seen to remain positive, although I can tell you that at times it was very difficult and hugely frustrating.'

He declared in advance that a draw would be a good result, and that he intended to build on reliability from the back, where Moncur and McKinnon had begun to develop a good understanding. Trying to gain the psychological upper hand, the Belgians had decided to take the game to Liege, where they would be assured of a strong partisan support from the local cosmopolitan mining community of French, Italians, Greeks, Turks and Algerians, creating a very hostile atmosphere. The pitch at Standard Liege's ground was tight and threadbare, set in depressing surroundings. Belgium's wily manager, Raymond Goethals, had selected six Standard players and stated ahead of the game that a draw would be good for them, predicting that Scotland would qualify. Brown was not swallowing that, saying that he expected a hard, relentless game. He was criticised for his defensive stance and for a defensive selection.

Heavy rain fell for hours prior to kick-off, with many convinced it would be called off. But it went ahead and was played in appalling conditions on a hazardous, waterlogged pitch, resulting in a 3–0 win for the hosts. This loss was heavily criticised by the press, one headline stating, 'Shame Night for Scotland'. Afterwards Brown stated that he had no excuses and that the better team had won, although he felt that McKinnon's own goal that opened the scoring was 'cruel luck'. A double by Anderlecht's outstanding Paul Van Himst completed the scoring. When asked about the country's future in the competition, he replied, 'I'll sleep on that one.'

Scotland's path to the European Nations' Cup finals had taken a significant wrong turning, which Brown was acutely aware he needed to put back on track, the next tie being a demanding one away to Portugal in two and a half months' time. In the intervening period, the only fixtures he had available to him were an under-23 and a league international, both against England, necessarily of limited value. Brown reckoned, after these games, that he had gained some useful information, noting the emergence of Jim Brogan of Celtic and Davie Robb of Aberdeen as candidates for the Portugal match. He also remained hopeful of fixing up a game for 7 April, a fortnight ahead of Portugal, which he and others considered a 'must'.

However, once more, no game could be arranged for that date. Again, Brown's team planning was hit by a raft of withdrawals – no Bremner, Lorimer, Gray, McLintock, Kelly (Arsenal) and Jardine. John Greig, who Brown wanted to bring in as a replacement, was also unavailable. To prepare as well as possible, he assembled his squad at Largs on the Sunday before flying out the next day for the Wednesday evening tie in Lisbon. Despite recent tribulations, Brown was upbeat about Scottish prospects, declaring 'we will go for goals'. Rumours were emanating from the Portuguese camp that their players were boasting of how they would beat the Scots 2–0. Whether it was because of that is not known, but their coach announced that while a win would earn them £120, in the event of their losing the players would not be paid anything. This prompted Brown to claim the moral high ground and respond, 'We're playing for the jerseys.' Scotland based themselves at Estoril, as had Celtic before their 1967 European Cup win, which Brown hoped might serve as inspiration.

On the night, Portugal were comfortable 2–0 winners at Benfica's Stadium of Light after a poor Scottish performance. In after-match comments, Brown criticised some of his players for a lack of basic ability. He thought they played well within their limitations, but that there was a lack of fight and control in midfield. He added that the work they had done on different moves had not been carried into practice during the match. The result attracted some trenchant criticism, with demand for an 'all tartan' team of home-based Scots again raising its head in the wake of the continuing unavailability of English-based players. This result was a huge setback to Brown's already slim prospects of reaching the European finals, and his position as national manager, as he realised, was being undermined. Already, the subject of his continuing in the role was being widely debated, and he appreciated the precariousness of his position. He hoped that the forthcoming Home Internationals would allow him the chance to regroup and aspire to a positive result in the next tie, against Denmark in June. Unfortunately, that was not to be.

The first game, against Wales in Cardiff, was overshadowed by the players' angry reaction to a recently published SFA annual report, which was highly critical of some of them, particularly for the poor result against Belgium, in what might be considered a 'blunderbuss' approach. Its timing and terms were not constructive, amounting to indiscriminate accusation, and Brown had to hold what were described as 'clear the air talks' with his squad ahead of the match. 'A number of the players were understandably quite upset, as part of the report implied a lack of application and spirit. Although results had been disappointing, including the Belgian one, there had never been any lack of effort by the players, and I had to do my best to repair the damage, which I think I succeeded in doing. Certainly I felt after our talks that the spirit in the camp was good.'

Brown was determined to put the Welsh defence under pressure, as their renowned central defence partnership of Terry Hennessey and Mike England were not playing, and therefore selected an attack-minded team. For the first time for a long time, his team featured no Rangers players, which was considered controversial. Unfortunately, heavy rain fell for hours beforehand, rendering Ninian Park a mudbath, and a fairly undistinguished game ended in a scoreless draw. At one point, it had looked likely that English World Cup referee Jack

Taylor would call it off. Brown was content, in the circumstances, with a draw. He was particularly pleased with Eddie Gray, and with Bobby Moncur and Frank McLintock in central defence, who he said had 'developed a good understanding opposed to two of the best strikers in the game, Ron Davies of Southampton and John Toshack of Liverpool'. After the match, his squad dispersed to reassemble at Largs on the Monday morning for the Tuesday evening game against Northern Ireland.

Unavailable to him were Bremner, Johnstone, Cormack and Robb. Against the team that should have been Scotland's weakest opponents, they put on a lacklustre display, losing 1–0 through a Greig own goal – the first post-war Northern Irish win at Hampden Park. There was a noticeable lack of penetration, and the Russian coach, Konstantin Nikolaev, who was there to assess Scotland ahead of their game in June, would have seen little to concern him. Adding to Brown's worries was a lengthy post-match injury list. About the only crumb of comfort for him was he thought his team had played with plenty of endeavour, although he recognised that much more would be required in the final game against England at Wembley. Scotland's big problem was an apparent inability to score goals, having failed to hit the net now in four consecutive matches, and with that in mind preparation for Wembley focussed on shooting practice.

Nor were these two mediocre results ideal preparation, as Brown was only too aware, and criticism of him was becoming more and more pointed.

From the Scots' training base at Brent Bridge, Brown did his best to sound positive, saying, 'My team will attack and our problems can be overcome. We need a break, we need one goal. This can be the day.' Skipper Moncur declared he was very impressed by the spirit in the camp, and that if a match could be won by that alone he would predict a win.

Only three members of the Scottish team had played previously at Wembley: Greig, Bremner and McLintock. Jimmy Johnstone was fulfilling an ambition in making his Wembley debut, and neither he nor his team-mates seemed unduly bothered about the bomb scare at their hotel on the eve of the match, which had disrupted their night. Unfortunately, come kick-off, the Scots' optimism and positivity did not transfer to the pitch, and a poor display resulted in a 3–1 defeat, much to the vocal anguish of their aggrieved support. Their chants of 'Brown must go' and worse intensified when, near the end of the game, he replaced Tony Green of Blackpool with Drew Jarvie of Aberdeen. Green had been playing well but was suffering severe cramp and, as he confirmed later, was incapable of continuing, so vindicating Brown's decision. But, by this stage, the fans were furious and screaming vitriolic abuse at him – the same man whom they had lionised only four years previously at the same venue, underlining the fleeting nature of a football manager's success and the fickle nature of fans. As well-known football writer John Rafferty put it in *The Scotsman*, 'Not even politicians could tolerate this and neither may he.' At the end of the match, Sir Alf Ramsey, not noted for any particular affection for the Scots, put a compassionate arm round Brown's shoulder as he accompanied him back to the dressing rooms, offering consolation.

Press reports did not spare Brown and the team, with articles posing the question of who should replace him. Chairman of the international selection committee Jim Aitken commented, 'The manager's future is in the balance, he carries the can.' Maintaining his dignity, Brown responded that he was not stepping down and that he still had a job to do, which he was getting on with – namely preparing for the next European tie, against Denmark, and the friendly against Russia. He accepted the fans were entitled to show their feelings and could not be blamed for doing so. He added, 'I credit myself with having enough moral fibre not to let this affect me.' There was no doubt, however, that within himself he knew his time as national manager was drawing inexorably and uncomfortably to a close.

The Danish game was to be played in Copenhagen on 9 June, with the Scots party continuing on from there for the friendly in Moscow against the USSR on 14 June. The trip was a somewhat dispiriting prospect, given that there was no realistic chance of European qualification and the Moscow fixture was a nothing-at-stake friendly, taking place at a time of the year when some players would rather have been on family holidays on a beach somewhere. These factors were reflected in the number of players who were unavailable for the trip. Brogan, Cormack, Greig, Martin Buchan, Jarvie, McLintock, Bremner, Lorimer, Jimmy Johnstone, Bobby Hope and Green were all unable to go for varying reasons – a team in itself!

Although by now Brown was well anaesthetised to call-offs, the problem reached new heights on this occasion or, better put, plumbed new depths. Even he, normally positive and diplomatic in the face of these difficulties, was forced to admit, 'We're struggling now.' Parodying the scenario, a cartoon appeared supposedly depicting the Scottish team's plane flying off to Copenhagen with a couple of players parachuting out of it, above a caption reading, 'They're still pulling out!' Despite the problems, Brown was his usual professional self in his preparation with the squad at their training base in the seaside resort of Vedbaek, 15 miles from Copenhagen, where they stayed in the prestigious Marina Hotel. He observed that the players were training well and were keen to prove the critics at home wrong, and was impressed by their morale. For the first time, Denmark were fielding several professionals who played abroad, alongside their amateurs drawn from teachers, clerks, insurance officials and factory workers. Although only prestige was at stake, the game was a sell-out, with the Danes making confident noises as to how they would win easily. Their team featured three who had played in Scotland: Sorensen, ex-Morton goalie; Arentoft, also ex-Morton; and Berg, ex-Dundee United. On the eve of the game, one of Brown's team, Kilmarnock's Tommy McLean, was signed for Rangers by manager Willie Waddell, who had flown out specifically to seal the transfer. It is unimaginable nowadays that a transfer would be completed during preparation for an international. As a footnote, this gave rise to a trivia question as to which player played for Scotland before representing his club team. Although there was a risk of the player being distracted, this did not happen to McLean, who was Scotland's best player in a 1–0 defeat at the Idraetspark Stadium, where Brown had played for Rangers years before.

The goal was scored by Finn Laudrup, father of the famous Michael and Brian, the latter who, of course, played in Scotland for Rangers. This defeat was not well received by the press, with one headline reading, 'Scots Hit New Low'. Reports made it clear that Scotland had been well outplayed, although keeper Clark, Stanton and, as mentioned, McLean emerged with credit. Brown knew he had only been able to field an under-strength team, but also realised that would not appease his critics. In an interview after the match, he said he envied his Danish counterpart, who had been able to call on players from several countries in Europe, while regretting that his own choice had been significantly restricted. He was also careful to add that he could not fault his players for lack of effort. Jim Aitken delivered a measure of support in a statement criticising clubs for a lack of co-operation. Brown's reaction was realistic and not one of 'sour grapes', but the reality was that the last slim vestige of possibility of European qualification had now disappeared, and it was a subdued party he led on their way to Moscow.

This would be the second time Scotland played the USSR under Brown's charge. The game was approached with a degree of pessimism given the background, and many feared the worst for Scotland. He commented in Moscow, 'Obviously I can't feel very happy about taking on the USSR in the present circumstances. There have been so many problems with this trip.' Brown recalled it was an interesting place, and that it was fascinating to be able to visit the Kremlin and see the State Circus. The Lenin Stadium, where the match was to be played, he found an impressive arena. But he soon discovered things in Moscow were a bit different from home in these Cold War days. He remembered that on the first floor of their Metropole Hotel, near Red Square, a large Russian lady was permanently stationed, monitoring their every movement. The hotel wanted to know in advance the numbers for meals, and, irrespective of the number who actually appeared, the number that had been 'ordered' were provided. To train, it was necessary to book the facilities for a specified period of time. Brown recalled that halfway through a 'reserved' session of an hour, heavy snow began falling, causing him to lead his players indoors – only to be refused entry as the 'reserved' period had not yet expired and they had to remain outside until it did!

Scotland did much better than expected on the rain-sodden pitch of the Lenin Stadium in front of a crowd of about 15,000 Muscovites, restricting their opponents to a 1–0 win. Because of personnel difficulties, it was an all 'home Scots' team other than Wolves centre-half Francis Burns. Brown was pleased with their play, especially what he described as 'their neat passing', and felt the loss of the goal, an error by keeper Clark, was unlucky. 'We were unlucky to lose and merited a draw. I was pleased with the new players brought in late,' he added. Certainly the home crowd seemed to agree with that, applauding the Scots more than their own team. At the post-match reception, Brown was conscious of there being little fraternisation between the teams and minimal conversation between the two parties, largely because of the language difficulty. He also recalled it as memorable for the presentation by the hosts to each player of a small model sputnik as a gift, which he thought eclipsed the tartan rugs handed over by the Scots!

Hibs legend Pat Stanton was the Scottish team captain in that game, Brown's last as manager, and recalled a special trip. 'We had what might be thought of as a "patch-up" squad but still had some very good players. Bobby had us well organised, and I thought we played well against the Soviets, certainly better than had been expected. It was a real privilege to visit Moscow then, and I have to say some of our preconceptions went out the window. We were expecting somewhere really cold and everyone going about in fur hats, but people were going about in T-shirts and it was hot! Our hotel was just next to Red Square, and we had a tour of the Kremlin, which was a beautiful place. Surprisingly, at least for us, there were a lot of tourists going about, and we certainly felt free to have a wander during the day without feeling uncomfortable. I remember having a walk about Red Square with one of my team-mates who was wearing a Superman T-shirt, not then available there, and I noticed this was attracting envious glances as if someone might try to take it, but nothing happened. A couple of things stick in my mind. There were two liaison-type hotel staff assigned to us, and if you wanted a coke it was not a simple case of asking and getting one. The liaison guy had to go speak to a waiter, who went to speak to someone else, and after about 20 minutes your coke appeared. The other thing was some of our guys had bought some heavy metal music LPs in Copenhagen, which were not available in Moscow. One of our liaison guys was into that type of music, so the guys gifted him the LPs, after which it was noticed the cokes began arriving much quicker! We also had a visit to the underground, and what struck me was there was no litter, no graffiti – the place was immaculate. It was quite something to be there at that time, and I found it hugely interesting. Another thing I remember was at the post-match function, speaking to their captain, the famous centre-half Albert Shesternev of CSKA Moscow, who by then had about 85 caps. He was one of the few players with any English, and he came over as a really nice guy.'

From what had seemed like a prospective date with failure, the scratch Scottish team emerged with considerable credit for their showing, the press generally of the opinion it had been Scotland's best performance for some time. The damage had been done in the preceding European ties and Home Internationals, and it was no surprise when on the return flight, Aitken, sitting next to Brown, told him that he thought his selection committee would be in favour of a change of manager. Brown had been thinking for some time that this was inevitable.

The truth was that he was no longer enjoying the job as he had done previously. The run of poor results, combined with the amount of criticism and personal abuse he was receiving, meant the negatives were outweighing the positives. He was also acutely aware that given the perpetual problems he had to endure over availability of players, he was in effect being asked to do the job with one hand behind his back. While some of the press appreciated his difficulties, it did not prevent others from calling for his head, nor did it dilute the hostility towards him from fans. When the next international selection committee meeting took place in July, he was advised, as anticipated, his services were no longer required. The six-month notice clause in his contract was activated, and he received six months' salary in lieu of notice.

Although results latterly meant there was an inevitability about this decision, it was clear from Mr Aitken's downbeat demeanour afterwards that the Association had not found it an easy one to make, given their harmonious relationship with Brown. When asked by a reporter if a new appointment would be made soon, he shrugged off the question, saying it had already been a hard enough day.

Brown commented, 'It was a weight off my shoulders and something I knew was coming for some time. I thought the job was becoming almost impossible to do – at any rate, in the way I wanted to do it, with all my first-choice players available. Unfortunately, a number of clubs, especially English ones, put their interests before Scotland's, which eventually added up to a whole lot of frustration for me. The first part of my time in the job was more successful than the second part, and I put that down to the increasing difficulty I had in getting players available. For example, I was never able to field my Wembley '67 team ever again. However, I know I gave the job my very best shot and can never be accused of a lack of commitment or professionalism.

'Of course, it would have been better to leave on a higher note, but football management is a fairly singular profession. I would have loved to have had players together for longer before games. In those days you got two or three days, unlike now, when the manager has them for a week. Having said all that, I do not regret it for a minute. I had some fantastic experiences, and there truly was never a dull moment, whether that be for better or worse!

'Practically speaking, I was the country's first full-time manager with completely unfettered control of player selection. I know the myth exists that wasn't the case completely because the selection committee continued to function, but I can categorically state that I had total control of selection. Before that, the way the committee operated was that several players would be nominated for each position, with each of the selectors having a vote, and the player receiving the most votes was chosen. As you can appreciate, that was rather a "pot luck" approach to selection and certainly not one I was going to endorse.

'In my opinion, the committee and I co-existed very amicably during my time as manager. We were respectful of one another and didn't cross the line between our different roles. In day-to-day terms, they and the secretary, Willie Allan, were the conduit between me and my ultimate employer, the SFA, and I had to engage with them as such. Generally I found them supportive, and relations between us were cordial. They would hold their meeting first, after which a bell would ring in my office indicating I was to join them. Once I did, we would discuss a variety of topics – often, for example, my report on the previous match, which players I was looking at for selection, contact with club managers and the media, my ideas for the next game, identification of potential future opponents and the like. Identification of players for the team was my sole responsibility, although, as you'd expect, I consulted with club managers and officials over their players. It was necessary to build up goodwill.

'As for the highs during my time, Wembley 1967 has, of course, to be up there – a truly memorable occasion. I was criticised for my selection of Ronnie Simpson in goal and Ronnie McKinnon at centre-half, but I was enormously pleased that my choices were vindicated. The World Tour that followed soon after Wembley was something I enjoyed hugely: having the opportunity to visit all these countries and get to know the players over a period of time as well as having them available 24/7 was highly beneficial. And, although this may sound curious, the night in Hamburg in the game against West Germany in October 1969 was also a high. Although we lost the match unfairly in my view, we played really, really well and deserved better. The build-up to the game was extremely high profile and tense, and on the night itself it was almost impossible to avoid being caught up in the white-hot atmosphere – it was really something else. To have come so close was agonising, but it was a completely absorbing occasion. And, of course, qualification for the World Cup was more difficult then, as only 16 teams did so. One offshoot of these games with West Germany was I enjoyed an excellent relationship with their manager, Helmut Schoen, whom I met several times over the years, including in Mexico during the World Cup. Through him I met Beckenbauer and Overath and also became friendly with their team doctor, who actually gifted me a German tracksuit when they played us in Glasgow in 1968.

'In terms of lows, the worst was clearly the Wembley defeat in 1971, when the fans turned against me – that was certainly not an experience you wanted to repeat. And also, my last two games, the defeats in Denmark and Russia, were among the lows, although our performance in Moscow, all things considered, was good. But these were the games that precipitated my losing the job.

'My most impressive national captains were John Greig, Billy Bremner and Bobby Moncur. Greig was inspirational, very reliable, and would give you 150 per cent every time. I'm not surprised he was voted "the Greatest Ever Ranger". I had the greatest respect for him. Bremner was another who would give you his all and then some. Fiery, a great tackler and accomplished distributor of the ball. And Moncur was also very good, a fairly quiet individual who was very reliable and an extremely effective captain.

'As for individual players, Jim Baxter stood out – what an artist! He could run a game by himself, especially in a team that was on top, although he was not so effective in a struggling team. Denis Law was outstanding, but injuries curtailed the impact he had when I was in charge. Eddie McCreadie was a superbly cultured full-back and ahead of his time. Others who did well for me included Bobby Lennox, Alan Gilzean, Billy McNeill, Jimmy Johnstone and Willie Henderson. Those last two were quite different in style – Johnstone a dribbler and Henderson more direct, using his pace. I had no problems with Johnstone: he certainly was a character, but underneath it he was quite a humble guy. I always remember he used to address me as "sir". When we were based at Largs before internationals and I produced the tactics board, he used to say to me beforehand not to ask him any questions, to avoid embarrassment if he gave the wrong answer. I asked Jock Stein how he coached him, and he replied "His brains are brand new", i.e. he's a natural, just let him express himself.

'Non-Scottish players whom I admired included Beckenbauer, a fantastic player as adept at defending as at setting up attacks. The Brazilians of that era were outstanding: Pele, of course, Gerson, Carlos Alberto, Rivelino, etc. Bobby Moore was a player I admired very much, always calm, never flustered and again, I think, ahead of his time. The Charlton brothers were also outstanding, Bobby, the iconic centre-forward, often the breaker of Scottish hearts; while Jack, underestimated I think, was a pillar of the defence, rugged and dependable. George Best was another hugely talented and exciting player. After one of our games, he gave me his Irish top which I gave to one of my daughters, who wore it for years before it was thrown out. I sometimes regret I did not keep it myself and frame it, as it would be very valuable today!'

Content to be relieved of what had become his burdensome duties, Brown threw a party that same evening in his house in Helensburgh, and the next day began looking forward to life outside football.

Chapter 12

Family Life and Business Career

FOR months before his contract was terminated, Brown and his wife, Ruth, had been giving some thought as to what he would do once the inevitable happened. Although steeped in football, he was nevertheless content to contemplate giving up a career in it and take on a business venture. He well knew football was a precarious livelihood and was keen to take steps to ensure his family's security and future. The welfare of his family had always been uppermost on his agenda, and he was aware that not only had his time at the SFA involved him in regular absences from home, but also his public persona and high profile had inevitably reflected at times on the family.

He was extremely fortunate in having a close and supportive family: his lovely wife, Ruth, and three wonderful daughters, Carolyn, Alison and Gillian, born in 1949, 1954 and 1958 respectively. Ruth, as already noted, was from Devon. After marrying Bobby, she was happy to settle in Scotland, although she and the family enjoyed regular summer holidays in

Devon, often with their caravan. Initially the Browns lived in Cambuskenneth near Stirling, before moving to Stanley, where they enjoyed a pleasant lifestyle, with Carolyn and Gillian attending Perth Academy and Alison at Morrison's Academy in Crieff. Leaving there was always the wrench it threatened to be, but was a step that had to be taken.

When Brown left on the 'World Tour' with the Scotland party in May 1967, it was agreed that Ruth would sell their home in Stanley and look to buy a house in Bearsden or Milngavie near Glasgow. On his return a month later, he was met by Ruth at Prestwick Airport to learn that their house in Stanley had sold within 48 hours of being advertised, but she had not yet succeeded in buying another. From Prestwick they went to Glasgow, where, over a coffee in the North British Hotel in George Square, they scanned the property pages of the *Glasgow Herald*. As nothing caught their eye, they decided to take a trip to Helensburgh, an attractive town on the Clyde coast familiar to both, about 20 miles from Glasgow, to check out what properties may be available. Famous as the birthplace of John Logie Baird, the inventor of television, it was an affluent place, still popular with summer visitors, and boasted lots of amenities including a lovely location overlooking the Firth of Clyde. It was also within easy striking distance of Glasgow, thanks to a recently improved train service, and all in all appeared to have a lot to offer.

As they walked along Millig Road, a short way up the hill, to the north of the town's seafront, they were aware of a young man nearby, casting regular glances in their direction. When they asked him if he was looking for someone, he replied that he was expecting to meet a couple coming to look at his family home nearby, which was up for sale. Although the Browns were not the couple in question, he nonetheless agreed to show them the house in an adjoining street, 'West Gable' in Rowallan

Road. As soon as they saw it, both Bobby and his wife knew this was the house for them. It was a large Victorian semi-detached property on two floors, with five bedrooms, several public rooms and a conservatory, set in extensive grounds accessed by its own driveway. They decided to stay the night in the town to pursue their interest, as the owner was due to return later that evening. When Bobby called him, he confirmed the prospective viewers had never shown up, and he agreed to meet the Browns that evening in the house. An agreement to buy it was reached there and then, with a handshake sealing the deal, and the next day Bobby arranged for his lawyers to complete the formalities. He would later comment, 'Moving to Helensburgh was the best move I ever made.' As he still lives happily in the town today, 50 years later, the truth of that remark is self-evident.

The whole Brown family were delighted with their new home and soon began to integrate into the local community. Eldest daughter Carolyn had by now left school to begin her nursing training in Edinburgh, while Alison and Gillian continued their education, initially at the local Hermitage Academy. Ruth was a very active lady with a broad sweep of interests, including being leader of the local Garelochhead Brownie troop, interior design and decoration, furniture restoration, cooking, gardening and walking the family dogs. While living in Stanley, she had attended night classes in electricity in the home and won the title of top handywoman housewife of the Women's Electrical Association in Britain. She was a night-class enthusiast and, soon after moving into Helensburgh, began attending a pottery class. In the little free time she had, she also helped to landscape the large garden and create a rockery and fishpond at the new family home. Ruth's links with her family's roots in Devon were maintained for many years through her and the family spending a month's annual holiday there each summer. The annual excursion to this beautiful part of the world was eagerly looked forward to and provided many happy memories. Bobby's friendship with a local farmer allowed him to use a field at Gara Rock near Salcombe to station his caravan. From there, the family would often set off on beautiful coastal walks nearby, with the southerly location usually bringing warm weather. With so many activities in which to participate and places to visit, a month passed very quickly. The village of Salcombe in south Devon was one of their favourite spots. Situated in a designated Area of Outstanding Natural Beauty, it is a highly attractive unspoilt harbour town overlooking the Kingsbridge estuary.

* * * * *

About a year prior to leaving the SFA, Brown had met a Glasgow music hall owner and businessman, Mr A.E. Pickard, who had property interests in Helensburgh. In the course of conversation, it emerged that he owned a building on the seafront in the town, which was in poor condition and had been condemned by the local council. By this stage, Ruth and a friend of hers, Mrs Catherine Weatherstone, had been considering opening a gift shop primarily to cater for the many summer visitors and holidaymakers. After viewing Mr Pickard's property, they agreed to rent a shop space from him once the necessary permission was obtained from the council. It was refurbished and began trading initially in inexpensive gifts. As it went well, Ruth and her business partner opened another next door, which dealt in more upmarket goods such as jewellery, clocks, onyx items and Lladro ware. It prospered too, and led to their opening a third adjoining shop specialising in the sale of pine furniture, then very popular. The three shops all traded as 'Whichcraft of Helensburgh'. Bobby was also taking an interest in the business and from time to time would accompany Ruth and her partner to the various trade fairs they attended here and occasionally in Europe. Having been impressed by Whichcraft's success, he and his business partner, Douglas Weatherstone, thought Mr Pickard's building had potential worth developing. Subject to being able to secure the necessary permissions from the council, they planned to open a coffee shop at street level and refurbish the various flats upstairs for letting purposes. Pickard agreed to sell them the building, and the necessary consents were granted by the council, conditional on their renewing the roof and modernising the flats, which they did.

Plessey Electronics were then opening a factory in nearby Alexandria and required accommodation for employees. These flats were ideal for their purposes, and a letting contract was entered into with the company. The coffee shop opened up, called the 'Copper Cauldron', and soon became popular, offering tea, coffees and snacks. By now, Bobby had left the SFA, and this represented a world away from football but one he found very absorbing. The next idea he and his business partner had was to open a restaurant. Bobby had always had an interest in cooking, but was realistic about his limitations. Acknowledging that, and aware that if he were to enter the restaurant trade it would be necessary to know more about cuisine, he enrolled on a course at Clydebank College. There the former Scotland football supremo, the only male alongside 30 ladies in the class, learned the essentials of good cuisine, how to baste and how to reduce, how to liquidise and how to make soufflés, how to prepare a balanced menu and the wines to accompany them and so forth. He wanted to have a fall-back position that he could, if required in an emergency, step into the kitchen.

The next step was the acquisition of the old bakehouse lying to the rear of the Whichcraft shops, across a pend, for conversion to a restaurant. He and his partner had decided to create a Victorian theme for it and accordingly named it 'Now and Then'. It also had a small patio area suitable for al fresco dining, weather permitting. Douglas, with his interest in antiques and background as a French polisher, was invaluable in sourcing items to set an appropriate atmosphere, such as grandfather clocks, balloon-backed chairs and antique Pembroke tables. Waiting staff were attired in period dress, and Bobby was front of house 'meeting and greeting', while also acting as sommelier, resplendent in velvet jacket and bow tie. Business went well, and it became very popular, particularly with the submariners from the nearby Faslane base. On their return from periods away on exercises, the crew would often book the whole restaurant for themselves to enjoy a special meal. As the restaurant's success grew, Bobby found himself working increasingly long hours. He still helped during the day in the Copper Cauldron, and from about 5pm onwards was on duty in Now and Then, at times until midnight or later. Another factor he had to contend with about this time was the closure of the Plessey factory, which brought an end to their letting contract. The flats therefore had to be let on short-term tenancies, which began proving problematic, and they decided to sell all of the flats.

After about four years, the intensity and long hours involved in making the restaurant a success had begun to take its toll on Bobby's health. Fatigue and diminishing energy became regular companions, which was concerning to someone who had always been very fit and active. He consulted his doctor, who advised him that, because of the stress he was experiencing, he should consider retiring from the business for the benefit of his health. The doctor also explained that a personal friend of his had recently presented with similar symptoms but had chosen not to follow the advice, and sadly had since died. In these circumstances, Brown decided to accord his health priority and withdraw from the businesses altogether, after which he and his partner sold them. The restaurant still operates today under a different name, but in a more scaled-down version.

Unfortunately, in 1978, Ruth became ill with a rare form of blood cancer, which required ongoing treatment over several years. Much of this was carried out at the Western Infirmary in Glasgow, where it became apparent that the provision of a blood processor unit to assist in the diagnosis of rare blood diseases would be of tremendous benefit. Accordingly, she was instrumental in setting up the Ruth Brown Blood Cell Processor Fund to raise funds to purchase the equipment for the hospital – and succeeded, through a number of activities, in raising the impressive figure of £15,000 to enable that to happen, at a time when charity appeals were not so widespread as now. She was delighted to be able to present the equipment herself to the hospital. Ruth and Bobby were hugely grateful to all who contributed, many from the Helensburgh area but also from all over the world, which they found extremely touching. This was a very difficult period for the family, who were highly appreciative of the excellent care afforded Ruth, especially by her consultant, Dr Rowan. According to Bobby, Ruth continued with an active lifestyle for as long as she could and remained philosophical and positive throughout. Sadly, she lost her fight with the illness and died on 12 November 1983 aged 59, a shattering blow for Bobby and the family.

Because of Ruth's attachment to the Salcombe area, after her death Bobby arranged through the local council for the erection of a bench in her memory at East Portlemouth, on the other side of the estuary overlooking Salcombe, at what was her favourite view. The commemorative plaque reads 'ERECTED TO THE MEMORY OF RUTH BROWN OF HELENSBURGH SCOTLAND WHO DIED ON 12. 11. 1983 AND WHO LOVED THIS AREA. FOR THE PLEASURE OF OTHERS.' Each year since then, Bobby has received phone calls from people, unknown to him, who have seen the bench, saying how much they like it.

After selling his business interests and restoring himself to full fitness, Bobby remained keen to continue working in some capacity. Having had some involvement in his wife's shops, he had made a number of contacts, especially through attending trade fairs. He could see that most retail outlets purchased their stock from wholesalers whose range of goods tended to be uniform and rather limited. It occurred to him that he could cut out the wholesaler and deal directly with these outlets, to source a wider range of products for them from the manufacturers. He therefore set himself up as a self-employed agent, supplying a range of quality goods to shops all over Scotland. However, given his health concern, his daughters insisted he restrict himself to three days' work per week, which also suited him.

He looked back fondly at this period in his life, 'I thoroughly enjoyed this work, meeting lots of different people and covering nearly all parts of the country. I dealt in a number of items such as Toni Raymond Pottery from Devon, Capo di Monte figures, Lladro ware, clocks, Copenhagen Porcelain jewellery and copper items. Copper goods at that time were fashionable, and people liked copper models of, for example, Edinburgh Castle and the Walter Scott Monument. Pictures etched in copper with a clock on one side were also much in demand then. I remember meeting an Orkney retailer at Birmingham trade fair, who was delighted to purchase from me copper models of Orcadian scenes such as Scapa Flow, The Italian Chapel and St Magnus Cathedral in Kirkwall, which was very good business. As well as the Scottish mainland, I also travelled to Orkney and the Shetland Islands, which was a great experience. Football helped open doors for me, I have to say. People were always keen to have a chat with me about my time in the game, and I was happy to respond. I remember on my first trip to Shetland, I flew from Wick to Sumburgh Airport with myself and my bag of goods wedged in more or less behind the pilot's seat. It was a 20-minute flight at about 750 feet. From the airport, I took the bus into Lerwick, which seemed to take for ever as it stopped frequently. As a result, it was about half past five in the afternoon when I made my first call at the town's main shop. The shop assistant recognised me, as it so happened he was the secretary of the Lerwick Rangers Supporters' Club! We started chatting about football and ended up having a good night out. He told me to return to the shop the next morning to speak to the buyer, which I did, and succeeded in selling him all my stock!

'I made a lot of friends through my agency and enjoyed a lot of repeat business. It was completely different from being involved in football. There was a definite "buzz" in doing well at it, and at the same time there was decent money to be made out of it. A number of us used to enjoy going to trade fairs and making contacts, networking I suppose you'd call it today. There would be about 15 agents, and we'd go to fairs in Aberdeen, Dundee, Aviemore and elsewhere. The biggest was at Birmingham, and another big one was held at the Kelvin Hall in Glasgow. I was on the move a lot, and, as I say, I really enjoyed it. As time moved on, imitation goods from abroad started coming on to the market and reduced the demand for what I was selling. I was also getting no younger, and once I reached 78 I thought that was about time to call it a day, after some 15 years or so at it.'

He remains very close to his three daughters, now all adults with families of their own. Carolyn, a qualified nurse, did her training in Edinburgh and latterly was a practice nurse in Ayr for 25 years until retiring in 2011. She is married to Tom, who owns and runs a retail furniture business in Kilmarnock where she occasionally helps, as she also does on buying trips abroad. They have a large extended family of five children and eight grandchildren.

Alison is married to Richard, a former submarine commanding officer who now manages the Royal Warrant Association. Bobby fondly recalled having 'one of the best lunches of my life' at the bottom of Loch Long, when he joined Richard and the crew on a 'family day' during one of Richard's tours of duty in a submarine based in Faslane in the 1970s. Today, they live close to Winchester, where they moved with their three children after leaving Scotland. Since moving south, Alison has worked in the charity sector, focussing on people with learning disabilities.

Gillian graduated in English from the University of Warwick and qualified as a teacher at Moray House College of Education, Edinburgh. She is still teaching and is married to John, who works in the oil and gas industry. They have two grown-up children. Bobby very much values the relationship with his daughters and their families and always looks forward to seeing them. He also maintains a close relationship with his sister, Nan, a retired teacher now aged 89, whom he visits regularly in Denny, where she still lives.

Away from football, Bobby enjoyed a number of pursuits through the years. He used to enjoy an occasional game of golf and cricket, which he played purely for fun, although had his circumstances been different, he could have aspired to being an accomplished performer on the cricket square. The great outdoors was a lifelong interest, and he used to love hillwalking and climbing trips all over Scotland, during which he reckons he climbed over 40 Munros. He occasionally took parties of Helensburgh youngsters on overnight excursions into the hills as part of their Duke of Edinburgh awards courses. He firmly believed that these outdoor activities helped develop their self-discipline. When living in Stanley, he was an enthusiastic fisherman and always enjoyed walking the various family dogs. Caravanning, including the annual trip south, was another regular family activity, and he enjoyed skiing occasionally. Over the years, with his friend Katharine Ferguson, a close friend of Ruth and the family, he has spent holidays in the Far East, including Singapore, Hong Kong, Malaysia and Borneo as well as Devon. Latterly they have also enjoyed regular trips to the same hotel in Lagos in Portugal's Algarve, where walking the coastal paths and frequenting local restaurants were high on their list of activities.

In Helensburgh, he became a member of the local Rotary Club and took part in their community and charity fund-raising activities. A constant through his adult life has been his religious faith and involvement with the church, which continues to be important to him. He attends Sunday services regularly at St Michael's Episcopal Church in Helensburgh, where he is the oldest member, having joined 50 years ago. His association with the Episcopal Church started through Ruth at the time of their marriage. Although professional football and church involvement tend not to be mentioned in the same sentence, he was never deterred from following his faith.

He is also the oldest member of his church's rambling club and still actively involved. The club stages rambles every second Saturday, starting early morning and finishing with afternoon tea, a sociable aspect at the core of their activity much enjoyed by Bobby. Until about a year ago, he was managing five-mile walks although latterly he has contented himself with two to three miles. One of the bonuses of living in Helensburgh for him and fellow ramblers was being able to catch a direct train in the morning to Corrour in Rannoch Moor, adjoining Glencoe, enjoy a day out in the hills and catch a return train to be back home by mid-evening.

Bobby, as is evident, still enjoys an active and independent life and aims to continue in the same vein.

Chapter 13

Full Time

ALTHOUGH Bobby's formal connection with football finished in 1971, he has continued to follow the game closely. In the mid-1970s, he scouted in the west of Scotland for former club Plymouth Argyle for about a year, but increasing business involvement made it difficult to continue. As the last surviving member of Rangers' 'Iron Curtain' defence and their historic first Treble-winning team, he is a welcome guest at Ibrox, where he occasionally attends games. He is the oldest surviving Ranger, having made his debut for the team more than 70 years ago. Recent events at the club have left him sad and disappointed, like many others. For him, it was unbelievable that this could happen. During the Struth era and after, the club was consistently successful, one of the wealthiest in Britain; its players were among the best paid in the country, and it was looked on as part of the establishment. However, he is optimistic for the future while accepting it will take a few years to re-establish themselves to their previous status, as he related.

'The club needs stability to progress. The support is tremendous and has stuck by them through all the difficulties.

Things, of course, have changed since my day, but we had a phenomenal support back then. Apart from Old Firm matches, Ibrox used to be packed for the visits of the likes of Hibs, Hearts, Aberdeen and others, with crowds of 90,000 and more. What a feeling it was running out on to the pitch there in front of these crowds – it used to make the hairs on the back of my neck tingle! You just hoped everything was going to go alright. In those days, almost every club in the country had outstanding players – just think of Hibs and their 'Famous Five', Hearts with their 'Terrible Trio' and so on: they weren't confined then to your Rangers or Celtics, the talent was more evenly spread throughout the teams, and that brought in the fans. There was more genuine competition. Now, of course, there is so much more money in the game, and that tends to be concentrated in the hands of only a few clubs, creating more of a gap between the top and bottom. For my part, I don't regret at all not playing in the modern era; I think, if anything, we had a better time of it than players today. Financially, we didn't do so well, although I have no complaints over my earnings with Rangers. I just think we had more enjoyment then. We weren't so hidebound by tactics; the players identified strongly with their clubs and tended to stay with them for years, as opposed to moving around every odd season. I think that led to better team spirit, and fans related to that and maybe respected us more for it. There was no "celebrity culture" among players in those days like there is now. I can tell you there's no way Mr Struth would have tolerated that at Ibrox! Bad behaviour and insubordination led in only one direction – out the door! Players then were part of their local communities and by and large lived what would be considered "normal lives".

'I certainly appreciate my good fortune in playing for Rangers at that important time in their history. We had some great times, were very well looked after by the club and went on some smashing trips. Thanks to Rangers, I was able to start married life with a new house and no mortgage, and was well paid throughout. Because I was ten years at Ibrox, I received two benefits of £750 each, substantial sums then, which you got instead of a testimonial. Queen's Park was also a tremendous experience for me and gave me a really good grounding in the game. It was a privilege being part of the fine traditions of the club, and the camaraderie was first class. I'm also extremely proud, in the best sense of the word, to have represented my country several times and of being the last amateur to be capped by the full Scotland team while playing for the Spiders. Similarly I'm proud of being the country's oldest internationalist. The only thing that disappoints me a little about my Scotland playing career is that you weren't awarded caps for the wartime internationals and Victory Internationals afterwards, particularly as nowadays you can win a cap for being on the field as a substitute for five minutes. The SFA did, however, present me with a an inscribed silver cigarette case to mark my wartime internationals "as an amateur among professionals". And I have to say I'm truly grateful for the good fortune I did have.'

* * * * *

Brown was much appreciated by many figures in the football world. Celtic great Bobby Lennox speaks highly of him: 'Bobby was first and foremost a really nice guy. I first came across him after he picked me for Wembley 1967 and hadn't met him before that. Like a lot of managers then, tactics wasn't something he dwelled on, but he knew how to knit players together into a team and succeeded in creating a very happy atmosphere. He did his job well, he didn't put undue pressure on you and was well liked.'

Colin Stein, of Hibs, Rangers and Coventry fame, was another player who didn't know Brown before being selected by him to make his Scotland debut against Wales in 1969. He commented, 'I thought he was a great manager, a real gentleman. We had a mutual respect for one another – he was good with the players and never a bawler and shouter as some managers at that time were. Instead he'd have a word with you one-to-one to get his point across, and I liked his style.'

Frank McLintock of Leicester City and Arsenal played under Brown five times for Scotland and was travelling reserve at Wembley in 1967. 'I hadn't met him before the Scottish squad assembled at Hendon before the 1967 game, although I had heard of him as a former Rangers and Scotland player. I was fully involved in the team's preparation for Wembley, but in the two days we had there was a limit to how much you could do. Bobby was a very likeable, smiley guy who was fairly quiet, certainly compared to some managers of the time. Myself and the other reserves, Stevie Chalmers and Bobby Ferguson, were gutted not to get on, but the team played very well, and we at least played our part in the celebrations later! The win was a great feather in Bobby's cap. He believed in his selection and they repaid his faith. Although at the time we "Anglos" got some stick, questioning our desire to play for Scotland, I was always chuffed to bits to play for my country. Bobby certainly never subscribed to that view of the "Anglos", as his teams always featured a number of us.'

Pat Stanton earned seven Scottish caps during Bobby's spell as national manager and was captain in his final game, in Moscow in 1971. He recalled, 'Bobby was a very pleasant man and someone I enjoyed speaking to. He was fair to players and didn't ask you to do something you couldn't do. If the team didn't perform, he took the flak and didn't blame the players, which they appreciated. Generally he had a nice, easy-going manner and mixed well with us. Sometimes, though, if a manager gets labelled "nice", players being players, some may try to see how far they can get with him. But in my opinion Bobby had an edge to him which discouraged any player from pushing his luck. It was always clear who was in charge, although he didn't go in for one-to-one confrontations. In my book, he had our respect, and I never heard any backchat. Occasionally a disciplinary issue would be delegated to the trainer to deal with, but that was how it worked back then. I used to see my first manager at Hibs, Walter Galbraith, on a Monday and then not till the Saturday, with the trainer doing the hands-on work during the week! Despite his pleasant manner, Bobby had a strong winning mentality: winning was very important to him. Another thing I remember about him is that he was always very smartly dressed. I thought a lot of him.'

Alan Herron was a well-known football journalist who covered Bobby's period at the helm for Scotland. He remarked, 'In my opinion, Bobby did reasonably well in the circumstances. His main problem was the number of call-offs he had to endure from his squads. I know he would sit by his phone on a Saturday night sick with worry, waiting on the inevitable calls. Some clubs were definitely keener on progressing in European competition than having their players representing Scotland. The Scotland manager's job has never been an easy one, but he did all right. Some of my colleagues were critical, particularly John Mackenzie, known as "The Voice of Football". At times his criticism could be vociferous, and I remember an occasion after a press conference when, understandably, Bobby had had enough of this and turned to Mackenzie, saying, "Right, you and I into a boxing ring with the gloves on and let's sort this out!" Suffice to say "The Voice" did not accept the invitation! On a personal level, I had a good relationship with him and found him co-operative and courteous with the press. I also remember him as a player – a very stylish and effective keeper, always immaculately turned out on and off the pitch.'

Bobby Moncur was another of Bobby's captains with good memories of him. 'He was a gent, honest, upfront and altogether an excellent guy. I had great faith in him. He told me he wanted me to do exactly what I did at Newcastle United, organising the team. When he made me captain, I wasn't the most popular choice as there were bigger names than me in the squad. I remember being so pleased and at the same time thinking to myself, "Bloody hell, he's made me captain of Scotland!" But it was brave of him to do so, and I like to think I did my best for him.'

Jim McCalliog also thought highly of him, as he commented, 'The first time I met Bobby was when he picked me for the under-23 game against England at Newcastle, about a month before the Wembley 1967 game. I took to him immediately – he seemed a lovely, happy, smiley man who obviously knew his football, and I was chuffed to meet him. When he picked me for the Wembley match, my first cap, I was thrilled – I thought to myself, "This is Utopia!" I remember thinking that if he thought I was good enough, that gave me the confidence to believe that I was. He was very good with the players then, going round them individually, having a word. I was the only player in the Wembley team to go on the "World Tour" a month or so later and got to know him quite well. He was always very professional and very attentive. At times he perhaps gave the impression of being overawed, but that can happen if you're not a shouter and bawler, which he wasn't. I actually think he was a pretty confident manager, and as far as I was concerned he was great for my confidence. I certainly enjoyed playing under him.'

Alex MacDonald also had a lot of time for Bobby. 'He was a gent, an absolute gent. I admired him because of his great reputation from his playing days, and that meant I listened to him and tried to learn from him. He was always immaculate, built an excellent team spirit and ran a happy ship, which is not easy to do with all the different types you have in a football club.'

Renowned football commentator and pundit Chick Young considers him 'an absolute gent. I did a radio interview with him a couple of years back and found him a fascinating subject. We actually spoke for hours after the mike had been switched off, and I could have listened to him for days. He is quite a remarkable man, and his sharpness of mind for his age is incredible. As I say, he's an outstanding gent and one who commands great respect.'

Denis Law, the only Scottish player ever to be voted European Footballer of the Year, said in relation to him, 'Bobby Brown was a really nice guy who was very proud to be manager of his country. He was a terrific bloke and one of the best. That was a great team he picked for the Wembley 1967 match, and that's a game he'll always be rightly remembered for.'

* * * * *

Bobby has been awarded a number of distinctions, reflecting his success in the game. He is extremely proud to have been inducted into the Rangers Hall of Fame in 2009. In 2013, he was very touched when the club's Supporters' Trust hosted a Tribute Dinner to him at Ibrox, marking the occasion of his 90th birthday, and produced a commemorative booklet. At the Scotland v. Croatia game in November 2013, he was a guest of the SFA and introduced on the pitch to the crowd at half-time, where he was presented with a silver quaich inscribed: 'To Bobby Brown, In Recognition Of Your Outstanding Contribution To Scottish Football.' On another occasion, Tony Higgins, president of PFA Scotland, visited him at home to make a presentation of a crystal decanter and whisky glasses for 'Services to the Game'.

And, in 2015, he was particularly pleased to be inducted into the Scottish Football Hall of Fame. On that occasion at Hampden, namesake Craig Brown was present and thought Bobby's appearance 'brought the house down'. As he recalled, 'Bobby gave a speech and afterwards did a question-and-answer session. He spoke brilliantly, his humour and sincerity shone through and everyone thought he was the star of the evening. In a way I had more of a connection with him than some, although at a distance, as my father, Hugh, was his PE teacher. I know he thought the world of Bobby and what he went on to achieve. In my opinion, as manager of Scotland he did a fantastic job at a difficult time when many good teams were around. His record stands up well in comparison to others, particularly when it is kept in mind that most of his fixtures were against major footballing nations. The Soviet Union then, for example, was one country, which meant there were no games against its subsequently independent nations, some of which were – initially at least – considered weak. It always seems a bit unfair to me that when you refer to a player having so many caps, that figure is not broken down by an analysis of results, whereas that does happen with the manager. I know Bobby was very well regarded by others in the game, and deservedly so in my view. His feat in winning at Wembley in 1967 was unforgettable, and generally he was a great ambassador for the game.'

While understandably pleased to have received these accolades, he is also happy to have achieved what he has without compromising his ideals or integrity. Although it may seem clichéd, he was always his own man through his football and business careers, and in this regard differed from some of his contemporaries. He enjoyed an independence of mind that allowed him to resist Mr Struth's overtures to switch to full-time football, and then later to walk away from the game to pursue a totally different path in business. Astuteness informed his financial arrangements while a Rangers player, and enabled him to be alert to business opportunities and maximise their potential. Without being reckless, he was decisive, was confident in his own judgement and was unafraid of risk. Those qualities, allied to his faith and engaging personality, equipped him well for success in both sporting and business spheres, and continue to drive his enjoyment of a fulfilling and active life.